Bias

Books by Dr. Clifton Wilcox

Scapegoat: Targeted for Blame
Groupthink: An Impediment to Success

Bias

The Unconscious Deceiver

Dr. Clifton Wilcox

Copyright © 2011 by Dr. Clifton Wilcox.

ISBN: Softcover   978-1-4653-4261-4
         Ebook   978-1-4653-4262-1

All rights reserved. No part of this book may be reproduced or transmitted in any form or by any means, electronic or mechanical, including photocopying, recording, or by any information storage and retrieval system, without permission in writing from the copyright owner.

This book was printed in the United States of America.

To order additional copies of this book, contact:
Xlibris Corporation
1-888-795-4274
www.Xlibris.com
Orders@Xlibris.com
102270

CONTENTS

AUTHORS NOTE..9

CHAPTER ONE
The Need to Belong..11
Minimal Group Studies 12
Group Identity...16

CHAPTER TWO
Implications for Ingroup Bias...19
Evidence for the Belongingness 20
The Need to Belong..21
The Need to Belong in Social Psychological Theories...............21
The Role of the Need to Belong 23
The False-Consensus Effect 24
Intergroup Discrimination in the Minimal Group Paradigm.....27
Similarity-Attraction Effect 29

CHAPTER THREE
Instrumental Intergroup Contact 32
Superordinate Goals with Instrumentality 34
The Mutual Intergroup Differentiation Model.........................35
The Effect of Cooperative Success or Failure 36
Instrumentality in Diversity Research 36
Reinforcement Theory 38
The Common Ingroup Identity Model.....................................39
Factors that Influence Instrumentality 41

CHAPTER FOUR
In Group Bias.. 45
Ingroup bias 46
Measurement of Ingroup Bias 47

Behavioral measures of ingroup bias. 47
Evaluative performance measures of ingroup bias. 47
Evaluative trait measures of ingroup bias. 48
Moderators of Ingroup Bias 50
Group reality 50
Relative ingroup size 50
Group status 52
Evaluation relevance 53
Group permeability 55
Ingroup Bias Moderators 56
Minimal Group Paradigm 57
Cognition and Affect 59
Defining Cognition 60
Defining Affect 60
Cognition and Affect in Other Intergroup Phenomena 61

CHAPTER FIVE
Hind-Sight Bias 63
"I Knew It All Along" 65
"How Do I Feel About It?" and Specific Emotions 66
Counterfactual Emotions: Disappointment & Regret 67
Emotion Appraisals 68
Disappointment and Regret 68
Regret and Satisfaction 69
Where Disappointment and Regret Collide 69
"Am I Responsible?": Specific Emotions and Hindsight Bias 71
"I'm not responsible!"—Disappointment and Relief 71
"I am responsible!"—Regret and Satisfaction 72

CHAPTER SIX
Bias and the Expert: Is Expertise Friend or Foe? 74
Bias and Expertise: Is There a Curse of Knowledge? 79

CHAPTER SEVEN
Juror Bias 91
Personality characteristics and attitudes 94
Locus of control 96
Belief in a Just World 96
Authoritarianism 97

Attitudes toward the Death Penalty...........98
Due Process and Crime Control Attitudes...........99
Assessing Due Process and Crime Control 100

CHAPTER EIGHT
Gender Discrimination 104
Stereotypes: Explicit Measures of Bias 107
Internalizing Negative Stereotypes...........107
Negative Stigmatization, Group Membership, and Self-Esteem 109
Explicit Measures: Automatic versus Controlled Cognitive Processing........111
Prescriptive and Descriptive Gender Stereotypes........... 114
Gender Stereotypes and Negotiation 119
Gender Stereotype Bias: Target Familiarity and Other Criticisms 121

CHAPTER NINE
Portrayal of Sex Differences in Popular Culture...........126
Sex Differences in Research 127
Factors in Perception of Sex Differences 128
Facial Expressions as Displays of Emotion 129
Conclusion 151

CHAPTER TEN
Conflict...........153
The Conflict Spiral 154
Structure of the Spiral 154
Potential Mechanisms of the Conflict Spiral...........155
Fear...........156
Dehumanization 158
Disagreement and Perceptions of Bias...........159
Interpersonal Conflicts...........160
Large Scale Conflicts 161
Perceptions of Bias and Conflictual Action...........162
Large Scale Conflict 163
The Bias-Perception Conflict Spiral in Negotiation 164
Support for the Role of Bias Perceptions in Conflict 166
Bias-Perception Conflict Spiral for Conflict
    Intervention and Prevention...........166
Non-Counter-arguing Listening...........167
Temporal Distance 168

Non-Counter-arguing Listening as an Intervention in the Bias-Perception
    Conflict Spiral 169
Why Listening? 170
Perceiving Social Situations 171
Why Temporal Distance? 173
Effects of Time on Judgments, Decisions, and Behavior 174
Multiple Selves 175
Psychological Distance 176
Conclusion 178

CHAPTER ELEVEN
Bias: Extreme Prejudice 179
Bias Crime Data and Trends 181
Offender Characteristics 182
Victim Characteristics 184
Bias Crime Incidents Characteristics 184
Bias Crime Trends 185
Summary of Data and Trends 185
Bias Crime Motivation 186
Classification 187
Summary of Motivations and Classifications 189
Brief Discussion of Aggression 189
Expressive and Instrumental Forms of Aggression 190
Homicide Research 191
Situational Variables 194
Multiple Offenders/Victims Literature 195
Summary 198

AFTERWORD 201
REFERENCES 203

AUTHORS NOTE

Bias arises from various processes that are sometimes difficult to distinguish. These processes include information-processing shortcuts, motivational factors, and social influence. In groups, individuals have a tendency to evaluate their own membership group (the ingroup) more favorably than a non-membership group (the outgroup). This differential group evaluation is known as ingroup bias.

Research on ingroup bias has a long history in social psychology. Early researchers believed that ingroup bias was largely a function of motivational processes, whereas later researchers believed that ingroup bias was largely a function of cognitive processes. Currently, researchers are more predominantly focused on the cognitive explanations, and affective processes are increasingly being used to explain ingroup bias.

This book is grounded in the structure of intergroup relations, out group relations, sex relations, gender, and violence. This book will provide an integrative theoretical approach that: (a) identifies underlying dimensions of intergroup behavior active/passive, facilitative/harmful), and their roots in (b) dimensions of stereotypes (competent/incompetent, warm/cold) and (c) corresponding prejudiced emotions (admiration, contempt, envy, pity); and (d) identifies ambivalent clusters of stereotypes, prejudiced emotions, and discriminatory behaviors. In the end, we will see that bias perceptions play an important role in the escalation of conflict by leading individuals to behave in a more conflictual manner through aggression and competition, rather than cooperative and peaceful.

Mundus Vult Decipi
(The world wants to be deceived)

CHAPTER ONE

The Need to Belong

Psychologists have long understood that forming relationships with other people satisfies a number of basic human needs, and research has shown that people from different cultures have a strong drive to cultivate and maintain associations with others.[1] One way individuals connect with others and derive a sense of belonging is by affiliating with a group. However, although group membership can confer a number of advantages to those within a group, it might also lead to prejudice against those outside the group. Indeed, membership in a group often appears to be a catalyst for the kind of negative attitudes that lead to wars, genocide, hate crimes, political and economic oppression, and other hostile discriminatory behaviors.[2]

Given the devastating social conflict that seems to come at the hands of group-based prejudice, a great deal of work in psychology and beyond has focused on investigating the underlying processes and consequences of social categorization.[3] Over the years, different perspectives have emerged regarding the role that mere categorization plays in fueling prejudice and discrimination. On the one hand, some have argued that affiliation with an ingroup (a group to which one belongs) *by definition* engenders antagonism and aggression toward an outgroup (a group to which one does not belong). For example, in his discussion of the nature of ethnocentrism, Sumner concluded that the positive sentiments typically attributed to one's ingroup are paralleled by feelings of negativity and hostility toward outgroups.[4] That is, prejudice against outsiders is an unavoidable aspect of identifying with an ingroup. This perspective fits with the evolutionary principle of adaptive conservatism, which holds that people are predisposed toward distrusting anything unfamiliar or different.[5] As a result, it may be that anyone outside the familiar bounds of the ingroup is viewed with dislike and suspicion.

In contrast, social psychologists have generally rejected the position that ingroup love and outgroup hate are reciprocally related.[6] For instance, drawing on the postulates of Allport, Brewer proposed that, at a fundamental level, ingroup favoritism and outgroup derogation are orthogonal constructs that arise under distinct circumstances.[7] Since humans are social beings who require the cooperation of others for long-term survival, Brewer argued that people are characterized by an obligatory interdependence.[8] In order to survive, individuals must rely on others for information, assistance, and shared resources—and be willing to share each in return. This kind of cooperative system requires that people trust one another, but it is potentially dangerous to trust indiscriminately. Forming ingroups, however, is one way of creating an environment where the risks of non-reciprocation are minimized. By limiting the extension of trust only to mutually acknowledged ingroup members, people are more likely to cooperate with those who will return the favor. In this view, trust is not extended to outgroup members—but neither is any form of fundamental hostility. Rather, it is argued that additional factors, such as a sense of moral superiority or perceived intergroup threat, must be present to elicit negative attitudes toward the outgroup.[10]

Due to the importance and primacy of the ingroup, the process of group formation is believed to involve a differentiation of the ingroup from the outgroup, rather than the outgroup from the ingroup.[11] So, if one were to imagine a baseline situation where an individual sees himself/herself as distinct from an undifferentiated group of others, creating ingroup and outgroup boundaries would lead to a realignment of perceptions such that ingroup members would be drawn psychologically closer to the self (less differentiated from the self than before), but the distance between the self and outgroup would remain constant. Based on this logic, when groups are formed, ingroup members are seen as more positive, but outgroup members are viewed no more negatively than they had been before group labels were introduced.[12]

Minimal Group Studies

In an effort to understand group bias in its most fundamental form, much research has explored the link between categorization and prejudice using an experimental tool known as the *Minimal Group Paradigm*.[13] Because the dynamic between most real-world ingroups and outgroups is confounded with a number of factors (e.g., a prior history of conflict or ongoing competition for resources), it is often difficult to determine if existing intergroup prejudice or discrimination is based on categorization per se or some other variable(s). The Minimal Group Paradigm was developed as an attempt to examine prejudice and discrimination in a "pure" setting free of the elements that frequently accompany real groups.[14]

In the most commonly used form of this procedure, participants are brought into the lab and assigned to one of two groups, ostensibly on the basis of some arbitrary characteristic. In some studies, for example, participants are led to believe that their placement in a group is based on a tendency to over-or-underestimate the number of dots presented in a visual perception task or a preference for paintings by the artist Klee to those of Kandinsky.[15] In actuality, group membership is determined by random assignment. To ensure that the groups created in the lab remain minimal, the researchers also isolate each participant so that he or she has little or no interaction with members of either the ingroup or outgroup. Thus, participants have no pretext other than their group label to form impressions of ingroup and outgroup members.

After being categorized into one of two minimal groups, participants are most commonly asked to rate ingroup and outgroup members on various evaluative dimensions or divide specific resources (e.g., points, money) between ingroup and outgroup members.[16] Across a substantial number of studies using the Minimal Group Paradigm, participants have tended to rate ingroup members more favorably than outgroup members and give more resources to ingroup targets than to outgroup targets.[17] The dramatic implication of these results is that prejudice and discrimination appear to be elicited from group categorization alone.[18] By simply being placed into groups, even ones that have no apparent meaningful basis, people seem willing to view or treat certain people differently from others.

The findings from the original Minimal Group Paradigm studies provided the foundation for the development of Tajfel and Turner's *Social Identity Theory*, which states that people perceive their group as better than the outgroup in an effort to feel good about themselves.[19] In addition, this work helped spur a long-standing interest in the consequences of categorization and the cognitive processes involved in stereotyping and prejudice.[20] However, despite the contributions of the initial Minimal Group Paradigm studies and those that followed, the specific nature of the bias observed under minimal group conditions remains ambiguous. In particular, although a *relative* preference for the ingroup over the outgroup has been well established, it is unclear whether this bias is driven by ingroup favoritism, outgroup derogation, or some combination of both.[21] This is because the experimental designs used in existing Minimal Group Paradigm studies make it difficult to definitively determine the direction of this effect. In a typical Minimal Group Paradigm experiment, participants are asked to rate or distribute resources between an ingroup and outgroup target, but no appropriate control group is included to decompose the relative bias in attitudes or behavior that emerges.

Instead researchers have primarily used different measurement approaches to try to infer the nature of the bias. For example, one of the most common dependent measures used in Minimal Group Paradigm studies is the allocation matrix.[22] Here, participants are presented with a two-row matrix of values representing resources (e.g., money or points) to be divided between two other individuals in the experiment. Participants indicate how much they wish to allocate to each target by circling one column of the matrix, and the values are arranged so that choosing a particular column over others represents a specific distribution strategy. Through repeated allocations, general orientations in the way participants award resources to ingroup and outgroup members can be derived. Four orientations are possible:

1) Fairness and parity—equally distribute resources to ingroup and outgroup members,
2) Maximum joint profit (MJP)—maximizes resources given to both ingroup and outgroup members,
3) Maximum ingroup profit (MIP)—award highest absolute number of resources to ingroup members regardless of what is given to outgroup members, and
4) Maximum differentiation (MD)—maximize difference in resources in favor of the ingroup over the outgroup, but at a cost to maximum ingroup profit.[23]

In general, participants tend to choose allocation strategies that favor ingroup members over outgroup members.[24] However, the matrices are designed in a manner that confounds certain orientations.[25] Specifically, participants are always asked to choose between columns that reflect one orientation and columns that confound two other orientations. For example, the dominant allocation strategy that emerges is one based on choices that confound the *maximum ingroup profit* and *maximum differentiation* orientations. This makes it difficult to determine whether participants are motivated to favor the ingroup, discriminate against the outgroup, or possibly both. Despite this ambiguity, however, the allocation strategy that confounds *maximum ingroup profit* and *maximum differentiation* has confusingly been defined in the literature at times as *ingroup favoritism*. [26]

Some researchers have also tested to see if categorization can lead to outgroup derogation by having participant's rate group targets on negative dimensions or distribute negative outcomes to group members. [27] The thinking here is that if participants feel hostile toward the outgroup, they should rate the outgroup more negatively than the ingroup and allocate more negative outcomes (e.g., punishments) to the outgroup than the ingroup. When such measures are used, however, the bias typically observed in Minimal Group Paradigm studies disappears or is much less pronounced. [28] This apparent reluctance to directly disparage or harm the outgroup has contributed to the belief that categorization per se is insufficient to arouse outgroup prejudice. [29] It is important to note, however, that even if participants' assessment or treatment of the outgroup is not negative in an absolute sense, it is still possible for them to hold a bias against the outgroup. That is, the formation of social categories could result not only in a boost in positivity toward the ingroup, but also a decrease in favorability toward the outgroup.

This decrease in outgroup attitudes would indicate a clear bias against the outgroup, even if evaluations of the outgroup were neutral or positive in absolute terms. In addition to providing evidence of intergroup bias in the Minimal Group Paradigm on conscious, explicit measures of attitudes and behavior, some research has also examined attitudes using implicit measures designed to capture automatic evaluative reactions to groups. [30] Notably, research using these measures has shown that a relative preference for the ingroup over the outgroup also exists at latively automatic level. Moreover, as was the case with explicit measures, a number of studies suggest that the bias observed on implicit measures is driven entirely by ingroup favoritism. For example, Otten and Wentura, found that participants made fewer errors in categorizing positive words when they had been subliminally primed with their ingroup category label than when primed with the outgroup label. [31]

Furthermore, the percentage of errors committed when participants were primed with neutral words was significantly greater than when the ingroup was primed but was no different than when the outgroup was primed. These results were interpreted as evidence of 1) an implicit preference for the ingroup over the outgroup and 2) is driven solely by ingroup favoritism. That is, implicit positivity is extended to the ingroup, whereas the outgroup is associated with neutrality. However, although the outgroup might be implicitly evaluated as neutral in an absolute sense, it is still possible that the inclusion of a control group could reveal evidence of bias against the outgroup. That is, priming participants with a control group category label in the Otten and Wentura procedure could have yielded error rates that were significantly smaller than the outgroup prime error rate (and perhaps even the same as the ingroup prime error rate). [32] This pattern of results would indicate that although the outgroup may be considered objectively neutral (i.e., similar to a neutral prime), the difference between implicitly measured ingroup and outgroup attitudes is based in part (or perhaps entirely) on outgroup prejudice.

Otten and Moskowitz found evidence of implicit ingroup favoritism using a paradigm measuring spontaneous trait inference. [33] The authors showed that reading sentences describing behaviors performed by a minimal ingroup member facilitated the inference of positive, but not negative, traits implied by the sentences. In contrast, reading sentences about behaviors performed by a minimal outgroup member did not facilitate the inference of implied traits, regardless of the valence of the behavior. This pattern of results was interpreted as evidence of implicit positivity toward the ingroup and a lack of implicit negativity toward the outgroup. However, as noted earlier, a bias against the outgroup could still exist, even if the outgroup was not viewed negatively in absolute terms. For instance, reading about positive behaviors performed by a non-affiliated person could facilitate the inference of positive traits, which would indicate prejudice against the outgroup. Indeed, if the degree of facilitation of positive traits was the same for control and ingroup targets, then one would conclude that the implicit intergroup bias was driven solely by outgroup prejudice.

Group Identity

From ethnic cleansing in Nazi Germany to contemporary terrorist attacks, many of the most tragic instances of social conflict across human history plausibly can be linked in some way to group identity and bias. In recognition of this relationship, one of the most vibrant and enduring research traditions in social psychology focused on the investigation of the fundamental processes and consequences of social categorization.[34] A critical finding from this domain is that categorization per se is sufficient to elicit intergroup prejudice and discrimination. That is, group membership, even when it is based on some arbitrary pretext, can lead people to favor those in their ingroup over those in the outgroup.[35] Importantly, social psychologists generally believe that this bias is fueled by ingroup favoritism and not outgroup derogation, unless other hostility instigating factors are present, such as competition for resources.[36]

However, prior studies that have attempted to examine this phenomenon within the confines of a "pure," minimal group setting have relied on methodological designs, procedures and dependent measures that make it difficult to tell if the relative bias is indeed solely the result of ingroup favoritism or if some degree of outgroup derogation also plays a role. In particular, most prior research has not employed an appropriate control group to help discern the direction of the minimal group effect, or if a control group was used, other factors in the experimental design rendered the results ambiguous.

Of the two types of bias, ingroup favoritism seems to carry more weight in driving the effect, which fits with current theories regarding the underlying motivations and consequences of social categorization.[37] But the fact that outgroup derogation also contributes to the bias suggests that the seeds of group-based conflict can take shape as soon as groups are formed—and without the influence of other factors known to incite outgroup prejudice.

This finding is not often anticipated by researchers, but neither is it necessarily contradictory with existing theory. For example, the tenants embodied in the social identity theory assert that individuals are inherently motivated to elevate and protect the status of the ingroup.[38] Devaluing the outgroup, at least a little, would seem to be one effective way of pursuing these goals. Also, the fact that outgroup derogation was evident on both explicit and implicit measures suggests that the results are likely not due to experimenter demand and points to the fundamental nature of outgroup bias. That is, mere categorization is sufficient to elicit prejudice against the outgroup at a relatively automatic level. This finding is critical given that some of the best evidence that intergroup bias in the minimal group situation is based on ingroup favoritism alone comes from Minimal Group Paradigm studies that employ implicit measures.[39]

Existing literature suggests that greater identification with the ingroup leads to more positive ingroup attitudes and a larger intergroup bias across a variety of domains.[40] However, because prior research has not included an effective control target in the Minimal Group Paradigm, it has not been possible to directly examine the relationship between ingroup identification and ingroup favoritism.

Although ingroup identification has received considerable attention in the literature, few studies measure participants' degree of identification with the outgroup, and no study has attempted to link this variable with intergroup attitudes in the Minimal Group Paradigm.[41] Rather, in rare cases when this variable has been captured, it has been used as a manipulation check of the effectiveness of the minimal group induction.[42] But previous research exploring the impact of taking a negational vs. affirmational group identity suggests that outgroup identification is a plausible antecedent of outgroup bias. Specifically, Zhong found that inducing participants to focus on a group membership they did not hold (negational identity) led them to derogate that outgroup, presumably because they were inclined to psychologically distance themselves from the outgroup.[43] However, it is possible that the outgroup bias observed in their studies was due to demand from their identity manipulation, and researchers were interested in determining if some people spontaneously dis-identify with the outgroup and whether lower levels of outgroup identification would predict outgroup derogation.

CHAPTER TWO

Implications for Ingroup Bias

Human beings are driven by an innate desire to form and maintain interpersonal relationships.[1] From this perspective, people seek relationships with others to fill a fundamental need, and this need underlies many emotions, actions, and decisions throughout life.[2] Presumably, the *need to belong* is a product of human beings' evolutionary history as a social species. Human beings have long depended on the cooperation of others for the provision of food, protection from predators and elements, and the acquisition of essential knowledge.[3] Without the formation and maintenance of social bonds, early hominids presumably would not have been able to cope with or adapt to their physical environments.[4] Thus, seeking closeness and meaningful relationships has long been vital for human survival.[5]

Presumably, the survival value of interdependence has evolved into a set of internal mechanisms that propel human beings into social groups.[6] These mechanisms predispose all humans to relate to others, to experience affective distress when social relationships are denied or dissolved, and to experience pleasure or positive affect from social contact and relatedness.[7] The need to belong is defined as the desire for frequent, positive, and stable interactions with others and is fulfilled primarily through affiliation with and acceptance from others.[8] In line with the idea that the need to belong is a basic motivation, a person's needed to belong increases following rejection and decreases following social inclusion or acceptance.[9] If the need to belong is threatened, people may go to extraordinary lengths to affiliate with others, be liked by others, and belong to groups.

Many patterns of group behavior and close relationships can be easily understood as serving the need to belong.[10] Because of the importance of this fundamental need, people should show a strong motivation to ease social interactions and maintain positive relations with others. Indeed, most people behave in ways that enhance their chances of inclusion and minimize their chances of exclusion in groups and relationships.[11] However, the central theme here is that the need to belong is likely to affect a much wider range of psychological phenomena than has previously been appreciated. This assumption is loosely consistent with current theories of social cognition that suggest that people's needs and desires can influence a broad range of cognitive and behavioral processes, including attention, evaluation and interpretation, memory, aggression, risk-taking, conformity, and pro-social behavior.[12]

Evidence for the Belongingness

The concerted efforts people make to develop and maintain social bonds suggest that the need to belong represents a fundamental human need. As Baumeister and Leary noted, people develop social bonds with relative ease and under diverse and seemingly adverse circumstances.[13] Thus, contrary to what one might expect; having things in common is not a requirement for the formation of close relationships. Apparently, mere contact with others is sufficient to promote friendships and other strong social attachments. Furthermore, people are eager to extend and quite reluctant to break social bonds, even when relationships are maladaptive or harmful.[14] Moreover, there is a seemingly universal tendency for people to respond with distress and protest to the end of a relationship, a pattern that is cross-culturally consistent across the lifespan.[15]

Baumeister and Leary have argued that the need to belong as a fundamental human motivation can be observed in the ways in which social relationships shape cognition.[16] People are likely to spontaneously categorize others in terms of relationship categories, are influenced by interpersonal concerns when making causal attributions, and differ in how they process information related to close versus distant others.[17]

Similarly, the potential for future relationships or interactions is likely to influence the way in which people process information about others. Information is processed more thoroughly, and is interpreted differently when it pertains to potential interaction partners.[18]

The strong emotions people experience when belongingness needs are fulfilled, or when they are threatened, provide further evidence for the belongingness hypothesis. Many of the strongest emotions people experience, both positive and negative, are interpersonal in nature.[19] Life events elicit stronger and more lasting emotions if they relate to close others than if they relate exclusively to the self.[20] In general, forming and maintaining social bonds is positively correlated with happiness in life and positive life outcomes.[21] People who have close connections with others are happier, and mentally and physically healthier than people who do not.[22]

The Need to Belong

For decades, psychologists have argued, explicitly or implicitly, that a great deal of human behavior is socially motivated. However, it is only in the past decade or so that researchers have specifically connected the need to belong to the specific social judgments and behaviors that have been of central interest to social psychologists.[23]

Thus, only a limited number of studies have directly examined the cognitive and behavioral implications of the need to belong. Primarily, this research has looked at the negative consequences of a lack of belongingness. These consequences include anxiety, loneliness, anger, substance abuse, reckless driving, and losing one's sense of control.[24] This research shows that social exclusion is correlated with crime and antisocial behavior, self-defeating behavior, cognitive impairment and even psychotic behavior.[25] In addition, research shows that social exclusion leads to considerable decreases in feelings of self-esteem. Indeed, research on the socio-meter hypothesis suggests that people's self-esteem is directly related to the extent to which they feel included and accepted by others. That is, high self-esteem comes from believing that others want to develop and maintain long-term relationships with the self. Conversely, low self-esteem arises when people experience actual or perceived rejection or fear that they will end up alone in life.[26]

The Need to Belong in Social Psychological Theories

Many prominent social psychological theories have a clear social motivational component. Indeed, most of the motives underlying behavior are social in nature and reflect human beings' innate desire to form and maintain social bonds. Fiske proposed that five core social motives facilitate the formation of social groups, enhancing people's physical and psychological survival.[27] According to Fiske, these five core needs include the need to understand, to be effective, to find the world benevolent, to maintain self-esteem, and to belong. Among these motives, the need to belong is presumably the most important for social survival. Fiske has even argued that the need to belong may serve as the foundation for the other four motives.[28]

Consistent with this view, many social psychological theories are at least loosely consistent with the premise that people are driven by an intrinsic need to belong. For example, classic theories of roles and norms propose that an individual's social behavior is driven by the desire to maintain his or her connection to social group members.[29] Role theories explain people's behavior as a function of their positions in social structures and the expectations linked to those positions. Similarly, norm theories describe various unwritten rules that govern social interaction and group life.[30] Both these perspectives suggest that the reason people subscribe to socially ascribed roles or comply with unwritten rules is the basic desire to be part of a group in which acceptance is maximized and social friction is kept to a minimum.[31]

According to Fiske, more domain-specific theories are also related to belongingness motives, as they affect behavior within groups, relationships between individuals, and processes within the individual.[32] Within groups, normative influence processes reflect the effect of reference groups on individuals. Along similar lines, obeying authorities or submitting to seemingly legitimate social hierarchies can allow people to maintain a basic sense of belongingness.[33] More broadly, ingroup identification facilitates belongingness among ingroup members as do pressures toward group cohesion.[34]

Between individuals, reciprocity norms that contribute to the predictability and fairness of social interactions are also facilitated by belongingness concerns.[35] Even more to the point, communal norms reflect explicit and implicit rules that emphasize cooperation and care for others. That is, people learn that one must sometimes restrain from selfish inclinations for the sake of pursuing the goal of social acceptance. Similarly, patterns of self-presentation and interpersonal redress and excuse making seem to be rooted in belongingness needs.[36] From this perspective, people's strategic manipulation of the self to gain social rewards such as approval represents a clear example of the influence of the need to belong; whereas, Jones and Pittman, argued that self-presentation is more typically grounded in a desire for power or social influence.[37]

Although the need to belong is presumably universal, it is highly plausible that there are individual differences both in the degree to which people desire social acceptance and in the manner in which people believe it is easiest to achieve it.[38] Thus, for example, research on individual differences in (a) social desirability biases and (b) rejection sensitivity assumes that whereas all people are concerned with avoiding social rejection, some people are especially fearful about whether others will meet their needs for acceptance and belonging and respond more intensively to actual or perceived social rejection.[39] Along similar lines, research on self-monitoring could be construed to suggest that, relative to low self-monitors, high self-monitors might be more sensitive to situational norms and are more likely to seek acceptance from others.[40]

The Role of the Need to Belong

Although some research has shown that serious forms of social exclusion may lead to antisocial responses like aggression, there is evidence that less serious forms of social exclusion stimulate a desire to affiliate and reconnect with others. Several studies have shown that individuals who are ostracized, excluded, or rejected by others behave in ways that will increase their inclusionary status.[41] These behaviors range from working harder in group settings, to conforming to group perceptions, or being more sensitive to information about others. For example, Williams and Sommer found that women responded to ostracism by increasing their efforts on a subsequent group task.[42] Similarly, Williams, Cheung, and Choi observed that ostracized individuals were more likely than others to conform to the opinions of other people.[43] Thus, these studies show that in response to social rejection, people seek to reconnect themselves with their social worlds. In addition, Gardner, Pickett, and Brewer found that individuals who experience social rejection are more likely to remember socially relevant information.[44] Thus, belongingness needs appear to guide the processing and retention of motive-consistent information.

Recently, Carvallo and Pelham argued that to maintain a basic sense of belonging people are eager to convince themselves that they rarely experience the same discrimination experienced by fellow ingroup members.[45] According to Carvallo and Pelham, it threatens one's need to belong to believe that other people routinely discriminate against oneself.[46] Accordingly, people should be motivated to believe that they rarely experience personal discrimination.

Conversely, the desire to feel connected to ingroup members should increase people's perceptions of discrimination directed at their groups. This reasoning was supported in three different studies. In Study 1, people who scored higher than average in the need to belong reported experiencing lower levels of personal discrimination (but higher levels of group discrimination). In Study 2 an experimental manipulation of the need to belong had a very similar effect. Finally, Study 3 showed that the need to belong influenced perceptions of personal discrimination in attributionally ambiguous situations. Women who were more highly motivated to be accepted by a highly traditional male confederate were less likely to attribute his negative evaluations of their work to prejudice.

These findings suggest that people strive to fulfill the need to belong not only by attempting to maximize actual acceptance from others but also by structuring their beliefs about the self and others in ways that allow them to feel that most people like and accept them.[47] In short, the drive to seek social acceptance should be accompanied by mechanisms for enhancing the subjective perception that one will, in fact, be accepted rather than rejected by others.[48] Thus, the drive for social acceptance (i.e., the need to belong) can color people's judgments of others in ways that indirectly allow people to fill this need.

As suggested by Fiske, the basic need for belongingness may fuel different behaviors designed to promote and maintain one's connectedness with social groups.[49] However, all the behaviors investigated so far appear to be related exclusively to instances of direct or perceived social rejection. Thus, it may appear that the influence of the need to belong is likely to apply only in situations in which connectedness with others is threatened or one seeks to regain social acceptance or inclusion. Contrary to this view, the belongingness perspective suggests that the motivation for connectedness and acceptance from others plays an important role in a wider range of behaviors. Therefore, researchers should expect to observe the influence of the need to belong in social behavior that is not directly linked to social rejection.

The False-Consensus Effect

The false consensus effect refers to an egocentric bias that occurs when people over estimate consensus for their own beliefs, attributes, and behaviors. Ross, Greene, and House described this bias as people's tendency to "see their own behavioral choices and judgments as relatively common and appropriate to existing circumstances while viewing alternative responses as uncommon, deviant, or inappropriate." [50] For example, people who prefer foreign films over American films or endorse Democratic candidates over Republican candidates estimate that a higher percentage of their peers prefer foreign films and endorse Democratic candidates compared with peers who prefer American films and endorse Republican candidates. Thus, the bias is typically established by comparing the perceptions of those who endorse a position with the perceptions of those who do not.

The typical paradigm for examining the false-consensus bias is simple. People are asked to report their attitudes or behavior on a dichotomous measure (e.g., *yes* or *no*, *agree* or *disagree*). They are then asked to estimate the percentage of their peers who would respond one way or the other (sometimes the order of these two ratings is counterbalanced). Individuals are said to show evidence of false consensus when their estimate of consensus for their own position exceed the estimate for it made by those who endorsed the opposite position. Thus, the bias is typically assessed in relative rather than absolute terms. [51]

Studies demonstrating the false consensus-effect usually employ a single target group.

Participants, usually college students, are asked to focus on "peers," "students in this class," "students at this college," "college students in general," or "adults." A meta-analysis of 115 tests of the false-consensus hypothesis revealed that the effect is highly reliable and of moderate magnitude. [52] The false consensus bias is relatively small (1) when the target population is highly inclusive (e.g., the general adult population), (2) when the number of items judged is large (e.g., 40 or more attitude items), and (3) when consensus estimates follow personal statements of endorsement, rather than the reverse. [53]

Researchers have proposed several processes to explain the false consensus effect. For example, Ross and colleagues suggested that the phenomenon results from selective exposure and availability of information when estimating consensus. [54] People are generally surrounded by similar others. This selective exposure to similar others results in a biased sample of social information. Thus, instances of similarity or agreement between self and other are more readily retrievable from memory than instances of dissimilarity or disagreement. Presumably, this availability increases estimates of consensus for one's preferred position. [55]

Focus of attention or causal attributions processes provide yet another explanation for the false consensus effect. Presumably, focusing one's attention on one's preferred position, rather than an alternative position, leads to relatively high estimates for the occurrence of that position.[56] When a perceiver focuses attention exclusively on a preferred position, perceived consensus should increase because that position is the only one in immediate consciousness. In contrast, when perceivers focus their attention on alternative positions, consensus estimates for one's own position tend to decrease.[57] Similarly, when people believe that their positions are influenced by external forces, they are more likely to estimate higher consensus for their attitudes and behavior. In contrast, when people view their own positions as stemming from their own personal characteristics or experiences, they make less biased estimates of consensus.[58]

Several motivational explanations have been offered for the false consensus effect. For example, perceiving false consensus between self and particular targets may help maintain self-esteem, maintain or restore cognitive balance, and reduce tensions associated with anticipated social interaction.[59] Perceived consensus for one's position also validates the correctness or appropriateness of that position.[60] This is particularly likely to be the case when consensus estimates are based on ingroup, rather than outgroup members.[61]

Self-justification processes provide another motivational explanation for the false consensus effect.[62] Research shows that those who prefer unpopular activities or engage in undesirable health habits (e.g., smoking), overestimate consensus for their own preferences.[63] Thus, the false consensus may reflect a need to perceive social support for one's position. The false consensus effect may also reflect one's attempts to psychologically associate the self with valued individuals or groups. This view is supported by findings that show the false consensus effect is greater among ingroup than outgroup members.[64] Similarly, the false consensus effect is stronger when target groups are attractive rather than unattractive.[65]

Three of the motivational explanations listed above are loosely supportive of the need to belong perspective. To be more specific, the idea that false consensus reduces social tension is consistent with the view that overestimating consensus for one's beliefs, attributes, and behaviors facilitates and promotes social interactions and bonding. Similarly, false consensus may provide consensual validation and reinforce the belief that one's views are accepted by others. Finally, the self-justification perspective is also loosely consistent with the idea that the false consensus effect may be grounded in the need to belong. People are able to enhance the connectedness with others if they believe that others support their views and attitudes. In short, from the perspective of the need to belong, individuals may often strive to achieve a sense of belongingness by convincing themselves that other group members share their own attitudes. Just as an individual's standing in a group is often threatened when one questions group beliefs or defies group norms, one's standing is presumably increased when one's attitudes or behavior satisfy the goals, norms and expectations of important reference groups. [66]

Intergroup Discrimination in the Minimal Group Paradigm

Many experiments have shown that people favor members of their own group and discriminate against members of other groups even in minimal intergroup situations.[67] This research, in which experimenters use variations on the minimal group procedure, provides evidence that merely being categorized into an experimental group is sufficient to induce favoritism for the ingroup over the outgroup. [68] In all these experiments, participants are first divided into groups according to trivial or arbitrary categories (e.g., preferences for the paintings of Klee or Kandinsky), and then asked to allocate resources (e.g., points or money) between members of their own group (ingroup) and members of another group (outgroup)—using allocation matrices known as Tajfel matrices. [69] Overall, ingroup favoritism in the minimal group paradigm is a well-established phenomenon, but the exact reasons for this favoritism remain unclear. [70]

According to social identity theory, ingroup favoritism results from motivational processes, whereby people try to maintain positive distinctiveness in social comparisons by increasing the status of their groups when these groups form part of their social self-concept. This process not only allows group members to differentiate their ingroup from outgroups, but also serves the function of enhancing their self-esteem. [71] Thus, ingroup-favoritism may result from people's tendencies to enhance the self-concept by enhancing the image of the ingroup.

Contrary to this view, recent research suggests that the ingroup favoritism effects observed in the minimal group paradigm are produced by an automatic evaluation effect in which the ingroup label acquires its positive meaning either because of its mere association with the self or because of an automatic process of ingroup conflict and competition. [72] In a similar vein, Cadinu and Rothbart proposed that ingroup favoritism results from self-anchoring and differentiation processes. [73] That is, people generalize their self-image to the ingroup. At the same time, the outgroup is seen as different from the ingroup, and thus less favorable. According to such view, participants views of the ingroup are automatically influenced either by their positive conceptions of the self, their negative conceptions of the outgroup, or both. In Tajfel's original language, because self and ingroup are regarded favorably, and because outgroup is regarded less favorably, the principle of differentiation will lead inevitably to ingroup bias.

Hertel and Kerr have proposed a normative account to explain intergroup discrimination in the minimal group paradigm.[74] These researchers argue that ingroup favoritism reflects a social norm or a "social script prescribing favoritism or loyalty to one's group as expected and socially approved behavior."[75] Presumably, these social scripts are learned from previous social experiences that reinforce social loyalty and punish the lack of it. According to Hertel and Kerr, participants in minimal group situations lack contextual cues to guide their allocation choices.[76] Therefore, people are likely to search their memories for appropriate normative scripts that give meaning to the situation and provide clear guidance.[77]

Consistent with a normative explanation of ingroup favoritism, Gaertner and Insko have demonstrated that people believe that group members are mutually obligated to reciprocate one another's beneficial actions—and that this reciprocity expectation might underlie ingroup favoritism.[78] Their research suggests that that the norm of group loyalty observed in Hertel and Kerr's research is moderated by self-interest such that members of minimal groups favor their group only when they can personally profit from the allocations of other ingroup members.[79]

A normative explanation is also evident in two additional lines of research. First, Jetten, Spears, and Manstead have shown that members of minimal groups display more ingroup favoritism in the allocation of resources when on a previous trial other ingroup members allocated more resources to the ingroup.[80] Finally, Blanz, Mummendey and Otten have shown that the tendency for members of minimal groups to discriminate when allocating positive outcomes (but not negative outcomes) can be explained, in part, by the normative appropriateness of differentially exposing ingroup and outgroup members to negative outcomes.[81]

A normative account of the minimal group paradigm is consistent with the need to belong perspective. Individuals rely on groups for a sense of belongingness that translates into feelings of support, security, and safety. That is, individuals require connectedness and belonging to groups in order to function optimally as valued group members. But relying on groups also implies an obligation to the group. For example, group members are expected to act in ways that promote and help the group or other individual group members. Any action that is designed to please the group should enhance one's standing in the group and make one more valued in the group. This process, in turn, should increase people's sense of belongingness. In sum, if the need to belong lies at the root of ingroup favoritism, manipulations of the need to belong should moderate ingroup bias. More specifically, ingroup bias should be stronger when the need to belong is increased and weaker when it is satiated or reduced. Alternatively, if ingroup favoritism is strictly a mechanism for enhancing the self-concept, it seems unlikely that manipulations of the need to belong would influence the magnitude of ingroup bias.

Similarity-Attraction Effect

One of the most robust phenomena in social psychology is the similarity-attraction effect.[82] Across a variety of populations and manipulations of similarity, increased similarity to a target is associated with interpersonal attraction to the target.[83] The similarity effect has been observed in studies with schoolchildren, undergraduates, and married couples.[84] Moreover, the effect is robust for a number of different types of information, including personality traits, attitudes, demographic characteristics, and physical attractiveness.[85]

Most research on the similarity-attraction effect has looked at attitudinal similarity.[86] Presumably, the reasons behind this focus on attitudes have to do with both their liability with which the effect is obtained for attitudes and the ease with which a bogus others' attitudes can be experimentally manipulated. Typically, participants' attitudes are assessed in a preliminary session and the simulated attitudes of a bogus target are presented to the participant at a later time, often during a single experimental session. Research shows that attraction increases in a more or less linear fashion with the proportion of shared similar attitudes between participants and bogus targets. Research also shows that the importance of attitudes and opinions on the attitude-attraction relationship is more likely to be observed when the attitudinal items are heterogeneous in their importance, and when specific items of greater personal importance to a participant are particularly likely to yield agreement.[87]

Based on cognitive and reinforcement models, two different lines of research provide alternative explanations for the similarity-attraction effect.

An example of a cognitive model is the information integration model. [88] According to this model, attraction results from a weighted composition of the information one compiles regarding a target. This model is based on the view that individuals regard themselves and the attitudes they possess mostly positively.[89] Therefore, an evaluator would infer favorable information about a target that holds similar attitudes as oneself. [90]

From this point of view, the similarity-attraction effect is the result of an integrated summary of the target's desirable and/or undesirable qualities. Kaplan and Anderson point out that people tend to infer from attitudes additional information about a target. [91] That is, if we are told that a target shares many attitudes with the self; we tend to like the target more because we expect the target to possess other positive attributes as well. In short, others who hold attitudes that are similar to ours are assumed to possess positive personality qualities. [92]

Reinforcement models probably provide the most widely accepted explanations for the similarity-attraction effect. Byrne and Clore's reinforcement-affect model, for example, proposes that a target who possesses similar attitudes is reinforcing because the target's attitudes provide consensual validation of one's own attitudes. [93] This consensual validation, in turn, helps to satisfy the *effectance motive*, "a learned drive to be logical, to interpret the environment correctly, and to function effectively in understanding and predicting events." [94] In short, this model proposes that similar others make us feel good, and right whereas dissimilar others make us feel bad and potentially wrong.

Aronson and Worchel proposed an alternative reinforcement model known as *inferred evaluation*. [95] According to this model, most people assume that similar others will like them. People assume that a person who agrees with them will also like them. This assumption of reciprocated liking is based on people's past histories of reinforcement. From this perspective, assumed liking from the target serves as a stimulus for reciprocal liking, thus giving rise to attraction. In short, there is an implicit expectation on the part of people that targets who share their attitudes and opinion will like them. Since people tend to like those who like them, this inferred evaluation hypothesis can account for the similarity-attraction effect.

Both the idea that similar others validate one's beliefs and the idea that people expect similar others to like them are consistent with the need to belong perspective. [96] Thus, similar others assure us that they are very likely to like us and thus indirectly assure us that others in general will probably like us. Thus, similar others are likely to fill the need to belong.

[97] As suggested by Byrne, people who are similar may find each other's company highly reinforcing, which may help people to form and maintain long term relationships. [98] Thus, it is possible that one main route through which people can fill the need to belong is by gravitating toward similar others. [99]

To the degree that this is true, attraction to similar others may be even stronger when one's sense of belongingness is thwarted or threatened. If people perceive similar others as more likely to provide social acceptance and support, then people should be more likely to seek out similar others when striving to restore their sense of belonging. Alternatively, if the only reason for the similarity-attraction effect is the assumption that similar others possess positive qualities, it seems less likely that attraction to similar others would increase when one's belongingness needs are not met or threatened.

CHAPTER THREE

In 1954, Allport introduced the contact hypothesis, stating that intergroup contact reduces intergroup bias, and proposed that bias will be less when intergroup contact is supported by authorities, groups are equal status, and they cooperate to achieve common goals.[1] Conventionally, people refer to these four moderators as *Allport's conditions of contact* and meta-analytic evidence indicates that when these four features are present bias is reduced more than when they are absent, although the difference in effect sizes is admittedly small.[2] Research has supported the contact hypothesis using multiple outgroups, situations, and cross-cultural populations, and shown that bias reduction is enhanced with increases in the duration and frequency of contact.[3]

Instrumental Intergroup Contact

In 1958, Sherif argued that bias reduction is more effective when groups have goals which are "compelling and highly appealing to members of two or more groups in conflict but which cannot be attained by the resources and energies of the groups separately."[4] The famous Robber's Cave study demonstrated that super-ordinate goals can reduce intergroup bias.[5] In the Robber's Cave, Sherif pre-selected boys to be as similar as possible to participate in a summer camp, and then randomly divided them into two groups of campers.[6] After creating a series of competitions that led to severe intergroup conflict, they introduced a series of goals that were unachievable without intergroup cooperation, and intergroup bias decreased subsequent to the cooperation.[7]

Unfortunately little attention has been given to Sherif's idea that bias is reduced more when group members feel they need each other to achieve a goal, than when they cooperate believing that their group would be more successful working alone. Most research simply imposes upon two groups the task of solving some problem, without considering whether each group's members may feel perfectly competent to generate a solution by themselves, such that there is no incentive to work with the other group. The term "instrumentality" is used to define the situation Sherif identified, where group members have a compelling reason to work with the outgroup because the outgroup's contribution is perceived to increase the probability of achieving the desired goal.[8]

Instrumental contact occurs when group members perceive that intergroup contact increases the probability of goal achievement, while dysfunctional contact occurs when group members perceive that intergroup contact reduces the probability of goal achievement. Goals can range from the more critical (e.g., when the Red Cross and the government work together to identify and provide for disaster victims) to the less critical (e.g., when a sports team's offense and defense work together to win a game). Alternatively, the goal can simply be enjoyment (e.g., when families go on vacation together). Regardless of how critical the goal is; if group members perceive that contact with another group will increase the likelihood of goal achievement, bias toward that group will be reduced more than when contact is perceived as dysfunctional.

While contact could also theoretically be instrumentally-neutral, such that it may be perceived to have no effect on the probability of goal achievement in the real world it is unlikely that group members will believe that working with another group has no effect on the probability of goal achievement. If the outgroup has no unique and relevant skills, ingroup members' attitudes toward the outgroup will likely influence their perceptions of instrumentality. If ingroup members have positive attitudes, they are likely to believe that working with the outgroup provides more people to perform goal-related tasks, which will decrease task completion time, increasing the perceptions of instrumentality. Conversely, if ingroup members have negative attitudes, they are likely to believe they will have to labor to combine the output from both groups, which will increase task completion time, decreasing the perceptions of instrumentality.

An illustration of how contact can be instrumental and reduce bias comes from Aronson's work on the jigsaw classroom.[9] The purpose of the jigsaw classroom is to maximize cooperation between majority and minority groups (e.g., Hispanics and Whites or the mentally healthy and mentally ill) and create a situation in which ingroup members must work with outgroup members in order to do well in the class. In the jigsaw classroom, students are assigned first to learning groups, where each group learns a different part of new material. For example, if students are learning about countries, each learning group may learn about a different country. After each group has learned the new material, the members are re-assigned to new heterogeneous (with respect to majority and minority group membership) teaching groups, in order to maximize intergroup contact. In each teaching group there is a single representative from each learning group and each representative teaches the other students about the material he or she learned in his or her respective learning group. Contact is instrumental because each member of the teaching group must rely on the other members in order to learn all the material. In other words, majority and minority students cannot succeed at the goal of doing well on the test without learning from each other. Research has shown that after being in a jigsaw classroom students express less bias and develop more cross-group friendships than students in a regular classroom, providing initial evidence that instrumental contact reduces bias. [10]

Superordinate Goals with Instrumentality

Upon initial examination, it may appear that the concept of instrumentality is not distinct from Sherif's concept of superordinate goals, and although there are similarities, there are also differences. [11] Both concepts involve groups cooperating on tasks because both groups' chances of success are increased by working together. Indeed, cooperation during the Robber's Cave study conforms to the definitions of both superordinate goals and instrumentality. The two groups of campers worked together (finding leaks to the camp's water supply, pooling their money together to rent a movie, and pushing a van carrying their lunch) because without their collective efforts they would not have been able to reach their goals.

One of the important differences between superordinate goals and instrumentality is that the concept superordinate of goals does not address what happens when groups cooperate, but their members believe that intergroup cooperation will decrease the probability of achieving their goal. This circumstance is addressed explicitly by instrumentality in terms of dysfunctional cooperation. Specifically, this perspective proposes that dysfunctional cooperation will exacerbate rather than reduce bias. Thus, researchers (including Sherif) have not distinguished between instrumental and dysfunctional cooperation and their influences on bias. Specifically it is proposed that instrumental cooperation reduces bias, and dysfunctional cooperation increases bias.[12]

A less important distinction between the concepts of instrumentality and superordinate goals lies in whether a group could achieve the goal by itself with enough time but that intergroup cooperation would facilitate goal achievement. According to Sherif, superordinate goals exist when the two groups could never attain the goal without their collective efforts.[13] According to instrumentality, a group may have the resources to achieve a goal on its own, but if working with the outgroup decreases the time or effort necessary to achieve the goal cooperation would be regarded as instrumental.

The Mutual Intergroup Differentiation Model

An early study examining the Mutual Intergroup Differentiation model provides support for the possibility that whether contact is instrumental influences bias.[14] The Mutual Intergroup Differentiation Model proposes that group members feel distinctiveness threat if the in— and outgroup are not different from one another along important and salient dimensions during intergroup contact. To reduce distinctiveness threat group members will manufacture intergroup differentiation (i.e., increase the salience of important intergroup differences), resulting in intergroup bias.[15] To test this model, letters and science majors were divided into distinct groups by their majors. The groups were given two pages of information with the task of re-writing the information and adding graphs, after which their work would be combined.

In the no differentiation condition, intended to create distinctiveness threat, each group was given one page of information and told to re-write the text and prepare the graphs. Thus both groups were given identical and undifferentiated assignments. In the differentiation condition, each group was given a different task: the sciences majors created graphs, and the letters majors re-wrote the text. Therefore in the differentiation condition, the groups were highly differentiated because each group's work was distinct from the other group's work. Groups in the differentiated task condition expressed less bias toward the outgroup than groups in the undifferentiated task condition.

Although the results are consistent with the Mutual Intergroup Differentiation model's predictions, they are also consistent with instrumentality's predictions. Contact was instrumental in the differentiation condition because each smaller group used its specific skills to the whole group's advantage to improve the quality of the final product (i.e., the sciences majors worked on the numbers and the letters majors worked on the text). Contact was dysfunctional in the no differentiation condition because both smaller groups' assignment were partially beyond their expertise (i.e., each had to work on text and graphs) and the participants may have thought they would need to spend extra time and energy combining both distinct group's contributions into one final product. Therefore, the findings also support instrumentality's prediction that when contact is instrumental, bias will be reduced more than when contact is dysfunctional.

The Effect of Cooperative Success or Failure

Research on the effect of intergroup success and failure on bias supports the possibility that instrumentality matters because when groups succeed at a cooperative task intergroup bias is decreased relative to if they fail. [16] People are motivated to think positively about themselves and their groups, and therefore after failure the participants probably expressed more bias because they blamed the other group for the collective failure. [17] If group members believed that working with the outgroup is what caused the failure, by definition group members would have perceived the cooperation as dysfunctional. This research supports the idea that dysfunctional cooperation increases bias, however, the researchers did not directly assess whether groups attributed the failure to the outgroup. Additionally, the research design does not allow us to draw any conclusions about whether there is an effect of instrumental cooperation (i.e., there was no condition in which the group members believed that without the outgroup they would have failed).

Instrumentality in Diversity Research

Research on the effect of perceptions of diversity supports the possibility that instrumentality matters because the more members of diverse groups value diversity, the more they identify with their diverse group.[18] Previous research has shown that as ingroup identification increases, positivity toward the ingroup increases. [19] Taken together, these findings suggest that when members of diverse groups value diversity they are more likely to feel positively toward all the members of the group than when they don't value diversity. In other words, when group members feel that working with different others (for example, an outgroup) is beneficial, they will likely evaluate those different others more positively than if they feel that working with different others is harmful.

Casting van Knippenberg's conditions in terms of instrumentality provides further support for the instrumentality's possible benefits. Participants learned that two fictitious cognitive styles exist: "Type H" and "Type P", that the two thinking types generated different solutions to similar problems, and that they would be working on a task later with three other participants. [20] Participants in the pro-diversity condition learned that their workgroup's task was to generate as many unique solutions to a problem as possible. Participants in the pro-homogeneity condition learned that their workgroup's task was to generate as many overlapping ideas as possible, such that each contribution would only count if three of the four participants generated the same solution. Further, participants were either led to believe that their workgroup was either homogenous or heterogeneous with respect to thinking type. The results indicated that participants who believed they were in a diverse workgroup identified more strongly with the workgroup when they were in the pro-diversity condition relative to participants in the pro-homogeneity condition. Participants who believed they were in a homogeneous workgroup identified more strongly with the workgroup when they were in the pro—homogeneity condition relative to participants in the pro-diversity condition.

The manipulations of perceptions of the ingroup are diversity and diversity's value are also manipulations of instrumentality, and the results suggest that instrumentality matters. When participants felt that working with the outgroup would be instrumental (i.e., working with the opposite cognitive style would help achieve the goal of generating unique solutions), they identified more with the workgroup than when they believed working with the outgroup would be dysfunctional (i.e., working with the opposite cognitive style would undermine the goal of generating similar solutions). As higher levels of ingroup identification lead to more positive evaluations of the workgroup, van Knippenberg's research implies that the more working with another group is considered instrumental, the more positively the other group will be regarded. [21]

Whether or not diversity itself is instrumental depends on the group's goals. Diverse groups tend to be more creative, and therefore if the group's goals are facilitated by creativity, working with diverse others should be instrumental. [22] However, there is a curvilinear relationship between diversity and creativity, such that at extremely low and high levels of diversity creativity is low, and at optimal levels of diversity creativity is maximized. This curvilinear relationship is due to the need for group members to be able to contribute unique ideas, but also for them to understand each other and have a certain degree of overlap between ideas and experiences. [23] When diversity is extremely low the number of unique ideas is reduced, and when diversity is extremely high understanding and common previous experiences are reduced. When diversity is at optimal levels the diverse group can generate unique ideas while still sharing enough of a common experience for understanding and agreement to exist. In addition to optimal levels of diversity inducing instrumentality, as detailed above, the extent to which diversity is valued will also contribute to whether diversity itself is perceived as instrumental, such that the more individuals value diversity, the more they will perceive working in a diverse group as instrumental.

Reinforcement Theory

The idea that instrumental contact will reduce bias more than dysfunctional contact is consistent with reinforcement theory. Reinforcement theory predicts that an association between the outgroup and the positive affect from experiencing a positive event is sufficient to increase liking toward the outgroup. [24] From a reinforcement theory perspective, attraction between relationship partners exists because people learn to associate positive events with a specific other, which causes them to have positive attitudes toward that other. [25] Reinforcement theory has been supported with research showing that when positive events are associated with a stranger, like a stranger delivering candy or good news about a test, liking increases toward the stranger, even when the stranger did not cause the event (i.e., the stranger was the messenger). [26]

Reinforcement theory also supports the possibility that instrumentality matters because both theories would predict that whether contact is instrumental or dysfunctional will likely impact how much groups working together feel like a single unit. Instrumentality theory predicts that the more group members believe working with the outgroup is necessary for goal achievement, the more likely they are to think of everyone as working together as a single unit to achieve the same goal. Reinforcement would also increase perceptions of the groups forming a single unit, as when people are in a positive mood (which must occur in order for reinforcement to occur) they are more likely to have broad and inclusive categorizations.[27] According to the Common Ingroup Identity Model, perceptions that two distinct groups form a single unit can have a large impact on evaluations and behavior toward outgroup members.[28]

The Common Ingroup Identity Model

Drawing from Allport's circles of inclusion, which shows that people can be categorized along ever-broader dimensions (e.g., families, neighborhoods, counties, nations, etc.), the Common Ingroup Identity Model posits that when others, who would otherwise be regarded as outgroup members, are categorized as sharing membership in a broader and more inclusive ingroup (including the self), bias is less than when categorization is narrow and exclusive.[29] There are three different representations that members could have that characterize the boundary between groups: separate groups, one group, and dual identity.

When a separate groups representation exists, people perceive that only membership in the distinct groups are important and salient, for example believing that only political party is significant when categorizing fellow countrymen (e.g., others are categorized as Republicans or Democrats). When a one-group representation exists, people perceive that a superordinate group encompasses both distinct groups, and only the superordinate group membership is important and salient, for example believing that only nationality is significant when categorizing fellow countrymen (e.g. others are categorized only as Americans). When a dual identity representation exists, people perceive that membership in both the distinct groups and the superordinate group is important and salient. Members of the distinct groups share an important and salient membership in the superordinate group, yet there are still unique and important characteristics that belong solely to each distinct group, for example, believing that both political party and nationality is important (e.g., others are categorized as Republicans or Democrats and as Americans).

Instrumentality theory would predict that when contact is instrumental a more inclusive representation is more likely because the groups only succeed by coordinating and working jointly, which causes the distinct groups' identities to become less salient and the superordinate identity to become more salient. Conversely, when contact is dysfunctional, a more exclusive representation is probably more likely because working together undermines goal attainment. If group members feel that the outgroup is preventing goal attainment they will likely attempt to disassociate from the outgroup, which causes the distinct group identities to become more salient and the superordinate identity to become less salient. Reinforcement theory would also predict that when contact is instrumental a more inclusive representation is more likely because when people are in a positive mood they are more likely to have broad and inclusive categorizations, and being in a positive mood is a necessary precursor to reinforcement (i.e., reinforcement occurs when people associate their positive moods with another person). [30]

Different representations of the intergroup context are likely associated with the language used in classifying members of varying groups. [31] When contact is instrumental people may be more likely to have inclusive categorizations and use the word "we," and conversely if contact is dysfunctional people may be more likely to have exclusive categorizations and to use the words "us" and "them". Compared to words like "them" and words like "we" have a more positive association; and therefore prime a stronger sense of similarity and collective self-identity. [32] This simple difference in language can have a profound effect on evaluations of intergroup relationships because relationships are rated as closer when "we", compared to "us" and "them", is used. [33] Therefore, as perceptions of instrumentality increase perceptions of an inclusive superordinate identity also likely increase, and as a result bias decreases and inclusive language increases.

While both instrumentality and reinforcement predict that instrumental contact will reduce bias, and that the relationship between contact and bias is mediated by one group representations, instrumentality's contribution to the beneficial effects of contact is likely greater than simply producing reinforcement. According to the theory of instrumentality, instrumental contact reduces bias because ingroup members believe that they would not achieve the goal without the outgroup members' contributions, which causes them to feel more positively toward outgroup members. According to reinforcement theory, instrumental contact would reduce bias because outgroup members become associated with a positive event (i.e., goal achievement), which causes them to feel more positively toward outgroup members. In other words, if reinforcement alone accounted for instrumentality's effects, outgroup members would only need to be present when ingroup members learn of their goal achievement, and not actually be integral to goal achievement. As the perception that the outgroup provided a necessary contribution is essential to instrumentality, reinforcement does not likely account for instrumentality's effects.

In summary, Deschamps and Brown's study of the mutual intergroup differentiation model, Worchel's research on the effect of failed cooperation, van Knippenberg's research on the effects of perceptions of diversity's value, and reinforcement theory all lend support to the possibility that perceptions of instrumentality will influence bias.[34] The extent to which contact is perceived as instrumental is likely to depend on two opposing factors: how much working with the outgroup increases the probability of goal achievement and the costs for doing so.[35]

Factors that Influence Instrumentality

What could be gained by working with another group? The nature of the intergroup task likely contributes to perceptions of instrumentality and Steiner's classification system for tasks can be used to evaluate how task type could influence perceived instrumentality.[36] He identified three dimensions along which tasks can be categorized: divisibility, maximization versus optimization, and interdependence.

Divisibility is determined by whether it is possible to divide the tasks into subtasks. For example, a flight crew preparing a plane for flight is a divisible task, whereas solving a simple Math problem is a unitary (i.e., non-divisible) task. When tasks are divisible, intergroup contact is more likely to be instrumental than when the tasks are unitary because with unitary tasks only one group is needed to generate the desired outcome and nothing is necessarily gained by adding more people. Further, if a task is divisible, each group might have unique skills that are applicable to completing the subtasks.

Maximization versus optimization distinguishes whether the task is best achieved by generating as much as possible regardless of quality (maximization) or generating a single high quality product (optimization). For example, political groups posting flyers for a rally is a maximization task, whereas a medical team diagnosing a patient's illness is an optimization task. Maximizing tasks are likely to be perceived as more instrumental for intergroup contact because two or more groups can usually accomplish more than one group (i.e., group size usually matters with maximizing tasks). With optimizing tasks, whether the outcome can be improved by contact with another group depends upon whether group members believe their group could produce an acceptable level of quality on its own. When the task can be categorized as divisible but also optimizing and each of the two groups possess different skills or expertise relevant to each of the subtasks, intergroup contact and cooperation may be perceived as especially instrumental. For example, architects and doctors working together to design the best possible hospital building is both a divisible and optimizing task.

Interdependence is composed of five categories and is determined by how individual outputs are combined to form the final output. Cooperation is more likely to be instrumental with additive, disjunctive, and discretionary tasks. When a task is additive, groups' separate products can be added together such that the more that is produced the better the group's outcome; for example, when organizations combine their separate resources to raise money for charity. When a task is disjunctive, a single product is chosen from all those produced to represent the overall group's product. A good example of this is when members of a fraternity choose the best flag football players among them to represent the fraternity. When a task is discretionary, groups can determine the best division of labor: for example groups choosing how to partition a job. When a task is averaging, the individual outcomes are averaged to create the group outcome: for example assessing a school's performance by averaging all of the classes' performances. When a task is conjunctive, the group's performance is determined by the worst performance: for example, an edited volume cannot go to press until the slowest authors submit their chapters.

Intergroup contact and cooperation are more instrumental with additive, disjunctive, and discretionary task types than with averaging or conjunctive tasks because either the group's outcome is certain to be better as with additive tasks, or the group can use outcomes from both groups' members as they choose as with disjunctive and discretionary tasks. Whether averaging and conjunctive tasks are considered instrumental for cooperation will depend on the outgroup's potential performance (i.e., is it likely that the outgroup will perform well?), because each individual outcome will have an impact on the overall outcome. Groups will have to evaluate whether working with the outgroup to complete averaging or conjunctive tasks will increase or decrease the chance of achieving the desired outcome. When the outgroup's contribution is excellent averaging and conjunctive tasks are likely to be instrumental, and when the outgroup's contribution is poor averaging and conjunctive tasks are likely to be dysfunctional.

What are the costs of working together with another group? Both the perceived harmony of the intergroup relationship and the effect of working together on the length of time required to complete the task jointly contribute to the potential costs of intergroup interaction. The better the quality of the relationship, the less of a sacrifice working together requires. When intergroup harmony exists, working together should be relatively smooth and therefore would not be costly. Conversely, the more conflict-ridden the relationship, the more uncomfortable group members will be when initially working together. Anxiety often occurs in intergroup interactions, which can create a desire to avoid outgroup members.[37] In instances of extreme intergroup hostility, group members may feel physically threatened by outgroup members, and could be sacrificing a sense of security to work together.

The effect of working together on the length of time required to complete the task depends both on the specific task required and the outgroup's relative competence. A good example is Steiner's typology to examine how features of the task could influence how long it would take to combine the output from two groups. Maximizing, divisible, additive, disjunctive, and discretionary tasks are likely to lend themselves to intergroup cooperation because the outcome can only improve by adding more people to work on the task. Whether completion time is reduced by working with another group on tasks that are unitary, averaging, conjunctive, or require optimization depends on perceptions of the quality of both group's work. If the ingroup has confidence in its own skills and believes that working alone would be sufficient to produce the desired outcome, working with the outgroup may be perceived as increasing completion time simply because it will take more time to coordinate activities or to combine the two groups' contributions. Conversely, if the ingroup believes that working with the outgroup could reduce task completion time, the higher the perceived quality of the outgroup's contribution the more likely contact will be perceived as instrumental.

In summary, research from different areas within social psychology supports the possibility that instrumentality may be an additional moderator of the relationship between contact and bias. Although Deschamps and Brown's study was meant to support the mutual intergroup differentiation model, differences in perceived instrumentality also explain the results.[38] Evidence from research on the effect of intergroup success or failure and on the effect of valuing diversity; has also supported instrumentality's potential moderating role.[39] Further, the task type, perceived quality of the outgroup's contribution, previous intergroup relations, and reward size likely influence perceptions of instrumentality.

It has been proposed that instrumentality may be an important moderator of the relationship between contact and bias; such that bias will be reduced the most when contact is instrumental and the least when contact is dysfunctional. Further, it has been proposed that instrumentality will reduce bias by improving attitudes toward outgroup members as they have become important contributors to a desirable goal, without necessarily changing attitudes toward ingroup members. When contact is instrumentally neutral, whether contact reduces or exacerbates bias depends on the pre-existing climate between the two groups.

CHAPTER FOUR

In Group Bias

In the Balkans, in the Middle East, in Northern Ireland, and in countless other locales throughout the world, ingroup bias continues to be a pervasive and serious problem. Ingroup bias refers to the tendency to evaluate one's own membership group (the ingroup) more favorably than a non-membership group (the outgroup).[1] Research on ingroup bias has had a long history in social psychology.

A classic example of empirical research is the Robber's Cave study by Sherif, Harvey, White, Hood, and Sherif.[2] In this field study young boys were put into competing groups, in order to examine the effects of intergroup competition on intergroup attitudes. Results showed consistent and sometimes extreme ingroup bias. However, intergroup interactions are not necessary for ingroup bias to occur. Billig and Tajfel demonstrated that ingroup bias also occurs in artificial laboratory groups, groups that were created by such minimal distinctions as the picking members using the game rock, paper, scissors or the flip of a coin.[3] This "minimal group" paradigm has often been used as a tool for studying ingroup bias.[4]

Creating artificial groups to study ingroup bias is a well-established methodology.[5] The value of artificial groups is based in part on the understanding that there are advantages to studying intergroup phenomena in a context that eliminates historical events or personal involvement that may cloud an understanding of the fundamental mechanisms of the phenomenon being studied. Tajfel and Turner stated that when laboratory groups are anonymous and have no interaction "these groups are cognitive and can be referred to as *minimal*."[6] As a result, employing artificial groups in the study of ingroup bias is often referred to as the *minimal group paradigm* based on the work of Tajfel and his colleagues. The intent underlying minimal group studies is to ensure equivalent cognitive and emotional significance, allowing for an examination of ingroup bias in its simplest and purest form. [7]

From real groups such as ethnicities in the Balkans, to groups as artificial as those created in the laboratory by Billig and Tajfel, individuals differentially evaluate their ingroup relative to an outgroup. [8] Understanding why this differential evaluation occurs are important given the extreme levels of ingroup bias that may occur in the real world. The predominant approach to understanding ingroup bias has centered on social cognition explanations. Tajfel stated that " . . . the etiology of intergroup relations cannot be properly understood without the help of an analysis of their cognitive aspects . . ." [9] These social cognitive explanations rely on perceptual aspects of group categorization as a key component of ingroup bias. However, Hogg and Abrams have noted that this purely cognitive analysis has difficulty in explaining the extremity of ingroup bias. [10] Hogg and Abrams suggest that a more complete understanding of ingroup bias must involve the subjective value of a group. [11] Therefore, two separate processes may be operating in ingroup bias: *cognitive processes*, the conscious intellective activities; and *affective processes*, an overall positive or negative subjective feeling.[12] There is much current interest in the relative contributions of cognition and affect to intergroup relations, but how these processes influence ingroup bias is not clear. [13]

Ingroup bias

Ingroup bias is a more favorable evaluation of the ingroup than the outgroup. [14] Ingroup bias was originally believed to be a negative evaluation of an outgroup based on affective or motivational needs of an individual. [15] In contrast to these early affective perspectives, later researchers postulated that ingroup bias was a purely cognitive phenomenon. For example, Tajfel stated that a "consideration of prejudice as a phenomenon in the minds rather than in the guts of men should take precedence . . ." [16] This cognitive perspective developed in part from minimal group research demonstrating that shared social history between groups was not necessary for ingroup bias to occur. [17] There are distinct advantages in using the minimal group paradigm when attempting to delineate the contributions of cognition and affect to ingroup bias.

Measurement of Ingroup Bias

Blanz, Mummendey, and Otten identified three types of dependent measures used in ingroup bias studies: behavioral measures, evaluative performance measures, and evaluative trait measures.[18]

Behavioral measures of ingroup bias.

In studies using behavioral measures researchers ask subjects to allocate points to both the ingroup and the outgroup on a series of resource allocation matrices. For example, Tajfel, Billig, Bundy, and Flament constructed six allocation matrices, each of which had the following general format.[19] Each matrix consisted of two rows of 14 numbers, with the numbers indicating points to be allocated to a group. Each row was labeled either "your group" or "other group." A box was drawn across the two rows for each set of 14 numbers. This process resulted in a matrix that included 14 different boxes, with each box having a differential resource allocation for the ingroup and the outgroup. The boxes had varying levels of points, with either the top row or the bottom row having a higher level of points. The structure of the matrices allowed subjects to maximize their own gain, minimize the outgroups' gain, or provide approximately equivalent resources to both groups. Subjects received the six matrices on six separate pages and checked a box to indicate their choice for allocating points. When researchers use resource allocation matrices ingroup bias is calculated as the difference between the ingroup and outgroup point allocations, with higher numbers indicating more ingroup bias (i.e., more positive evaluation of the ingroup).

Evaluative performance measures of ingroup bias.

In studies using evaluative performance measures researchers ask subjects to evaluate both their ingroup and the outgroup on the quality of the group process or group product.[20] For example, in Gaertner and Schopler's study subjects engaged in a "moon survival task" within their assigned groups.[21] Subjects then evaluated how good the solutions to the task were for both the ingroup and the outgroup. Similarly, Simon and Brown asked their school-age subjects to evaluate how good the ingroup and outgroup were at schoolwork. [22] When researchers use evaluative performance measures ingroup bias is calculated as the difference between the ingroup and outgroup performance evaluations, with higher numbers indicating more ingroup bias.

Evaluative trait measures of ingroup bias.

In studies using evaluative trait rating measures researchers ask subjects to evaluate both their ingroup and the outgroup on a series of evaluative traits such as "intelligent," and "kind." Occasionally researchers provide the traits on a bipolar dimension with semantic differential scales (e.g., "warm-cold," "stupid-intelligent"). For example, in Gerard and Hoyt's study subjects evaluated the groups using traits such as "warm-cold," "strong-weak," and "honest-dishonest." [23]

When researchers use bipolar trait evaluation measures ingroup bias is calculated as the difference between ingroup and outgroup trait evaluations, with higher numbers indicating more ingroup bias. Researchers more commonly provide the traits on a unipolar dimension with Likert type response scales (e.g., "warm," "intelligent"). For studies that use unipolar scales, some studies have used measures with only positive evaluative traits. For example Reichl used positive traits such as "cooperative," "practical," and "sincere." [24] When researchers use only positive traits the ratings for each group are summed and ingroup bias is then calculated as the difference between the ingroup evaluations and the outgroup evaluations, with higher scores indicating more ingroup bias . Other studies using unipolar scales have used measures with a combination of positive and negative evaluative traits. For example Thompson and Crocker used traits such as "friendly," "trustworthy," and "incompetent." [25] When a combination of positive and negative traits are used researchers reverse score the negative traits before the ratings for each group are summed. Ingroup bias is then calculated as the difference between the ingroup evaluations and the outgroup evaluations, with higher scores indicating more ingroup bias. Brewer suggested that the strength of the ingroup bias effect varies with the particular dimensions used to measure it, with positive dimensions such as "honest" eliciting the most ingroup bias. [26]

At present there are efforts to examine the relative contributions of cognition and affect to ingroup bias. These efforts focus exclusively on studies that measured ingroup bias with evaluative trait ratings. Evaluative trait rating measures lend themselves to an examination of the cognitive and affective components of ingroup bias that is not possible to examine with behavioral measures or with evaluative performance measures. Resource allocation measures may show ingroup bias because individuals cognitively believe that their group deserves more points, or because individuals affectively feel that their group deserves more points. Because the only information that may be gleaned from the individuals' behavior is the relative number of points allocated to each group, the process underlying that behavior cannot be extracted.

Evaluative performance measures may show ingroup bias because individuals cognitively believe that their group performed better, or because individuals affectively feel that their group performed better. Although it may be possible to extract the cognitive and affective components of the measures in these performance studies, there is a confound in these studies that would negate the utility of extracting cognition and affect. When groups engage in performing a task, there is in fact a difference between the two groups in their levels of performance. If a study finds "ingroup bias" it may be a reflection of areal performance difference between these groups, or biased attempts to accentuate the performance differences between these groups. If a study finds no difference in "ingroup bias" it may be a reflection of no difference in performance between the groups, or biased attempts to attenuate the performance differences between these two groups. Therefore, any attempts to delineate the relative contributions of cognition and affect in evaluative performance studies would suffer from the confound between group evaluations and group performance.

In studies that use evaluative trait ratings, it is possible to extract the cognitive and affective components of ingroup bias. Evaluative trait rating studies measure ingroup bias using discrete evaluative traits. It would be possible to extract the cognitive and affective attributes of each of each of these traits as an indicator of the contributions of cognition and affect to ingroup bias. For example, traits such as "friendly" and "honest" have a positive cognitive connotation, whereas traits such as "dull" and "stupid" have a negative cognitive connotation. Further, despite the similar cognitive connotation "dull" is less affectively intense than is "stupid." Therefore, it is possible to extract the cognitive and affective attributes of evaluative traits. The extraction of the cognitive and affective properties of traits has a long history in psychology. For example, Anderson examined the cognitive properties of traits, whereas Osgood, Succi, and Tannenbaum rated the affective properties of traits.[27] More recently, Rothbart and Park examined the cognitive properties of traits, whereas Whissell examined the affective properties of several words including traits.[28]

Moderators of Ingroup Bias

Ingroup bias occurs in studies using simple categorization into dichotomous groups even in the absence of shared history or competitive settings.[29] Ingroup bias is a reliable phenomenon of moderate magnitude.[30] In the first meta-analytic integration of the ingroup bias literature, Mullen found a moderate ingroup bias effect, with the ingroup evaluated more positively than the outgroup.[31] In a more recent meta-analytic integration Bettencourt found a weak ingroup bias effect.[32] Several moderators to the basic effect were discovered in both meta-analyses.

Group reality

A long-standing issue in the study of group dynamics is the possible difference between the study of real groups in natural environments versus the study of artificial groups in laboratories. Many researchers argue that studying artificial groups in laboratory settings allows for greater experimental control, enabling researchers to make causal inferences about the phenomenon being studied. However, this increased control may come at the expense of realism and the ability to generalize beyond the laboratory setting. Shaw discussed the possibility that results from artificial groups might be weaker than results from real groups due to the stronger potency of variables when studied outside the laboratory.[33] The general ingroup bias effect in Mullenet was weaker in artificial groups, than in real groups.[34] This general pattern of weaker ingroup bias in artificial groups was subsequently replicated by Bettencourt in 2001.

Relative ingroup size

One well-established aspect of group dynamics is that the relative sizes of the ingroup and the outgroup influence group processes and perceptions of the group. For example, Mullen and Hu examined the relative heterogeneity effect, i.e., the tendency to perceive greater variability among ingroup members than among outgroup members.[35] Results of Mullen and Hu's meta-analytic integration revealed that the perceived variability among the ingroup decreased as the size of the ingroup decreased.[36] Similarly, Mullen, Johnson, and Salas examined productivity in brainstorming groups.[37] Brainstorming refers to generating ideas within the context of a group. Results of their meta-analytic integration revealed that brainstorming productivity increased as the size of the ingroup decreased. In another study, Mullen and Copper examined the cohesiveness-performance effect, i.e., the expectation that a more cohesive group will perform better.[38] Results of Mullen and Copper's meta-analytic integration revealed that the cohesiveness-performance effect increased as the size of the ingroup decreased.[39] Finally, with regards to ingroup bias, Mullen examined ingroup bias as a function of relative ingroup size.[40] Results of their meta-analytic integration revealed that ingroup bias increased as the size of the ingroup decreased.

Taken together, the group size results presented above demonstrate clear and consistent effects of relative ingroup size. As the size of the ingroup decreases, the group is perceived as being more similar, becomes more productive, and engages in more ingroup bias. The importance of group size has been explained by both cognitive and affective factors. Mullen proposed from a cognitive perspective that a salient group is more likely to be cognitively represented at a prototype level whereas a non-salient group is more likely to be cognitively represented at an exemplar level.[41]

Individuals engaging in prototype representation perceive a category as an average of the members of that category, whereas those engaging in exemplar representation perceive a category as a collection of individual members of that category. "The group to which we pay the most attention, by virtue of its proportionate size, is the group which will be cognitively represented with the simplest strategy."[42] Therefore, ingroup bias may be stronger in smaller groups because the smaller group is more salient, and membership in that group is therefore more cognitively salient to its members. From an affective perspective, Brewer proposed that individuals have competing needs for similarity to others and distinctiveness from others. Brewer concluded that when the size of the group is too large, the groups "are not sufficiently differentiated to constitute meaningful social groups."[43] Therefore, ingroup bias may be stronger in smaller groups because the smaller group satisfies a need for similarity, and membership in that group is therefore more affectively meaningful to its members.

Group status

Different groups may obtain different levels of status based on existing (real group) status hierarchies such as gender or race.[44] For example, Sidanius and Pratto have shown that there is a high degree of consensus regarding ethnic group status within the United States, with Whites afforded the highest status and Latinos afforded the lowest status.[45] Interestingly, this consensus was present across many different ethnic groups including the lower status groups. Different groups may also obtain different levels of status in artificial groups. For example, Crocker and Luhtanen randomly assigned participants to receive either group success or group failure feedback after taking a bogus personality test.[46] The results demonstrated that the high status group (success feedback) engaged in ingroup bias whereas the low status group (failure feedback) did not engage in ingroup bias. These results contradicted Brewer's narrative review of the ingroup bias literature in which she suggested that lower status groups engage in ingroup bias whereas higher status groups may engage in outgroup bias.[47] Mullen's meta-analysis found that, in real groups, the ingroup bias effect showed a (non-significant) tendency to decrease as the status of the ingroup increased, whereas in artificial groups, ingroup bias increased as the status of the ingroup increased.[48] These results also contradict Brewer's suggestion. In fact, Mullen found that lower status groups engaged in outgroup bias, that is they rated the outgroup more positively than the ingroup.[49]

Bettencourt's meta-analysis replicated the pattern of results found in Mullen. In real groups, there was no effect of group status on ingroup bias. In artificial groups, ingroup bias was stronger in high status than in low status groups. Taken together, the group status results presented above demonstrate that individuals tend to afford different social groups different levels of status. The importance of group status has been explained by both cognitive and affective factors.

From a cognitive perspective status expectations theory suggests that expectations associated with a group include beliefs regarding the ability and skills of members of that group.[50] Higher status groups are believed to be more respected and competent than lower status groups.[51] Therefore both the high status group and the low status group will evaluate a high status group positively, meaning that the high status group engages in ingroup bias whereas the low status group does not engage in ingroup bias. From an affective perspective, social identity theory suggests that individuals receive part of their self-worth from their group memberships and therefore need to view their groups in a positive light.[52]

Therefore, high status groups should be able to engage in ingroup bias on any dimension.

However, for low status groups the social identity perspective appears to contradict the effects of status on ingroup bias. As discussed above low status groups tend to engage in outgroup bias, which would not satisfy the need to view one's group in a positive light.

System justification theory provides a solution to this contradiction. System justification theory suggests that all groups have a motivation toward ingroup bias, but that low status groups must deal with the reality of their lower social status.[53] Therefore, high status groups should be able to engage in ingroup bias on any dimension whereas low status groups should not be able to engage in ingroup bias on dimensions relevant to the status distinction.

Evaluation relevance

Researchers have examined how group dynamics are affected by the relevance of an evaluative task to the characteristics that define the groups. Brewer suggested that ingroup bias is more likely on evaluative traits relevant to the group categorization, and less likely on evaluative traits irrelevant to the group categorization.[54] For example, Wilson and Robinson asked participants to rate the ingroup and outgroup after engaging in a Prisoner's Dilemma game in which participants must choose to either cooperate or compete with each other.[55] The evaluative rating traits included motive traits (e.g., cooperative, fair), sociometric traits (e.g., likeable, friendly), personality traits (e.g., anxious, dependent), and ability traits (e.g., capable, intelligent). The strongest ingroup bias occurred on the motive traits, which were directly relevant to the experimental task, with the next strongest bias occurring on the sociometric traits. Ingroup bias did not occur on the personality traits or the ability traits. Brewer, Manzi, and Shaw asked participants to rate the ingroup and outgroup after a minimal group categorization experience that included a perceptual task described as an "intelligence test" predictive of career success.[56] Participants received bogus feedback about their group's performance, and then rated the ingroup and outgroup on ability traits relevant to the group categorization (e.g., able, intelligent) and social traits irrelevant to the group categorization (e.g., warm, kind). Results showed an interaction between evaluative relevance and group status. High status (success) groups engaged in more ingroup bias than low status (failure) groups on the relevant traits, but not on the irrelevant traits. Mullen's meta-analysis similarly demonstrated that for high status groups ingroup bias was stronger when the comparison dimension was more relevant to the group categorizations, whereas for low status groups ingroup bias was stronger when the comparison dimension was less relevant to the group categorizations.[57] Bettencourt subsequently replicated this result.

The evaluation relevance results presented above demonstrate that individuals will engage in ingroup bias to the extent that the evaluation of the groups is related to the categorization of the groups. The importance of evaluation relevance has been explained by both cognitive factors and affective factors. From a cognitive perspective Brewer discussed the importance of evaluation relevance through Tversky's feature matching model.[58] According to Tversky, the perceived similarity of two objects is a function of their common and distinct features.[59] Some features will be assigned more weight depending upon the context of the comparison. Therefore, two objects may be judged as dissimilar in one context but similar in another context. Additionally, two groups of objects may be judged to be dissimilar or similar depending upon the context.

When two groups of objects are judged, Tajfel and Wilkes demonstrated that the difference between the groups is accentuated to the extent that there is a relationship between the group classification and the judgment process.[60] In other words, when groups of objects are evaluated on properties related to the grouping of the objects, stronger differences between the groups emerge. Therefore, when the objects being evaluated are groups of people, the relevance of the evaluative terms is an important factor in ingroup bias. From an affective perspective, Tajfel and Turner discussed the importance of evaluation relevance in terms of social identity.[61] According to Tajfel and Turner, individuals satisfy a need to feel good about their groups through comparisons with other groups.[62] These other groups must be perceived as a relevant comparison group, and the social situation must allow for a comparison on relevant evaluations. Because not all group differences involve meaningful evaluations, comparisons on irrelevant evaluative traits would not help high status individuals to feel good about their group. However, in low status groups a comparison on the irrelevant traits is the only comparison that would allow low status individuals to feel good about their group, a strategy Tajfel and Turner labeled "social creativity."

Group permeability

Group membership may be ascribed or achieved. Ascribed groups are those such as gender or race that are fixed at birth. Achieved groups are those such as team or friendship that are attained through efforts on the part of the individual.[63] For ascribed groups the boundaries are always fixed; one either is or is not a member of that group and the group boundary is impermeable. However, for achieved groups there is the possibility that one's standing in relation to the group will change. An individual could become a member of an achieved group through efforts to attain that membership, and the group boundary is therefore potentially permeable. For some types of groups the boundaries are more permeable than for other types of groups.

For example, one can obtain membership in many religious groups and civic organizations simply by professing a desire to be a member of that group. However, to obtain membership in fraternities or to obtain U.S. citizenship there are indoctrination rites and examinations before group membership is conferred. Achieved groups therefore have varying levels of permeability of their group boundaries.

Tajfel and Turner suggested that low status group members may attempt to move into the high status group when group boundaries are permeable, in an effort to enhance their social identity.[64] Tajfel and Turner further suggested that when group boundaries are permeable, ingroup bias will be weaker in low status groups but stronger in high status groups. These contrasting effects will occur because low status group members are less likely to favor the ingroup (and denigrate the outgroup) if they are attempting to leave their ingroup for the outgroup. Conversely, high status members are more likely to favor the ingroup and denigrate the outgroup because the permeable group boundary threatens the cohesiveness of their group and therefore threatens their social identity. Researchers have provided some support for these predictions. Ellemers, Wilke, and van Knippenberg found that low status groups showed less ingroup bias when group boundaries were permeable than when impermeable.[65] Bettencourt's meta-analysis similarly showed that the difference in ingroup bias between high and low status groups was stronger when group boundaries were permeable than when impermeable.[66]

The results presented above demonstrate that when group boundaries are permeable low status groups will engage in less ingroup bias whereas high status groups will engage in more ingroup bias. The importance of group boundary permeability has been explained by both cognitive and affective factors.

From a cognitive perspective, Brewer discussed the importance of group boundaries in terms of the salience of group boundaries.[67] In her qualitative review of the ingroup bias literature Brewer suggested that the more salient the group boundaries, the more likely an individual will be aware of a reason for the group categorization (i.e., the more likely the individual will see distinctions between the groups).[68] The reason behind the categorization provides an impetus for ingroup bias. More recently Brewer proposed that individuals seek affiliations with others that do not engender a loss of individuality.[69] Although Brewer did not comment directly on ingroup bias, she did suggest that groups must "maintain clear boundaries that differentiate them from other groups.[70] In other words, groups must maintain distinctiveness in order to survive".[71] Thus if group boundaries are too permeable, the group members may engage in ingroup bias in attempts to redefine the group boundaries. From an affective perspective, Tajfel and Turner discussed the importance of group permeability in terms of social identity.[72]

According to Tajfel and Turner, individuals satisfy a need to feel good about their groups through comparisons with other groups. When low status groups compare themselves with high status groups, the resulting negative comparison does not satisfy the need to feel good about one's group. If the group boundaries are permeable, low status individuals may disassociate with their group and attempt to join the high status group, and therefore they would decrease their ingroup bias. If the group boundaries are impermeable, moving to the high status group is not possible, and therefore they would not decrease their ingroup bias. Conversely, when high status groups compare themselves with low status groups, the resulting positive comparison satisfies the need to feel good about one's group. If the group boundaries are permeable, individuals may associate more strongly with their group to defend the group boundaries, and therefore they would increase their ingroup bias. If the group boundaries are impermeable, defense of the group is not necessary, and therefore they would not increase their ingroup bias.

Ingroup Bias Moderators

Generally speaking ingroup bias is stronger in real groups, when the group size is small, when the group status is high, when the evaluation is relevant to the group categorization, and when the boundaries of the group are permeable. Based on the explanations that researchers have provided for these moderators, one common process that underlies all of these moderators is cognition.

Researchers have explained the effects of these moderators in terms of cognitive processes related to the representations of the groups, beliefs regarding the groups, feature recognition, and the salience of the groups. In all of these moderators, then, there may be a cognitive component eliciting ingroup bias. However, an alternative common process that may underlie all of these moderators is affect. Researchers have explained the effects of these moderators in terms of affective needs related to meaningful social groups, the self-worth that comes from these groups, and ways to deal with negative self-worth.

In all of these moderators, then, there may be an affective component eliciting ingroup bias. The evidence regarding these moderators, and previous theoretical integrations of these moderators, highlight the potential contributions of cognition and affect to ingroup bias. However, the relative contributions of cognition and affect to ingroup bias cannot be delineated based on a reading of the existing literature because previous ingroup bias studies have not systematically addressed the relative contributions of cognition and affect and because of the cognitive beliefs and affective feelings that already exist in real social groups.

Minimal Group Paradigm

Researchers choose ingroup bias in the minimal group paradigm for three reasons. First, the minimal group paradigm is the most common methodology for examining ingroup bias. Second, the minimal group paradigm provides methodological homogeneity across studies. Although there are slight differences between studies in the categorization process when creating minimal groups (e.g., dot estimation versus choice of painter), this variation is much less than the difference between studies that use real groups (e.g., Whites and Blacks versus homosexuals and heterosexuals). Third, the minimal group paradigm may eliminate any stereotypes and history of discrimination that exist between real groups.

Tajfel delineated the conditions of "minimal differentiation" between groups that came to be known as the minimal group paradigm.[73] These conditions are: a) no face to face interaction among subjects, within or between groups; b) anonymity of group membership; c) absence of any instrumental link between the basis for intergroup categorization and the response measure; and d) a response measure involving real and significant choices but of no direct utilitarian value to the subject.

Despite the clear description of the conditions that create a minimal group, subsequent research has often failed to adhere to these conditions. To be fair this lack of adherence is often in the service of testing a prediction regarding group interaction or competition. According to Reynolds, Turner, and Haslam interaction with either the ingroup or the outgroup, or even the knowledge of other's group membership, should be considered "quasi-minimal" groups. [74] Research supports the distinction between minimal and quasi-minimal. For example, Gaertner and Schopler found that interaction with the ingroup leads to stronger cognitive distinctions between the ingroup and the outgroup. [75] Doise and Sinclair found that ingroup bias becomes significantly stronger when ingroup members expect interaction, in part because subjects anticipate the possibility of engaging in ingroup bias at a behavioral level. [76] Because group interaction is enough to make a study quasi-minimal, studies that have groups engage in competition are clearly not minimal group studies. In fact, Gerard and Hoyt stated that studies that involve competition cannot be considered minimal group studies because competition itself is sufficient to account for ingroup bias. [77]

Although a discussion of "minimal" versus "quasi-minimal" groups may appear to be an academic exercise, the implications of a quasi-minimal methodology in the study of cognition and affect are quite real. Bodenhausen distinguished between "integral" affect and "incidental" affect in intergroup phenomena. [78] Integral affect is the emotion elicited by the social group itself. Incidental affect is the emotion elicited by situations unrelated to the intergroup context. When researching the study of cognition and affect, one of the goals is to understand the relative contribution of affect to ingroup bias. In Bodenhausen's terms, this goal would be to understand integral affect associated with ingroup bias. [79] In order to accomplish this goal it is necessary to eliminate incidental affect as a confounding variable. Citing the literature on the effects of affect on cognitive processes, Bodenhausen noted that if affect can influence social cognitive processing, then affect may influence the views of group members ."‥ for reasons having nothing to do with the group or its members". [80] If Bodenhausen is correct, then minimal group studies that allow incidental affect to occur may lead to ingroup bias based on situational cues unrelated to the group categorization process.

Minimal groups are defined as follows. First, the groups must have been created in the laboratory for the purposes of the study based on a relatively unimportant justification. For example, Rubin, Hewstone, and Voci asked participants to estimate the number of dots that appeared on an overhead transparency, and then ostensibly categorized participants as being in the over-estimator group or the under-estimator group.[81] This group distinction is based on a relatively unimportant justification, and the study is therefore a minimal group study. However, Rabbie, Benoist, Oosterbaan, and Visser formed laboratory union and management groups that engaged in negotiations regarding wages and vacation.[82] Although Rabbie created the groups for the purposes of the study, the nature of the project makes the distinction between the groups important, and therefore this study is not a minimal group study.[83] Second, the groups must have been created based on only one criterion.

For example, Eurich-Fulcer and Schofield asked participants to select one of two artists' paintings that appeared on a series of slides, and then categorized participants as being in the Klee preference group or the Kandinsky preference group.[84] This group distinction is based on only one criterion, and the study is therefore a minimal group study. Brown and Turner also asked participants to select photographs from a series of slides.[85] However, Brown and Turner categorized participants as preferring one of two photographers, and also one of two country scenes.[86] The combination of photographer and scene created a two factor crossed-categorization in which four different groups existed on the basis of two criteria. Therefore, Brown and Turner's study was not a minimal group study. Third, there must have been a minimum of interaction between the participants before ingroup bias was measured. For example, Andreapoulou and Houston categorized their participants into groups and then permitted no interaction between the groups before the evaluative ratings were completed.[87] Therefore, Andreapoulou and Houston's study was a minimal group study. However, Dion categorized his participants into groups and then required the groups to engage in an intergroup competition to win money before the evaluative ratings were completed.[88] Therefore, Dion's study was not a minimal group study.

Cognition and Affect

Researchers have argued that cognition and affect are independent processes, and the separation of psychological processes into their cognitive, affective, and behavioral components has been a longstanding tradition in social psychology. [89] The ability to examine thoughts and feelings as independent processes is somewhat contingent upon how one defines cognition and affect. [90] For the present purposes, cognition and affect can be distinguished as follows.

Defining Cognition

Despite the abundant use of the term cognition in social psychology, there has been relatively little effort directed toward defining what is meant by cognition. Averill has argued for two definitions of cognition, one that reflects intellective knowledge, and another that reflects all non-behavioral mental activity. [91] Averill's second definition follows the logic of Holyoak and Gordon, who pointed out that both cognition and affect can be rapid, automatic, and irrational. [92] From Holyoak and Gordon's viewpoint a distinction between the two processes is less important because both would be subsumed under one mental system. [93] However, as will be discussed below, evidence suggests that cognition and affect can be measured separately and that they have different effects on intergroup phenomena. Therefore, it appears that a definition of cognition needs to be more precise than just "all mental activity." Based on the definition used by Esses, Haddock, and Zanna, and on a compendium of distinguishable differences between cognition and emotion listed by Fiske and Taylor, in the present context the definition of cognition would be *intellective beliefs about a social target.* [94]

Defining Affect

Unlike cognition, the definition of affect has received much attention. While affect can be thought of as a broad generic term encompassing moods, emotions, and evaluations, most researchers suggest that affect is a subjective feeling that is not as strong as emotion. [95] Early researchers tended to use affect as a synonym for evaluation, but this use is problematic in part because it implies that an individual cannot evaluate social targets using intellective knowledge.[96] Affect has been defined as "an overall positive or negative subjective feeling", with "feeling states that may range from strongly positive to strongly negative".[97] Based on these definitions and also on the definition used by Esses, in the present context the definition of affect would be *subjective feelings about a social target.* [98]

Cognition and Affect in Other Intergroup Phenomena

Intergroup phenomena have often been explained with cognitively based theories and research, with varying emphasis on cognition in different periods including the current dominance of social cognition.[99] However, the heavy emphasis on social cognition has been questioned by social psychologists in recent years.

For example Bodenhausen stated that "although this cognitive analysis has been fruitful, it has become increasingly obvious that emotion is far too central a component of intergroup relations to be discarded by those who would understand intergroup phenomena".[100] Some efforts to demonstrate the importance of affect have led to mixed results. Jussim, Nelson, Manis, and Soffin examined the relative contributions of cognition and affect to bias in group evaluations.[101] In a series of studies, Jussim asked participants to evaluate a member of a socially valued group (e.g., heterosexuals) and a socially devalued group (e.g., homosexuals), and then examined the effects of cognition and affect on bias in group evaluations.[102] Evidence in two studies indicated that controlling for cognition did not eliminate bias, whereas controlling for affect did eliminate bias. However, two other studies in Jussim showed that controlling for cognition did eliminate bias.[103] This series of studies demonstrates that affect is involved in intergroup phenomena, but did not rule out the importance of cognition.

Research in other areas of intergroup phenomena has also found mixed evidence for the roles of cognition and affect. In a meta-analysis of illusory correlation studies, Johnson and Mullen coded studies for both the cognitive load and affective intensity of the evaluation measures.[104] Illusory correlation is the extent to which individuals perceive a relationship between two variables that does not exist. Illusory correlation studies examine the perceived relationship between group size and group behaviors. The typical result of these studies is that subjects recall more negative behaviors for the smaller group, despite no such relationship. Johnson and Mullen discovered that as either the cognitive load or the affective intensity of evaluation measures increased, the evaluation effect became weaker, suggesting that both cognition and affect are important in illusory correlation tasks.[105] Subsequent studies have demonstrated that cognition may be primary for some types of illusory correlation tasks (e.g., assignment), while affect may be primary for other illusory correlation tasks.[106]

As opposed to the mixed evidence discussed above, some evidence suggests that cognition may be the primary mechanism in intergroup phenomena. For example, Zanna, Haddock, and Esses assessed evaluations of four different social groups. [107] Zanna measured cognition and affect regarding each of the four groups and discovered that both cognition and affect were correlated with group evaluations. [108] However, multiple regression showed that cognition was a better predictor than affect of the evaluations for their more extreme social groups (Pakistanis and Homosexuals), suggesting that cognition may be the primary mechanism behind evaluations of at least some outgroups.

In contrast to the evidence for the primacy of cognition, other evidence suggests that affect may be the primary mechanism in intergroup phenomena. For example, Stangor, Sullivan, and Ford examined the roles of affect and cognition in evaluations of minority groups. [109] The researchers had participants indicate both cognitive beliefs and affective feelings about the minority group. Results of regression analyses indicated that affect was a better predictor of evaluations of minority groups when the simultaneous effects of affect and cognition were considered. Other evidence for the primacy of affect comes from Verkuyten. [110] Verkuyten asked participants to complete the Twenty Statements Test and a measure of ingroup preference. [111] The Twenty Statements Test asks subjects to list twenty answers to the question "Who am I?" Results showed no difference in ingroup preference between those participants who spontaneously listed ethnic group membership on the Twenty Statements Test and those who did not. However, participants who had rated their ethnicity as important showed significantly stronger ingroup preference.

These results suggest that mere ethnic group categorization may not be enough to elicit ingroup bias without considering the importance of ethnicity to the participants. In other words listing ethnicity (a cognitive categorization process) did not influence ingroup preference whereas rating ethnicity as important to oneself (a subjective affective process) did influence ingroup preference.

CHAPTER FIVE

Hind-Sight Bias

Consider the following excerpt taken from an interview between Matt Lauer, co-host of NBC's morning show "Today" and then Secretary of State Colin Powell:

> MR. LAUER: *Mr. Secretary, good morning to you.*
>
> SECRETARY POWELL: *Good morning, Matt.*
>
> MR. LAUER: *You know better than most people how difficult and deadly war can be.*
>
>   *You've served this country in different capacities in several wars. Did you ever think, sir, that we'd be sitting here a year and a half after the invasion of Iraq with 1,000 dead and almost 7,000 wounded and still no end in sight to the insurgency?*
>
> SECRETARY POWELL: *Well, of course, I couldn't have known that....* [1]

Once people know the outcome of an event they tend to feel that the outcome was both inevitable and foreseeable, this phenomenon having been coined *hindsight bias*.[2] There are times, however, when people do not show hindsight bias, as the above statement from the former Secretary of State Colin Powell illustrates. What would lead former secretary Powell to state so forcefully that he "couldn't have known" the direction that the Iraqi war would take? Why would he make such a judgment, when several senior State Department officials insist that former Secretary Powell had earlier advised President Bush that there were too few troops in Iraq, a concern that had been at the forefront from the time US troops entered Iraq in March 2003.[3] Former Secretary Powell has declared on numerous occasions that looking back to the beginning of the Iraqi war, the emotion that he feels most is regret that he played such a pivotal role in manufacturing support for US involvement in the war.[4] Could this emotion that former Secretary Powell continues to feel, regret, be a factor in his lack of hindsight bias? Would he have shown hindsight bias, and said instead, "We knew it would turn out like this," if the Iraqi war had ended as quickly and bloodlessly as the most optimistic predictions before the war and he instead felt satisfaction? Would he have said, "We knew it would turn out like this," if the outcome was the same, an ongoing and bloody war, but if he had not had been one of the principal people soliciting the US people's encouragement of the war and he instead felt disappointment?

The emotions we experience following the outcome of an event depends on our appraisals of the event, these being the specific pattern of evaluations and interpretations of the event factoring in elements above and beyond just the valence of the outcome.[5] Moreover, there is evidence that the emotional experiences people have mold the information that people use to make judgments of outcome likelihood, thereby influencing whether or not hindsight bias is evidenced.

Following negative outcomes, people tend to consider either how different things would have been had the state of the world been different, the disconfirmed expectancies that lead to disappointment, or people consider how different things would have been had they made a different choice, the bad decisions that lead to *regret*.[6] The positive complements to these two emotions have been relatively neglected, but help tell the full story of these emotions' influence. Following a positive outcome, when people feel their negative expectancies have been disconfirmed, they experience relief, and when people feel that they have made a good decision, they experience satisfaction. These two pairs of specific emotions differ on several appraisal dimensions, but what has been proposed that the most important difference is agency, which distinguishes whether the cause of the event outcome is the self, some other person, or the circumstance, not unlike cause attribution.[7] Disappointed and relieved people have circumstances-agency where they feel no responsibility for the outcome, while regretful and satisfied people have self-agency, so that they do feel responsibility for the outcome. It has been proposed that it is this distinction which leads to differential effects of these two pairs of emotions on hindsight bias.

"I Knew It All Along"

People tend to believe that they "knew it all along" and tend to exaggerate how inevitable the outcome was after they are informed of the outcome of an event. People's memory of the event and the factors leading up to it become distorted as knowledge of the outcome causes people to update the mental models they have of events. Fischhoff coined the term *creeping determinism* to refer to this readjustment. [8] New causal linkages are formed, and information that seemed important prior to outcome knowledge loses its salience, becoming de-emphasized. Hindsight bias effects are robust. [9] Hindsight phenomena has been observed in both laboratory and non-laboratory settings, and in domains as diverse as news events, historical events, findings of scientific experiments, almanac questions, brainteasers, political elections, medical judgments, legal judgments, and even for gustatory judgments. [10]

Why do people exhibit hindsight bias? Some of the possible explanations for the existence of the hindsight bias fall under the umbrella of motivational explanations, suggesting that hindsight bias is induced by our "hopes, fears, wishes, desires and apprehensions". [11] Evidence of self-serving motivations behind the hindsight bias has been proffered by making links to personality variables such as the need for predictability, the desire to self-present, and the need for cognition as well as situational factors such as monetary incentives, outcome favorableness, task involvement, and attributions. [12]

On the other hand, some explanations for the hindsight bias are purely cognitive, such as memory impairments and reconstruction biases. [13] Hoffrage and colleagues have proposed the

Reconstruction After Feedback with Take The Best (RAFT) model, where hindsight bias is described as a by-product of the adaptive process of updating event knowledge. [13] Given that specific emotions are associated with appraisals that take into account people's needs, goals, ability to cope with consequences, self-ideals, and social norms. [14]

Why is there such a quantity of literature centered on the hindsight bias? The practical implications of the hindsight bias are significant, and can have consequences as profound as death, and losing billions of dollars, or as mundane as performing badly on an academic quiz. The significance of the hindsight bias goes beyond just affecting a person's perception of the probability that an event should have occurred. Essentially, hindsight bias prevents people from learning from their successes and their failures. It causes people to feel overconfident in their abilities since they feel as if they could have predicted the outcomes of events. In a medical setting, students may overestimate their diagnostic abilities after reading case studies that document the decisions others have made and the outcomes that have resulted.[15] Louie gives an example of the ultimate cost of hindsight bias, citing Jon Krakauer's description of a tragic Mount Everest from his book *Into Thin Air* where several hikers lost their lives.[16] A possible explanation suggested for their deaths was the overconfidence of their guide who, having led numerous climbing expeditions in the past, may have taken unnecessary risks. Hindsight distortion would have led to him to think that he made correct decisions in the past and therefore under-compensate for the bad weather they encountered.

Fearing the touted "dark side" of the hindsight bias, researchers have, almost from its identification, tried to reduce or totally eliminate this bias. It was first believed that since hindsight bias is associated with increased confidence in the known outcome; that just thinking of many possible alternative outcomes would provide a remedy, but instead it was more often the case that a *back-fire effect* occurred and that the hindsight bias was intensified.[17] Manipulating subjective accessibility experiences was found to cause attenuation of the hindsight bias, whether this manipulation was cognitive or physiological.[18] This reduction in hindsight bias, termed the "it could never have happened" effect, was shown by participants in manipulations including those who had listed many thoughts about the known outcome and those who contracted their brows when considering the known outcome.

"How Do I Feel About It?" and Specific Emotions

Schwarz' Feelings-as-Information model suggests that the feelings that people have are important sources of information when judgments are being made.[19] When this model was first unveiled, the focal point was the effect of moods and mood inductions on unrelated judgments, comparing the types of judgments made after positive or negative mood inductions.[20] More recently, researchers have suggested that such a limited focus (1) does not fully account for the results that past research has found when examining the effect of simple mood inductions on judgments, and (2) is lacking the complexity and predictive power that bringing specific emotions into the picture would provide. [21] Consequently, the "Feelings" in this "Feelings-as-Information" model has been expanded to include emotions as well as moods. Schwarz and Clore distinguished emotions from moods based on differences such as how specific the affect-inducing targets are where emotions tend to be specific, intense, and caused by a particular event whereas moods tend to be more amorphous, and additionally based on duration where emotions tend to be more time limited. [22]

Emotional experience has been investigated extensively in the realm of judgment and decision making where (1) emotional reactions are predicted based on pre-outcome information of expected probability and magnitude of the outcome, and (2) behavioral choices are predicted based on the emotion elicited prior to people's choices. [23]

Research has expanded to look at the effect of emotions on certain types of judgments. Keltner, Ellsworth, and Edwards showed that even when their participants all felt affect of the same negative valence, when asked what forces were responsible for an ambiguous social event angry participants were more likely to blame dispositional factors than sad participants. [24] DeSteno and colleagues found that angry participants are more likely to stereotype outgroup members than sad or neutral participants. [25] Specific emotions such as anger, fear, and happiness have been found to impact perceptions of risk too, as well as the decision-makers' depth of processing. [26]

Counterfactual Emotions: Disappointment & Regret

Within the specific emotion literature there is a subset of emotions that cry out for a link to judgmental biases and specifically hindsight bias research. Hindsight bias has often been linked in the literature to counterfactuals, or alternatives to past reality, the idea being that when people consider how likely the known outcome was, they consider as well how likely the alternative outcome was. [27] The emotions of interest, disappointment, relief, regret, and satisfaction, were first called *counterfactual emotions* by Kahneman and Tversky because they are emotions that result when "reality is compared to an imagined view of what might have been". [28] In the case of disappointment and relief this alternate reality is one in which the situation was different; in the case of regret and satisfaction, this alternate reality is one in which the choices made were different.

Emotion Appraisals

Research to date on these emotions has concentrated on the appraisals that are yoked to disappointment and regret, and exploring the differences between the two patterns of appraisals; relief and satisfaction have been ignored in this literature. According to Roseman, there are nine appraisal dimensions, or factors which differentiate specific emotions.[29] These are: (1) *unexpectedness* (Was the outcome expected or unexpected?); (2) *situational state* (Did the outcome improve things or make them worse?); (3) *motivational state* (Is the outcome related to wanting to get less of something punishing, or more of something rewarding?); (4) *probability* (Is the outcome certain or uncertain?); (5) *agency* (What or who caused the outcome?); (6) *control potential* (Was there something a person could do about the outcome or nothing that could be done?); (7) *problem type* (Did the outcome reveal the basic nature of someone or something or did it not?); (8) *own power* (Did the person feel powerful or powerless?); and (9) *legitimacy* (Did the person think of themselves as morally right or wrong?).[30] The different appraisals that accompany the emotions of interest are discussed further below.

Disappointment and Regret

People who feel disappointment consider the outcome to be unexpected. They want something pleasurable, but are denied it. They are more likely to think that they are morally right, and that the outcome has been caused by circumstances beyond their control, or *circumstances-agency*.[31] Disappointment is associated with phenomelogical components such as feeling as if something is missing and lethargy. Behavioral components include inaction, and expressions such as weeping. Strategies for reducing disappointment would be to stop moving towards the goal, or avoidance.[32] Disappointment is further associated with imagining how things could have turned out if the outcome had not been worse than expected, or thinking situational counterfactuals.[33]

People who feel regret believe that they could have done something about the event, and that it was caused by them, or *self-agency*.[34] Regret is not associated with thinking about how things could have turned out in a different state of the world, but instead with how things could have turned out if a different choice had been made, or generating behavior-focused counterfactuals.[35] Indeed, Zeelenberg and Pieters underlined the difference between disappointment and regret by showing that disappointed customers are more likely to complain to others, while regretful customers are more likely to switch businesses.[36] Regret is associated with phenomelogical components such as feeling like you have made a mistake, feeling sick, or a sinking feeling. Behavioral components include wanting a chance to do things over or differently, and expressions include closing the eyes, stretching the lips and rolling them together. Strategies for reducing regret would be to correct or improve the outcome, or approach.[37]

Regret and Satisfaction

Similar to disappointment, relief is associated with disconfirmed expectations, but instead of having been denied a pleasant outcome, people experiencing relief feel that they have escaped an unpleasant outcome.[38] As the positive counterpart to disappointment, is the expectation that relief would be coupled with circumstances-agency as well, where people experiencing relief would feel that the outcome was caused by a state of the world that they had no control over. Furthermore, the expectations that relief would be similar to disappointment in avoid or inaction tendencies where people feeling relief would want to get away from the event. Phenomelogical components of relief include amelioration and calming, with behavioral components such as resting and relaxing, and expressions such as exhaling and sighing.[39]

Satisfaction is not linked to alternative states of the world where things could have turned out better, but instead to some "chosen alternative" that resulted in a desired outcome.[40] Thus the expectation with satisfaction, as the conceptual opposite of regret, would be associated with self-agency, where people believe that they did have some control over the past event. It is probable to expect too that satisfaction would approximate regret in approach or action tendencies, so that people feeling satisfaction would not want to get away from the event, but instead would want to go back and change things to make the outcome even better.

Where Disappointment and Regret Collide

Let us examine the appraisal dimension of interest more closely. What exactly is meant when referring to "agency"? Roseman defined agency as "who or what caused the motive-relevant event" and sectioned it into three elements: circumstances-agency, other person-agency, and self-agency. [41] The example Roseman gave to explain this concept pertained to a couple whose relationship has broken up. [42] An appraisal of circumstances-agency would be verbalized as "The difficulty of being in a two career couple caused the break-up." Another person-agency appraisal would be "My partner's in attention to the relationship caused the break-up." "My own inattention to the relationship caused the break-up," would represent a self-agency appraisal. According to Roseman, it is combinations of appraisals that influence the emotions felt. [43] For example, anger results when an event is appraised as having an outcome inconsistent with the motive, or being a failure and this outcome is seen as being caused by another person, or other person-agency. Disappointment and regret have similar motive-inconsistent outcome appraisals, but the outcomes that induce them are further appraised as respectively circumstances-agency and self-agency.

Van Dijk and Zeelenberg have conducted research with the goal of making a distinction between relief and disappointment. [44] They asked participants to recall and describe a situation where they felt disappointment, regret, sadness or anger. They then measured how much participants believed the different appraisal dimensions had contributed to their felt emotions. They found that in regards to the emotions disappointment and regret participants differed on five of the appraisal dimensions: unexpectedness, motivational state, control potential, legitimacy, and agency.

Although this is a viewpoint that has been challenged by researchers who have asked if a feeling of responsibility is really essential to the experience of these two emotions, disappointment and regret, where the spotlight is directed on regret. Zeelenberg and colleagues have noted that this difference is a robust phenomenon, especially when specific emotion measures are used, as opposed to omnibus happiness measures as have been used in studies from which contradictory conclusions were drawn. [45] Connolly contended that agency does not play a major part in the experience of regret. [46] In a series of experiments participants judged the happiness of two students registering for a required undergraduate course, Alan or Bob, who before the start of the semester had had an opportunity to change to another course section, or were randomly assigned to another section. The students' outcomes and the average outcome in other sections, or the possible alternative outcomes were manipulated. Using this methodology, Connolly did not find any effect of the responsibility or agency manipulation. [47] Zeelenberg replicated these studies and found the same null effect of responsibility using a happiness measure. [48] However, they demonstrated that if disappointment and regret were individually measured, the results were consistent with responsibility, or agency, being a defining factor of these two emotions. They found that when the student was randomly assigned to course sections so that self-agency was low and circumstances agency was high, and a negative outcome was the result, more disappointment was perceived for that student; when the student made a critical choice so that self-agency was high and circumstances-agency was low, and a negative outcome was the result, more regret was perceived for that student.

"Am I Responsible?": Specific Emotions and Hindsight Bias

No research to this point has looked at the influence of specific emotions on post-outcome judgment biases such as the hindsight bias. At the most specific emotions are measured, and are seen usually as a byproduct of the judgments made, not as a possible antecedent. [49] In attempting to bring emotions more fully under the umbrella of hindsight bias influences, a model was generated where it has been proposed not only that appraisals of agency lead to specific emotions and to specific patterns of hindsight bias, but furthermore that the emotions experienced can lead to certain appraisals which then lead to certain patterns of hindsight bias.

"I'm not responsible!"—Disappointment and Relief

Disappointment corresponds to an appraisal of a motive-inconsistent, unexpected outcome and circumstances-agency, so people do not feel responsible for the outcome.

Pezzo and Pezzo's sensemaking Model of Hindsight Bias predicts that after a negative, self-relevant outcome where there is high expectation-outcome congruence, there is little to no hindsight bias. [50] However, after an outcome where the expectation-outcome congruence is low and external reasons for the outcome are easy to generate, hindsight bias is evidenced. Pezzo and Pezzo explain this ironic prediction by suggesting that a negative, self-relevant, unexpected outcome activates a search for meaning. [51] This increased search for causal linkages between antecedents and the outcome eventually increases a person's belief in the inevitability of the outcome, resulting in greater hindsight bias if this sense-making process is successful. Disappointment is primarily defined as a disconfirmed expectation, as is relief. Pezzo and Pezzo's model, revised from an earlier model concentrates solely on negatively valenced events, and as such suggests no predictions for hindsight bias after emotions such as relief that occur following positively valenced events. [52]

On top of this search for meaning, it has been suggested that there are self-serving motivations that will influence whether or not hindsight bias is shown after disappointment or relief. Consider the agency that is associated with the specific appraisals of disappointment and relief: circumstances-agency. People who feel disappointment and relief do not feel responsible for the event that has occurred. They want to distance themselves from the outcome by coping, as in the case of disappointment, or moving on, as in the case of relief. They are not motivated to learn from the event in the case of failure, or to take credit in the case of success. The retroactive pessimism literature posits that after extreme disappointment people are motivated to show coping mechanisms in order to keep going on, and tell themselves that the negative outcome was meant to be and that there was nothing they could have done, effectively increasing hindsight bias; thus predicting hindsight bias after disappointment. [53] No predictions are made in the retroactive pessimism literature or any other literature for the possible effect of relief on hindsight bias. It has been posited that since people do not feel responsible for the outcome when they feel relief, they will not attempt to take credit, and they will want to get away from the situation, because they feel that the outcome easily could have been otherwise and negative. Here one could assume and predict no hindsight bias after relief.

"I am responsible!"—Regret and Satisfaction

Regret corresponds to an appraisal of a motive-inconsistent outcome where the choice made was bad, and self-agency, so people do feel responsible for the outcome. Louie predicts that people will take credit for successes by judging them as being more inevitable and that they will deny blame for failures by judging them as being less inevitable. [54] In her research, participants have to make choices which turn out to be favorable or unfavorable, and she finds that after success, people have more internal thoughts focusing on reasons for success, whereas after failure people have more external thoughts excusing failure. In one study, participants made an informed decision as to whether or not to purchase a company's stock after which they were given favorable or unfavorable outcomes with regard to stock performance.[55] Favorable-feedback participants showed increased hindsight bias while the unfavorable-feedback participants showed decreased hindsight bias, as compared to no-feedback participants.

According to Louie, motivation for this hindsight bias strategy is one of ego validation, or self-promotion.[56] Consider the agency that is associated with regret and satisfaction: self-agency. Participants who are regretful or satisfied do feel responsible for their outcomes. They are motivated to do over the experience and to make things right in the case of regret to redo the experience and continue to make things right in the case of satisfaction. What is the link between these two emotions, regret and satisfaction, and self-serving self-promotional motivation and hindsight bias? It has been suggested that for the self-serving motive to be salient to people, they must feel that they had control over the outcome they received, or were responsible for it.[57] In Mark, participants who made choices that led to negative self-relevant outcomes perceived the outcome to be unforeseeable in hindsight.[58] If this is the case, only regretful or satisfied participants should use a self-serving motive, unlike disappointed or relieved people. Regretful people would want to deny blame for failure, and it is predicted they would not show hindsight bias. This prediction would also be expected due to regretful people wanting to learn from their mistakes, so that they can "do over" the event in search of a more positive outcome. Satisfied people would want to take credit for their success, allowing them to say that the outcome was inevitable, and that they knew all along that they would succeed. It is predicted that satisfied people would show hindsight bias.

CHAPTER SIX

Bias and the Expert: Is Expertise Friend or Foe?

    Experts are called upon by courts of law, media outlets, and countless other parties in search of definitive answers to difficult questions. Viewers would be hard pressed to accept as fact the opinion of a local news anchor on the costs and benefits of stem-cell research. Jurors would be unlikely to factor into their verdicts statements made by a psychiatric hospital's custodian testifying about the imminent dangerousness of a patient. Experts hold a special place in the minds of lay people, who appreciate the unique knowledge experts possess. But, is expertise always worthy of the acclaim it receives? Shanteau described a dichotomy in the portrayal of expert competency in the literatures of different branches of psychology, noting that judgment and decision-making researchers tend to focus on experts' missteps, while cognitive science researchers paint a rosy picture of experts. [1] Researchers on both sides have explored numerous aspects of expertise, including specific qualities experts exemplify, the kinds of strategies experts use to solve problems in their areas of expertise, differences in the costs of information search between experts and novices, differences in the way experts and novices incorporate new information, and under what conditions experts are likely or unlikely to perform competently. [2] As noted above, some researchers have questioned whether expertise is always beneficial, or whether expertise can, in some instances, be detrimental.

    Consistent with conventional wisdom, expertise often affords individuals with substantial benefits over novices. For example, Spilich, Vesonder, Chiesi, and Voss demonstrated that participants high in baseball knowledge (high knowledge) were able to process more readily information presented about events in a baseball game than were participants low in baseball knowledge (low knowledge). [3] Spilich argued that high knowledge individuals have better knowledge than low knowledge individuals regarding the "goal structure" (e.g., scoring runs, preventing runs from being scored, winning the game), "game actions" (e.g., a pitcher throwing a "strike," the batter striking out, the left fielder catching a fly ball), and "sequences of actions" (e.g., the shortstop fielded a "line drive" and threw the ball to the first baseman for a "double play") that occur in baseball games. [4] Importantly, the authors posited that high knowledge individuals are better than low knowledge individuals at relating game actions and sequences of actions to the goal structure and successfully keeping in working memory "values" of the goal-related game actions (e.g., there are men on first and third base) in a way similar to the play-by-play updates given by game announcers. In order to test these hypothesized differences between high knowledge and low knowledge individuals, Spilich presented participants with a taped account of a half of an inning of a baseball game and asked participants to a) summarize what happened in the half-inning, b) recount as much of the half-inning as possible, and c) answer 40 questions regarding specific events contained in the half-inning account. [5] The results confirmed the authors' predictions. High knowledge participants recalled more and answered more questions correctly about events from the account than did low knowledge participants, and the specific events high knowledge participants recalled were more relevant to the goal structure of the game. Specifically, high knowledge participants recounted more events related to game actions that actually resulted in important changes in the goal structure of the game, while low knowledge participants more often recounted game actions that were unrelated to the goal structure.

Spilich also found high knowledge participants' statements to be more embellished than statements written by low knowledge participants; high knowledge participants made more inferences about the people and events described in the half-inning account (e.g., describing a pitcher identified only as "left-handed" and capable of striking out "quite a few batters" in the account as a "big, fast balling lefthander"). [6] In general, Spilich found evidence that high-knowledge individuals have an advantage over low-knowledge individuals in terms of the incorporation and recall of relevant, goal-related information. [7]

Larkin also discussed the benefits of expertise, focusing on the ways in which experts represent information in long-term memory, their perceptual knowledge, and their recognition capabilities in their areas of expertise. [8] Larkin described the typical experiment used to demonstrate expert performance in chess players. [9] In this paradigm, participants are shown a chess board containing a position with approximately 25 pieces on the board. After seeing the chess board for about 5-10 seconds, participants are asked to recreate the position from memory. While chess masters and grand masters perform this test with extremely high accuracy (approximately 90% accuracy), less-skilled players typically remember the placement of about 5 or 6 pieces. In the second phase of the experiment, pieces are randomly placed on the chess board, and the memory task is repeated. In this case, masters and grand masters actually perform worse than do the novice players. In the latter case, expert chess players fail to remember the placement of the pieces because they are unable to exploit the skill afforded by their expertise, namely their capacity to recognize and store "chunks" of multiple pieces set up in typical configurations. A chunk is a stimulus composed of multiple units that, due to repeated exposure, have come to be recognized as a single entity. While novices can only hold in short-term memory about 5 or 6 pieces at a time, experts can hold in short-term memory about 4 times as many pieces, since they can remember chunks of pieces in lieu of single chess pieces. When the pieces are randomly placed on the chess board, experts must use the same strategy as novices when memorizing the placement of the pieces, thus eliminating any advantage expertise typically provides. This demonstration illustrates a benefit of expertise: experts are able to recognize typical configurations of information in their area of expertise. Furthermore, experts store or "index" these chunks of information in long-term memory and are able to access them when necessary. In this sense, chess masters are similar to the high knowledge participants in the Spilich experiment described above. [10] Participants high in baseball knowledge had in memory representations of baseball goal structures and sequences of actions typically observed in baseball games. When they were presented with baseball information, high knowledge participants were able to act similarly to chess masters recreating a chess position from memory: high knowledge participants remembered more from the half-inning account than did low knowledge participants because high knowledge participants could remember sequences of actions in "chunks" typical in baseball games.

As Shanteau noted in his discussion of expert competence, experts are not infallible. [11] Examples of errors in expert decision-making abound in the judgment and decision-making literature and often are explained in the "heuristics and biases" tradition. [12] For example, Poses and Anthony examined erroneous probability estimates made by physicians and implicated inappropriate use of the availability heuristic and wishful thinking in physicians' over diagnosis of bacteremia in hospitalized patients.[13] Casscells, Schoenberger, and Graboys found that most of the 20 house officers, 20 attending physicians, and 20 fourth-year medical students polled were unable to arrive at anything near the correct likelihood of a patient having a particular disease, even though they were given the data necessary to arrive at the correct answer.[14] Caplan, Posner, and Cheney demonstrated that when anesthesiologists were given a scenario in which exactly the same standard of care was adopted by a doctor during intubation, but a negative outcome resulted that was either permanent or temporary, the anesthesiologists judged the doctor to have acted more inappropriately when the outcome was permanent than when the negative outcome was temporary.[15] These are only a sampling of the many examples of physicians' tendency to succumb to cognitive biases.[16]

In addition to examples of physicians displaying cognitive biases, judges have also been shown to demonstrate cognitive errors within their own profession. Guthrie, Rachlinski, and Wistrich tested judges' susceptibility to anchoring, framing effects, hindsight bias, egocentric bias, and use of the representativeness heuristic and found that judges are subject to all of these cognitive errors.[17] For example, two groups of judges were given a scenario regarding a personal injury lawsuit and were asked to state how much they would award the plaintiff in compensatory damages. The group of judges who saw an additional, but invalid, argument from the defendant that the case should be dismissed because it did not meet the $75,000 jurisdictional minimum said they would award the plaintiff $367,000 less than judges in the group who did not receive the defendant's argument. Even though the defendant's argument was invalid because the plaintiff clearly suffered damages far in excess of $75,000, and even though judges recognized that the defendant's argument had no merit (only 2% of judges said they would grant the motion to dismiss based on the defendant's jurisdictional minimum plea), the $75,000 mentioned in the plea nevertheless served as an anchor and affected the judges' awards.

While the abovementioned examples demonstrate that experts are indeed susceptible to cognitive errors in their areas of expertise, they do not implicate expertise as *responsible* for engendering the errors. However, Arkes and Freedman demonstrated that expertise can be detrimental in some instances; that is, certain properties of expertise can lead experts to make mistakes where novices do not.[18] In a study exploring the "paradox of interference," Arkes and Freedman showed that experts' ability to "go beyond the information given" led them to commit more errors than did novices in identifying new and old information. [19] Arkes and Freedman presented baseball experts and non-experts with one of four stories about baseball. [20] Two of the stories contained "synonymous targets" to be paired later with "synonymous distractors," which were synonyms of words used in the baseball story. The other two stories contained "inferential targets" to be paired later with "inferential distractors," which were inferences that could be drawn from the story, although they themselves were not presented. All of the stories also contained "control targets" to be paired later with distractors that bore neither a synonymous nor an inferential relationship to the target. Participants had to read the assigned story, take a 45-question baseball quiz (used to categorize participants as experts and non-experts), and then rate sixteen sentences on a scale indicating to what extent the participants felt they had read the exact sentence in the baseball story (i.e., whether the sentence presented was "old" or "new"). Some of these sentences contained the control, synonymous and inferential distractors. Results demonstrated that when control distractors were included in the sentences, baseball experts showed superior recognition accuracy than did non-experts.

However, when the sentences contained synonymous and inferential distractors, expert performance suffered. Specifically, when sentences contained synonymous distractors, experts were less likely than non-experts to judge the targets as "old" and the distractors as "new." When sentences contained inferences that could be drawn from the story but were not actually presented, experts were more likely than non-experts to judge the distractor as "old." The authors cleverly included as well an inference distractor whose inference would contradict what was presented in the story. In this case, expertise was beneficial; experts correctly identified the inferential distractor as "new" to a greater extent than did non-experts, since the experts recognized that the distractor was inconsistent with the events that took place in the story. Arkes and Freedman concluded that expertise is detrimental in some instances because experts can infer information that was not actually presented; this otherwise beneficial ability to make inferences leads to poorer performance when the tasks calls for veridical recognition of presented information. [22]

Related to Arkes and Freedman's findings is research on the relationship between confidence and expertise. [23] Since experts are able to make inferences about presented information, they may infer that related stimuli were presented when they in fact were not. [24] When such inferences are made, individuals may be unable to identify whether the information in question was actually presented or whether it was simply inferred from the information given; this is precisely what occurred with experts in Arkes and Freedman's study. [25] Arkes and Freedman suggested that if an expert is later presented with information consistent with the information he or she had inferred previously, the presented information may be erroneously perceived as *additional* evidence supporting the inference the expert has already made. [26] As evidence in favor of a particular conclusion accumulates, an inflated level of confidence may result.

In a study testing the effects of expertise on overconfidence, Bradley demonstrated that when participants were asked true or false questions, they preferred to guess rather than admit ignorance when the questions were in the topic area that the participant believed he had the greatest amount of expertise; this result is particularly disturbing in light of the finding that participants answered most of the questions in their area of expertise at or below chance frequency. [27] Furthermore, participants were unwilling to admit to their uncertainty regarding the correctness of their answers; as the rank of area of expertise increased, the degree of uncertainty with regard to the correctness of the answer decreased. More will be discussed about the implications of these results in later sections. While Bradley's demonstration of the effects of subjective expertise on overconfidence, he did not test the particular effect of expertise on confidence explicated by Arkes & Freedman (that expertise inflates confidence due to an erroneous sense of accumulating evidence for a particular outcome), Bradley nevertheless established a connection between presumed expertise and confidence. [28] The following section explores a specific task in which expertise may be harmful or beneficial: predicting the performance of less-informed others.

Bias and Expertise: Is There a Curse of Knowledge?

The task of communicating information to less-informed others is a daily occurrence for professionals in many different lines of work. Professors must teach inexperienced students about calculus, organizational behavior, the fall of the Holy Roman Empire, and countless other topics about which their students are otherwise relatively naïve. Physicians must explain to patients who have never learned about the intricacies of the nervous system why the pain in their lower back is exacerbated by running. Mechanics must relay to their mechanically unsophisticated customers why their car's engine is rattling, and financial planners must explain to their clients why it is good to have a diversified portfolio and safe to invest in government bonds. All of these situations require experts to relay information to non-experts in a way they will understand. As such, these situations require well-informed individuals to understand what less-informed individuals do and do not know and to correct for this knowledge discrepancy.

Anecdotally, it is clear that experts do not always succeed in their attempts to "dumb down" their communications enough for lay people to understand. Any student who has experienced complete confusion in a lecture in which he does not understand the terminology the professor uses to explain other concepts recognizes some professors' inability to discount their special knowledge in the name of teaching. Similarly, any customer who leaves the Ford dealership without knowing why his catalytic converter is making strange sounds, or what a catalytic converter even is, has been the victim of a mechanic's inability to put himself in the shoes of an individual who knows nothing about cars. In addition to anecdotal evidence, previous research has explored the problem of communication between more—and less-informed individuals. Nickerson noted that in order for individuals to communicate successfully to others, they first must gauge their own knowledge and then adjust this estimate for any special knowledge they have. [29]

In the case of a professor, he must assess his own level of knowledge, recognize that he has specialized knowledge that his students do not possess, and adjust downward to accommodate this difference. One potential problem with enacting this chain of events is that well-informed individuals may have difficulty identifying when they acquired the knowledge they currently possess. [30] If a professor thinks he "always knew" how to take the first derivative of a function, he will fail to recognize that this information is something he must teach inexperienced students for them to understand how to solve math problems in his course. In a similar vein, individuals tend to overestimate the commonality of their knowledge; a professor who thinks taking the first derivative of a function is "common sense" will also fail to teach his students this important lesson. [31] As a general finding, individuals mistakenly ascribe to less-informed others knowledge that they, themselves, possess, and this erroneous imputation of special knowledge can lead to break-downs in communication. [32]

In Hinds' discussion of the "curse of expertise," she identified reasons why well-informed individuals may find difficulty in adjusting their knowledge downward when communicating with less-informed individuals. [33] First, Hinds implicated the *availability heuristic* as being responsible for experts' inability to discount their knowledge.[34] The availability heuristic is a rule of thumb by which individuals estimate frequency or probability by the ease with which they can bring to mind instances of the stimulus in question. According to this explanation, experts can bring to mind easily instances in which they have dealt with the stimulus in an unproblematic way, leading the expert to overestimate the probability that others will be able to handle the stimulus in a similar trouble-free manner. Hinds also entertained the notion that *anchoring and adjustment* may contribute to the "curse of expertise."[35] Here, when attempting to identify what others know, experts are presumed to "anchor" on their own level of knowledge and "adjust" downward to account for special knowledge they may possess. According to Tversky and Kahneman, individuals typically fail to sufficiently move away from their original anchors; in the case of experts, then, Hinds suggested that it is the insufficient adjustment away from the anchor (one's own expert knowledge) that leads experts to overestimate what less-informed others know.[36] A final reason Hinds gave for experts' failure to discount their special knowledge is experts' tendency to oversimplify tasks in their area of expertise.[37] In the case of a calculus professor, such an oversimplification might lead the professor to say " . . . then you take the derivative of the function . . . ," while omitting the steps involved in this procedure.

Research on the hindsight bias is intimately tied to the task of predicting what less-informed others know. First investigated by Fischhoff, hindsight bias is the tendency to view past events as predictable or obvious after obtaining information about the outcome of the event.[38] When individuals are provided with outcome information but must make decisions without taking into account the outcome information, they are essentially attempting to put themselves in the position of less-informed others.

Regardless of whether an expert or non-expert is called upon to make such a judgment, the individual must be able to discount his current knowledge state in order to respond appropriately to the question at hand.[39] Previous research has demonstrated that experts and non-experts alike fall prey to the hindsight bias. For example, lay persons may view the results of an election as having been inevitable after learning who the victor is, the events included in president Nixon's itinerary for his trip to China might seem foreseeable to the general public after he actually engaged in the various activities, and seasoned physicians may think the correct diagnosis is obvious after they find out about a patient's true ailment.[40]

The inability to discount outcome information has important implications for the law as well, since legal verdicts by nature are decided after events have taken place and outcome information is available. [41] Legal situations are an interesting area in which to examine hindsight bias in experts and non-experts, since both groups are called upon to make decisions in the courtroom: jurors are non-experts and judges are experts. Guthrie, Rachlinski, and Wistrich examined the occurrence of hindsight bias in judges. [42] Guthrie gave 167 federal magistrate judges attending the 1999 Federal Judicial Center's Workshop for Magistrate Judges in New Orleans a scenario regarding a prisoner who filed an action against his state's Director of the Department of Criminal Justice. [43] The prisoner alleged that the prison provided him with negligent medical care, which the prisoner claimed was in violation of Section 1983. The district court dismissed the prisoner's claim because medical negligence does not violate Section 1983. In addition to dismissing the prisoner's claim, the district court also sanctioned the prisoner pursuant to Rule 11, which required that any future claims the prisoner wished to file be approved by the district's Chief Judge. This ruling was based on the fact the prisoner had filed similar medical negligence complaints in the past that were also dismissed, and he was therefore aware that medical negligence is not in violation of Section 1983. The prisoner proceeded to appeal the Rule 11 ruling. After reading the scenario, the judges in the experiment were assigned to one of three conditions. In the "lesser sanction" condition, the judges learned that the court of appeals ruled that the district court had abused its power under Rule 11 and ordered that a less severe version of Rule 11 be assigned to the prisoner. In the "affirmed" condition, the judges learned that the court of appeals upheld the district court's ruling of the imposition of Rule 11 on the prisoner.

Finally, judges in the "vacated" condition learned that the court of appeals ruled that the district court had abused its power under Rule 11 and removed the prisoner's Rule 11 sanction. After receiving this outcome information, the judges were asked to assign probabilities to the three possible outcomes of the appeal described above. The results showed that the judges were greatly influenced by the ruling of the court of appeals; the total percentage the judges assigned to the outcome that was "most likely to have occurred" was 172%. That is, the judges assigned much larger probabilities to the outcome they learned had actually occurred than did the judges who learned that a different outcome had occurred (note that if there were no effect of the outcome information, the total probability assigned to the "most likely to have occurred" category would have been 100%). Judges in this experiment clearly fell prey to hindsight bias.

Jurors, who are non-experts in legal decision-making, also demonstrate the hindsight bias. Casper, Benedict, and Kelly examined whether or not jurors could disregard testimony presented during a court case that had been deemed inadmissible by a judge. [44] Casper gave mock jurors a scenario in which they read that police searched the apartment of a victim and either found drugs in the apartment or did not find drugs in the apartment. [45] In a third group's scenario, there was no mention of the search or the drugs. Since the search was conducted without a warrant, the mock jurors were instructed not to let the outcome of the search affect their award to the victim. Even though the mock jurors were told to disregard the evidence presented about the search, the average amount awarded to the victim by each group of jurors differed depending on the outcome of the illegal search. Jurors who learned that drugs were found in the victim's apartment awarded the victim less money (M = $16,090) than jurors learning that no drugs were found (M = $24,834) or jurors who heard nothing about the search (M= $22,748). The mock jurors in this experiment were unable to disregard the outcome information and act as if they had never learned about the search.

Berlin discussed an interesting medical malpractice lawsuit in which hindsight bias was demonstrated by both experts and non-experts in the same case. The lawsuit involved a radiologist who was sued for malpractice because he failed to detect a tumor on a patient's initial chest x-ray. Three years later, the patient returned to the physician because he had been experiencing chest pains and weight loss. A second x-ray was taken at this time and revealed a malignant tumor. The patient died 16 months after the second x-ray was taken. Expert radiologists were retained by both the plaintiff and the defendant to serve as expert witnesses at the trial. The expert radiologists testifying on behalf of the defense agreed that the tumor was not visible on the initial x-ray, while the experts testifying on behalf of the plaintiff argued that the tumor on the initial x-ray was clearly visible. Interestingly, the defense attorney included an exposition of hindsight bias in his line of questioning. While the plaintiff's experts claimed that hindsight bias was not responsible for their assertions because they reviewed the initial x-ray without first seeing the second, positive x-ray, the defense attorney argued that simply being asked to review x-rays for a malpractice case would have signaled to the radiologists that they were looking for a missed tumor. Thus, the defense attorney maintained that hindsight bias was the major determinant for the plaintiffs' expert witnesses' opinions that the tumor was visible on the initial x-ray. The jurors in the case found the defendant guilty of malpractice. This case is an example of experts (the plaintiffs' expert witnesses) and non-experts (the jurors) falling prey to the hindsight bias; the former demonstrated the bias in their determination that the tumor was clear on the initial x-ray, and the latter may have been influenced by the knowledge that the patient was about to die as a result of the tumor. Jurors in medical malpractice cases are instructed to make decisions based only on the physician's standard of care at the time of incident and not on the resulting events, but jurors are often influenced by whether or not damages have occurred.

Like the radiologists described above, expert physicians have also been shown to demonstrate the hindsight bias. Dawson, Arkes, Siciliano, Blinkhorn, Lakshmanan, and Petrelli examined the occurrence of the hindsight bias in physicians' predictions of medical diagnoses. During a clinic pathological conference, an instructional session in which a discussant reports on a medical case and selects the diagnosis he deems most likely, Dawson asked half of the physicians in the audience to predict the probability that each of 5 possible diagnoses was correct. After these predictions were made, the audience members learned the patient's actual cause of death, and the other half of the physicians in the audience were asked to report the probabilities that they would have assigned to each of the 5 diagnoses before hearing the cause of death.

Dawson found that physicians who were afforded the information about the patient's actual cause of death assigned a much higher probability to the true diagnosis than did participants who assigned probabilities before learning the outcome information. While this study showed that experienced physicians were susceptible to the hindsight bias, the most senior physicians did not demonstrate the bias on the most difficult cases; these most experienced doctors could appreciate the rarity of the co-occurrence of two symptoms as indicative of the ailment responsible for the patient's death.

Although the abovementioned examples demonstrate that even experts can fall prey to hindsight bias, some recent research suggests that expertise can protect individuals from hindsight bias. In a virtual-reality batting task, Gray, Beilock, and Carr examined how well expert and novice baseball players would be able to predict the outcomes of their bat swings.[46] Using virtual-reality technologies, Gray was able to pause the simulation at the exact moment the bat hit the ball. At this point, participants were asked to predict where on the field the ball would land by clicking on a yellow cone on the screen and moving it to the location on the field they thought accurately reflected where the ball would land. If they thought they hit a homerun or foul ball, participants placed the yellow cone where they thought the ball would cross the fence or exit the playing field. After making these predictions, participants were given accurate feedback as to where the ball would have actually landed. After participants received outcome feedback, the virtual screen went blank and reappeared after 20 seconds. At this point participants had to mark again where they thought the ball would have landed without taking into account the outcome feedback. Results showed that the discrepancy between the placement of the yellow cone before and after participants received outcome feedback was greater for novice players than it was for expert players. The authors included an additional analysis that tracked hindsight bias as a function of expertise and current performance and found that it was when experts were doing well at the task that hindsight bias was reduced. While the results of this study are compelling, it is difficult to confidently generalize the results of this research to other hindsight studies for two reasons. First, this study tested a very specific skill (swinging a baseball bat and predicting the result of the swing) that may be idiosyncratic with regard to its relationship to hindsight bias. For example, expert baseball players have an enormous amount of veridical feedback regarding the result of each swing they take. In this sense, baseball experts asked to predict the outcome of a swing are like "super experts" as compared to experts tested in other domains in which feedback is much more imperfect and infrequent. Shanteau commented on this distinction, noting that experts whose domain of expertise involves repetitive tasks that produce reliable feedback tend to make more accurate predictions than do experts in tasks that involve unstable and unreliable stimuli. [47] Second, the evidence for visual or perceptual hindsight bias has been mixed. Winman, Juslin, and Bjorkman found a reverse hindsight bias in a perceptual task, while Harley, Carlsen, and Loftus found a positive hindsight bias in a perceptual task. [48]

Recall the abovementioned study conducted by Guthrie in which judges displayed hindsight bias in an appeals case. [49] While the authors demonstrated that even magistrate judges fall prey to the hindsight bias in their area of expertise, a second study failed to demonstrate the bias in judges. Guthrie discussed an experiment in which judges were presented with a case regarding probable cause. [50] The judges read a scenario describing a police officer who was patrolling a parking lot outside of a rock concert when he noticed a concert-goer nervously looking through the trunk of a BMW. A half hour later the officer became aware that the window to the car was rolled down and approached the car in order to close the window. Upon approaching the car, the officer smelled something he thought was likely burnt methamphetamine, and he proceeded to look inside the car only to find Visine, a map, and some empty beer cans.

After reading this first part of the scenario, the judges were randomly assigned to either a foresight or hindsight group. Foresight judges read that the officer called in a request for a telephonic search warrant, since he believed there was probable cause to search the trunk of the car. The foresight judges were then asked whether or not they thought there was probable cause to grant the telephonic warrant based on the scenario. Judges in the hindsight group were told that the officer searched the trunk of the car without a warrant and found ten pounds of methamphetamine and other drug paraphernalia, as well as a gun that was used to murder a drug dealer earlier that day. In the hindsight scenario, the officer proceeded to arrest the car owner, who was later prosecuted even though the defense attorney argued in court that the evidence found in his client's trunk was inadmissible on grounds that the officer did not have probable cause to search the trunk.

Hindsight judges were then asked whether they would admit the evidence from the warrantless search. The percentage of judges in the foresight and hindsight groups who thought there was probable cause to grant the warrant (23.9%) and who would have admitted the evidence procured from the search (27.7%), respectively, were not significantly different. That is, unlike the results of the other study by Guthrie in which judges did demonstrate the hindsight bias, judges in this probable cause case did not fall prey to the hindsight bias. Guthrie argued that the strict, rule-based nature of the probable cause problem in jurisprudence may have aided the judges in their decision-making process, shielding them from hindsight bias.[51] Indeed, Guthrie noted that many judgments and decisions judges make on a daily basis are made intuitively as opposed to analytically.[52] The addition of strict rules to the decision-making process may shift the judge's decision strategy from intuitive to analytical, thereby reducing the hindsight bias. Previous researchers have also demonstrated that analytical thinking (e.g., "consider the opposite") can help to reduce the hindsight bias.[53]

The jury seems to still be out on the exact relationship between hindsight bias and expertise. It has been argued that expertise exacerbates hindsight bias because experts *feel like* they know more in their areas of expertise than they actually do. Demonstrating that hindsight bias increases with expertise is interesting because it is counterintuitive. It would seem that those who are more knowledgeable in a particular area should be less vulnerable to biases in the area.[54] In fact, in their meta-analysis of previous hindsight bias studies, Christensen-Szalanski and Willham found that one moderator of hindsight bias is "expertise" or "familiarity" with a particular task.[55] The authors coded 128 experiments as either "familiar" or "not familiar" based on the types of questions that were asked in the experiments and who the participants were. For example, the abovementioned study by Dawson was coded as "familiar," since physicians were asked about medical diagnoses.[56] Christensen-Szalanski and Willham found in their analysis that there was an effect of familiarity on hindsight bias: the effect of hindsight bias was smaller for more familiar tasks.[57] This result supports the notion that those who known more in a particular area should be less susceptible to biases in this area but contradicts the hypothesis put forth in the current series of experiments; that is that expertise exacerbates hindsight bias.

Why might hindsight bias be more prevalent in experts than in non-experts? The Suchan effect may occur if people judge what they know based on the *domain* in which the question lies rather than judging based on the specific question being asked. In other words, an individual's perception of what he knows in a particular domain likely exceeds what one *actually* knows in that domain. This general effect is often expressed as a measure of overconfidence, and it has not only been observed in experts, but it also has been shown to vary with expertise.[58] For example, Dawson, Connors, Speroff, Kemka, Shaw, and Arkes demonstrated that physicians' confidence in their estimates of values pertinent to right-heart catheterization was unrelated to their accuracy of these estimates; the physicians were overconfident in all instances.[59] In fact, the more experience the physicians had, the more confident they were, but experience afforded no increase inaccuracy. Thus, more experienced physicians displayed greater overconfidence than did those who were less experienced. Bradley also found a relationship between confidence and expertise. He demonstrated that the reluctance to admit ignorance increased as subjective expertise increased even though accuracy in one's area of presumed expertise was below chance.[60] Participants also were unwilling to admit to their uncertainty regarding the correctness of their answers; as the rank of area of expertise increased, the degree of uncertainty with regard to the correctness of the answer decreased. Inasmuch as certainty in the correctness of one's answer can be expressed as the degree to which one feels like he "knows the answer," the effects of expertise on hindsight bias ("I knew it all along") should mirror the effects of expertise on overconfidence. Indeed, Bradley noted that participants showed "a reluctance to admit ignorance when one should, the reluctance being most pronounced in one's area of greatest expertise". [61] It is precisely this reluctance to "admit ignorance" that may contribute to an increase in hindsight bias as expertise increases; failure to admit ignorance is comparable to an individual's feeling that he "knew it all along."

It is interesting to note that in addition to individuals' feelings that their expertise extends far beyond the actual boundaries of one's expertise, individuals often think that others' areas of expertise are more inclusive than they actually are. Some common interactions between experts and non-experts may inform the discrepancy between what experts know and what experts think they know. Non-experts may not realize that there are in fact sub-disciplines that contribute to expertise in some areas within a domain without contributing to expertise in other areas within the same domain. If an individual has a cardiologist in his family, for example, the individual may be tempted to ask the cardiologist about a strange growth on his back simply because the family member is a physician. Again, the individual may overgeneralize the extent of the cardiologist's expertise, assuming that he knows everything about medicine because he has a medical degree. In some sense, however, the cardiologist's family member is not completely unjustified in asking the cardiologist about a medical condition, since the cardiologist most certainly knows more about medicine than does the family member, who has no medical training. The same goes for a teacher. Friends of that teacher may comment that "you're a teacher, you should know that" when the teacher does not know the answer to a particular question. That teacher may be a kindergarten teacher, and although that teacher is quite intelligent, that teacher should not be expected to know everything about U.S. history simply because he or she is a teacher. This general failure to recognize that expertise in a particular sub-topic of a domain does not denote expertise in the entire domain can contribute to discrepancies between what one knows and what one thinks he knows as well as what one knows and what others think he or she knows.

The hypothesis that greater expertise leads to greater hindsight bias stems from previous research demonstrating that greater confidence in one's answers is associated with greater hindsight bias, and that familiarity with atopic leads to greater hindsight bias. [62] Recall the discussion above regarding the effects of expertise on overconfidence. Bradley showed that overconfidence increased as subjective expertise increased. Werth and Strack demonstrated more recently that greater subjective feelings of confidence can lead to an increased "knew-it-all-along" effect. [63] Werth and Strack gave participants 40 extremely difficult questions (i.e., they only chose questions that no participants in a pretest answered correctly) requiring numerical estimates as answers. [64] Participants were also given one of two answers for each question: a low estimate and a high estimate of the actual numerical value. The participants were instructed to answer the questions as they would have had they not been given the answer, and they had to give confidence ratings indicating how confident they felt about each answer. Werth and Stack found greater assimilation to the provided estimates when participants had experienced more confidence in generating their answers. [65] The authors argued that this effect is the result of participants experiencing a sense of familiarity or a sense that "the question seems so familiar" that leads to confidence and, in turn, hindsight bias.

While Werth and Strack contended that greater confidence leading to greater hindsight bias resulted from participants feeling like the information was more familiar, they did not directly test this assumption. [66] In a second study, Werth and Strack manipulated perceptual fluency in an attempt to show that greater fluency similarly would lead to feelings that the question "seems familiar to me," but this second experiment still did not directly test the familiarity assumption. [67] In a series of eight experiments, Marks and Arkes explored the specific idea that familiarity leads to the hindsight bias. [68] The authors showed that participants were unable to discount information they read about the familiar Revolutionary War when taking a subsequent true or false quiz, but they were able to disregard information they read about the more obscure War of 1812 during a subsequent quiz. Marks and Arkes showed that *source confusion* was responsible for the difference in participants' ability to disregard essay information. [69] Source confusion refers to the failure to correctly identify the source of one's current knowledge. [70] Marks and Arkes (Experiment 3) found that familiar information is more susceptible to source confusion than is unfamiliar information, and it is this difference in source confusion that leads to participants' differential ability to discount these different types of information. [71]

Is there a mechanisms underlying hindsight bias by establishing a connection between expertise and hindsight bias? By definition, experts should be more familiar than non-experts with information dealing with their area of expertise. If hindsight bias is more likely to occur with more familiar information, then expertise, like familiarity, should be a determinant of hindsight bias as well. [72] As mentioned previously, some studies have already explored the connection between hindsight bias and expertise, but the findings thus far have been inconsistent and inconclusive. [73]

CHAPTER SEVEN

Juror Bias

Two individuals sit side by side, listen to the same information, and apply the same instructions to their task. Afterwards, they meet to discuss and realize that not only have they reached different conclusions, they have very different interpretations of the information. An American jury is composed of twelve of these individuals. The same reason that the jury system works in the United States is also why it may fail, and why it generates so much research. Asking jurors to hear a case is interjecting human nature into the legal process.

The emphasis on selecting an impartial juror is relatively new. When the use of juries first began, they were composed of individuals from the community expected to make informed decisions using their prior knowledge of the case, the irrespective areas of expertise, and the values and principles of the community. [1] These days this would be unacceptable. Frequently, information uncovered during an investigation is suppressed for legal or relevancy issues, without the jury hearing of its existence. In fact, the purpose of voir dire, or jury selection, is to reveal potential jurors who may possess biases about the case or those involved, or who know too much about the case and have already formed an opinion.

Possible effects of bias in the courtroom often drive suggestions to reform or limit the use of juries. [2] Research has shown that personality characteristics and attitudes can affect how a juror perceives trial information and decides a verdict. [3] For example, jurors who are pro-prosecution, and unable to set aside this attitude, may have a decision of guilt that begins at a level closer to conviction than to acquittal. Presumably, less evidence would be required to secure a guilty verdict in such persons than if jurors are pro-defense or apply no weight to their initial biases. [4]

Many of the differences in attitudes toward the legal system have underlying similarities; specifically, general attitudes about the state and purpose of the criminal legal system. The goal of the present paper is to show that those different viewpoints regarding the "is" and "ought" of the criminal legal system can be defined and measured, and have the potential to bias jurors. [5]

It should be noted that how a juror interprets a case might be quite different from how the jury interprets, and subsequently decides, a case. [6] The jury's decision is not a compilation of each juror's understanding of the evidence combined with the judge's instructions but more of an exploratory process during which jurors may come to interpret the evidence in a multitude of ways. Within jury deliberations, the greater the number of different interpretations of the case, the less chance there is of reaching a unanimous verdict. [7] Holstein found that where jurors agreed on a single interpretation of the case evidence they reached a unanimous verdict 100% of the time. [8] With the introduction of a second interpretation, the jury reached a unanimous verdict 72% of the time. The trend continues such that with the introduction of three or more interpretations, the chance of a unanimous verdict drops to approximately 28%.[9]

While deliberations are an important aspect, and perhaps a turning point in a trial, research has shown that the best predictor of final verdict is initial, individual verdicts. [10] Kalven and Zeisel were able to reconstruct the initial ballot count in 225 actual trials. [11] Almost 90% of the trials had a final verdict that was the same as the initial majority verdict. Interestingly, very rarely was the first ballot unanimous, meaning that the totality of a case's evidence was open to different interpretations.

As well, research has shown that while the biasing impact of certain extra-legal factors may be reduced after jury deliberations—such as attorney obnoxiousness (Kaplan & Miller, 1978), unattractiveness of the defendant and inadmissible evidence—this may not always be the case. [12] Kerr, Niedermeier, and Kaplan proposed that jury deliberations may decrease juror bias only in the more "extreme" cases—cases with very low or very high probabilities for conviction—but for trials with a moderate conviction rate, jury deliberations may have no effect on the impact of biasing information. [13]

In their study, Kerr and colleagues used a child molestation trial in which a man was accused of undressing a pre-teen boy. [14] They altered aspects of the trial to produce two different versions—one that generated a low rate of conviction (20-30%) and one that led to a moderate rate of conviction (50-60%). To simulate bias, the researchers gave mock jurors either highly prejudicial or somewhat innocuous "pretrial publicity" in the form of fake newspaper articles. In one condition, a newspaper article discussed how the defendant had been banned from a local Big Brother organization because of past indiscretions (high bias). The other condition used an article claiming that the defendant had been rewarded for his service in the organization (low bias). Mock jurors read the trial transcript and pretrial publicity before joining groups of 3-19 other individuals in order to deliberate on a verdict. If discussing the evidence of a case in a group situation helps jurors ignore biasing information and focus on the relevant evidence, post-deliberation verdicts in low and high bias conditions should be more similar to one another than pre-deliberation verdicts. Findings indicated that only in the low conviction condition did deliberations attenuate bias (9.9% difference in high bias versus low bias verdicts pre-deliberations to 3% post-deliberations). In the moderate conviction condition deliberations actually accentuated the bias (a 10.9% difference in guilty verdicts between the high and low bias conditions pre-deliberation to a 28.7% difference post deliberations).

Research such as that by Kerr is relevant because of the type of cases that actually end up going to trial; roughly 90% of all cases in the United States never go to trial, either because of the entry of a guilty plea or a dismissal of the charges. [15] One can assume that those actually reaching the courtroom are less likely to be cut and dried convictions or acquittals and are more likely to contain some ambiguity. [16] De la Fuente, De la Fuente, and Garcia found the same trend in their research; in a case with ambiguous evidence, the process of deliberations accentuated pre-deliberation, pro-defense, and pro-prosecution biases. [17] If this is the case, then assessing juror bias can be an excellent predictor of subsequent jury decisions.

In the 1960s, the Chicago Jury Project undertook the task of assessing jury effectiveness. Presumably, judges do their best to remain impartial and obviously have an excellent understanding of the law; therefore, if a jury is doing the same, its verdict should agree with what a judge would have decided. Kalven and Zeisel, the Chicago Jury Project researchers, asked more than 500 judges to recall jury trials over which they had presided. [18] Data for 3,576 jury trials were accumulated from the responses. Judges reported agreeing with the jury verdict the vast majority of the time, roughly 78% of cases. When asked about the cases in which they did not agree with the jury, judges expressed that they felt juror "sentiments"—attitudes, personality characteristics, use of extralegal information (including defendant attractiveness and lawyer competency), etc.—were influencing trial verdicts. [19] This is not to say that jurors are doing a poor job, or that they are unfit to decide facts of law, but when the evidence is ambiguous or open to different interpretations, jurors may turn to their "sentiments". [20] The term "sentiments" was used was because the jury was found to generally be more lenient than the judge. [21] Disagreements overwhelmingly took the form of the jury voting to acquit but the judge favoring conviction (19% of the remaining 22% of the cases). Kalven and Zeisel found that complexity of the evidence had nothing to do with the difference in conviction rates between judges and juries; they were just as likely to disagree on verdicts in cases with complex evidence as in cases with evidence that was easier to understand. [22] While some of the differences were due to knowledge one party had that the other did not (e.g., a judge knows about a defendant's prior record and of any evidence deemed inadmissible), it was clear that other extralegal factors were also influencing the jurors.

One example of extralegal factors would be the internal characteristics of the jurors. The idea of the "thirteenth juror", or the influence of personality characteristics, has been prominent in courtroom strategy for decades. The term stemmed from a 1945 book in which Judge Jerome Frank proposed that bias in the juror box took the form as "Mr. Prejudice" and "Miss Sympathy" and these effects on jurors needed to be assessed and dealt with in any jury trial. Based on responses from the judges interviewed, Kalven and Zeisel's research suggested that sympathy had swayed the jury in about 4% of the trials. [23] Recall that only 3% of the cases in which jurors and judges disagreed did the jurors vote to convict. One interpretation is that juries let prejudice sway their verdicts less than 3% of the time; assuming that judges and juries did not use prejudice as a deciding factor in any of the cases they agreed upon.

Personality characteristics and attitudes

A trial commands that a juror change or ignore any preexisting attitudes in favor of an equitable perspective. Even if this may not be possible, will the bias have any real effect on the verdict? The very best predictor of juror verdicts is always going to be the content of a case itself, such as physical evidence and eyewitness testimony. [24] No matter the bias an individual may possess, the best possible determinant of verdict is weight of the evidence. [25]

Juror bias in a case with very strong or very weak evidence is not likely to exert any meaningful influence over the verdict, but when trial evidence is somewhat ambiguous a juror may invoke personal beliefs and thoughts for assistance in interpreting information presented or deciding between competing evidence and testimony. In these situations, assessing juror bias may possibly yield important information about juror responses to that trial. [26]

In cases where attitudes may exert an influence, the best predictor of juror bias is attitudes toward specific, key elements of the case. [27] For example, when a lawyer has been accused of a drug related offense good predictors of guilty verdicts are attitudes toward drugs and attitudes toward lawyers.[28] In the same respect, attitudes toward rape is a good predictor of the verdict in a rape case and endorsement of myths about battered women is a good predictor of the verdict when such women are accused of murdering their batterers. [29]

Assessing individual biases is only half of the battle. The ability to predict behavior from attitudes has been a debated for decades and findings are mixed. [30] The problems arose when, contrary to widely held beliefs, researchers were finding that stated attitudes were not good predictors of behaviors. [31] In an attempt to find definitive answers regarding if or when attitudes could reliably predict behavior, Ajzen and Fishbein compiled a review of the available research.[32] Their analysis revealed that referencing general attitudes to predict a single, specific behavior is unlikely to produce the desired results. There are too many extraneous factors to account for in order to obtain an accurate prediction. Instead, Ajzen and Fishbein emphasized that if researchers wanted to use attitudes to predict behavior, they should focus on attitudes toward that behavior. Another option is to use multiple measures of a target behavior to represent an attitude.

Kraus performed a meta-analysis of 88 studies assessing the predictability of attitudes on future behavior. [33] What he found was a significant correlation between reported attitudes and future behaviors. As previously established, the more specific the attitude was to the future behavior, the stronger the relationship. Kraus found that the variability in study results was extremely high. He attributed this to five attitude moderators influencing the attitude-behavior correlation: attitude stability, attitude certainty, affective-cognitive consistency (the extent to which emotions and beliefs toward an issue match), direct experience, and the accessibility of the attitude. In the courtroom, assessments of juror bias may do well to incorporate questions about how long a juror has held his or her attitude or about any real-world experience a juror has that may be relevant to the case.

Information integration theories suggest that one of the initial components affecting juror decision-making is an a priori bias relevant to beliefs about the legal system.[34] In testing this theory, Kaplan and Miller pre-identified respondents as being supportive of either harsh treatment toward law-breakers or lenient treatment before exposing them to trial information. [35] This "general bias" of jurors played an important role in decisions of guilt, such that those pre-identified as harsh were more likely to convict and were more punitive than those identified as lenient were. While on the surface this may seem to violate Ajzen and Fishbein's contention that general attitudes are poor predictors of specific behaviors, the researchers showed that it was the attitudes effect on a larger range of behaviors that, cumulatively, were predicting verdicts. [36] For example, when asked to list three pieces of evidence that affected their decisions, harsh respondents were more likely to choose evidence incriminating the defendant, even if it deemed unreliable.

Perhaps the difference between individual jurors' interpretations of trial information is a result of differences in personality. Research supports three main personality characteristics that can have such an effect: locus of control, belief in a just world, and authoritarianism.

Locus of control

Julian Rotter developed the locus of control theory to differentiate between individuals who believe that they are in charge of their own behavior (internal locus of control) or that forces beyond their control are driving them (external locus of control). [37] People who have a high internal locus of control are likely to believe that individuals can control their behavior and its consequences. In contrast, those high in external locus of control believe that fate, luck, or people who are more powerful lead their actions, taking choice out of the equation. Jurors who have a high internal locus of control are more likely to see the defendant as responsible—i.e., "His actions are his choice; therefore, he didn't have to respond in that manner." [38]

Belief in a Just World

The just world hypothesis proposes that, in order to make sense of the world, people may grasp onto the idea that there is an inherent sense of justice in everything that happens. [39] In other words, people get what they deserve. The cognitive benefits to endorsing the belief in a just world include being able to categorize people and occurrences as "good" or "bad", or "right" or "wrong". The belief also gives one a sense of safety (e.g., if I am a good person, good things will happen to me) opposed to having to reconcile the fact that innocent people are victims of crime every day, regardless of their disposition.

A belief in a just world can affect a juror's verdict or perception of a case in two very distinct ways: blame the victim or be harsher on the defendant. [40] Common victims to blame are, unfortunately, women who have been raped and battered women. [41] Jurors with a strong belief in a just world may see the woman to be partially at fault (e.g., "She shouldn't have been out alone that late at night, wearing what she was wearing" or "She shouldn't have provoked him"). Blaming the victim is usually a last resort for people with a strong belief in a just world. If the world really is just, then a defendant who has committed a terrible crime should receive a terrible punishment; this idea leads just-world jurors to be harsher on the defendant than those jurors without a strong belief in a just world. [42]

Authoritarianism

The personality characteristic potentially most influential on a juror's verdict is level of authoritarianism. Authoritarianism is an ideology of complete and utter trust in authorities and a kind of blind obedience to the system, characterized by an adherence to traditional values and lack of tolerance for those who challenge these values or the status quo (e.g., homosexuals, atheists, hippies, etc.). [43]

Research on jurors rated as high authoritarians reveals that they are more likely to convict and impose harsher sentences than those low in authoritarianism. [44] The effect is even larger with legal authoritarianism, which is a strong adherence to legal authorities and a disregard for the civil liberties of the accused—an attitude that is much more specific to factors present in a trial than is authoritarianism. [45]

There is some evidence that people high in authoritarianism are more likely to rush to judgment when assessing a defendant and to base their decisions on gut, emotional reactions. [46] The one important exception is if the defendant has committed a crime that is consistent with the authoritarian perspective (e.g., breaking the law out of obedience to a superior) or is a person of authority him or herself (police officer, military officer, etc.) then the authoritarian juror may actually be more lenient.[47]

Besides personality differences, juror bias research has focused on the affects of specific attitudes. As mentioned, the more specific an attitude is to a case the more likely that attitude is to exert some sort of influence over the juror's task.[48] But research in the area has shown that specific attitudes (such as those toward the death penalty) predict more than just behavior relevant to that attitude (i.e., voting not guilty in order to avoid sentencing someone to death).

Attitudes toward the Death Penalty

Ellsworth and her colleagues have investigated attitudes toward the death penalty and the relation they have to verdicts and trial interpretations.[49] The criterion for a death-qualified juror, in a major case, is saying "No" in response to the following question: "Is your attitude toward the death penalty such that you would never be willing to impose it in any case, no matter the evidence?" If a juror answers "Yes" to this question during a trial's voir dire, he or she automatically excluded for bias. The presumption is that a strong opposition to the death penalty may lead a juror to vote to acquit in order to avoid sentencing a defendant to death.[50] The researchers thought that the jurors answering "No"—those remaining on the jury—were also biased, but in the opposite direction. In other words, those jurors who have been death-qualified are maybe more likely to convict.

Fitzgerald and Ellsworth used this Witherspoon standard and polled members of the community on their attitudes toward the death penalty.[51] Respondents who would have been excluded (roughly 19% of the sample) were more likely than those who were death-qualified to agree that letting a few guilty defendants go free was better than convicting an innocent person (63% to 44%, respectively). Death-qualified respondents were also more likely to agree that a defendant's failure to testify indicated guilt, that the insanity plea is a loophole, and that all laws should be strictly enforced. Death-qualified respondents also admitted that, even if instructed not to, they would consider a confession that was inadmissible—60% compared to 49% of Witherspoon "excludables." It seems that the attitude toward the death penalty predicts more than just how one responds in a capital trial. The researchers believed that the individual differences predicted by death-qualification were due to more general attitudes regarding the criminal justice system: due process and crime control attitudes. [52]

Due Process and Crime Control Attitudes

Packer's distinction between a due process and a crime control perspective suggests a template that society uses to assess the justice system. [53] He proposed that the state of legal affairs in the United States, and the ideological differences between its citizens, may be summarized as falling somewhere in between two extremes. At one end of the spectrum is crime control and with it the idea of the swift hand of justice and the other end is due process and a vigilant attempt to preserve individual rights.

For crime control, what is important is the finale and accordingly sanctioning those who commit crimes. The crime control model has a low tolerance for the adjudicative process. If a case has been thoroughly investigated then it is safe to assume the suspect is likely guilty. This "presumption of guilt" is what will allow the system to move in a more expeditious manner. [54]

According to this perspective, a perfect legal system would allow criminal investigations as much freedom as possible, demand efficiency and thoroughness in these investigations, advocate swift punishment if the investigation has deemed there is enough evidence to assume the individual in question is probably guilty (or expeditious exoneration if it is determined the defendant could not possibly be guilty), and employ adequate deterrents of future crime (generally in the form of harsh punishments).

It is incorrect to infer that the crime control perspective endorses wrongful convictions. Instead, it promotes extensive investigations of a crime in order to accurately exclude those who could not have committed the offense. But, it realizes that this may not always be possible, either because of limited resources or because of laws that restrict the investigative power of the police. In such circumstances, if those in charge of the investigation (police and prosecutors) believe the defendant most likely guilty, we should trust this judgment. Erring on the side of caution would be over-convicting rather than over-acquitting. Choosing policing over preservation of individual rights is a small price to pay for society's safety; after all, law-abiding citizens have nothing to fear.

On the other hand, the old adage that, "It is better for ten guilty men to go free than for one innocent man to suffer an injustice," is the foundation of the due process model. The tolerability for error is low. If there are any qualms about the guilt of an individual then that person should go free. In the crime control model, allowing investigators to use all necessary power to determine factual guilt is the goal of the legal system. The due process model makes a distinction between those who are factually guilty and those who are legally guilty. [55] Whether or not the individual actually committed the crime is secondary. What is important is whether, through legal means and by preserving individual rights, a valid adjudicative process finds that individual guilty.

A perfect due process system would consist of investigations stemming from solid evidence and carried out with the utmost respect for individual rights, an adjudicative process that carefully combs through and analyzes each aspect of a case for possible errors, and the never-ending possibility of review of a case if new evidence arises. The perspective recognizes that at every level, human error is a possibility and until we are sure that a case is completely devoid of any of the effects of human error (if this can ever truly be determined) that case is not "closed." There should be no limit to the number of appeals filed by those convicted of a crime.

Due process does not condone crime nor does endorsement of this perspective equal a view that crime is not a problem in society. [56] Instead, recognition of potential problems in criminal investigations (e.g., faulty eyewitness identifications and coerced confessions) and in legal proceedings (e.g., biased witnesses and inadequate counsel) suggests that we should never assume a case closed. Still, Packer suggests that the due process orientation, as he proposes it, is not void of affect, strictly concerned about preserving individual rights. He describe show a due-process leaning may promote anti-authoritarian views and a distrust of the players in the legal system.

Assessing Due Process and Crime Control

Even with knowledge of the two perspectives (and the face validity of the assumption that people differ along this dimension), attempts to evaluate whether the distinction actually exists have been scarce. The first step is to define exactly what one means by a due process and crime control distinction. Those addressing the topic have used Packer's outline of the models as a starting point. [57]

A simplistic view in assessing these biases is an assumption that we can define due process or crime control by their correlations with other attitudes; in other words, proposing the definitions of due process and crime control a posteriori from observing the relationships between attitudes concerning the death penalty, pro-prosecution or pro-defense standings, authoritarianism and conservatism. [58]

The research on death-qualified jurors indicates that attitudes toward the death penalty relate to attitudes toward other aspects of the legal system.[59] Death-qualified jurors are pro-prosecution, suspicious of defendants, distrusting of defense attorneys, and unlikely to favor due process initiatives in the criminal justice system. Fitzgerald and Ellsworth suggest that this shows attitudes toward the death penalty predicted whether a juror was due-process oriented (focused on preserving individual rights in the justice system) or crime control oriented (focused on swift, efficient justice). [60]

Unfortunately, while Fitzgerald and Ellsworth presented questions that appear to be representative of a due process ("It is better for society to let some people go free than to risk convicting an innocent person") and a crime control ("All laws should be strictly enforced, no matter what the results") perspective, each of the ten items was treated as a separate measure and not empirically combined to determine overall factor structure. [61] Analysis of their data actually shows the individual items purported to represent the constructs had only a small relationship with one another which is not what one would expect if the items are representing the same construct. [62]

Liu and Shure believed that the ideas of due process based on Packer's model did not clearly distinguish between due process as an ideological concept and due process as a basis for legal decision making.[63] The authors propose that what researchers have been calling due process or crime control actually represents social and political ideas of justice. While the previous literature referenced does not use the concepts of due process and liberalism or crime control and conservatism interchangeably, it does emphasize relationships between the legal attitudes of due process and crime control and death qualification and between the political attitudes of liberalism and conservatism and death qualification, leading to the tentative assumption that that those who are due process may be liberal and those who are crime control may be conservative. [64]

Liu and Shure suggest that the concepts are not necessarily related, specifically that due process attitudes do not always coincide with political liberalism. [65] The example they provide is the American Civil Liberties Union's—strong supporters of all that represents due process and preservation of individual rights—decision to support the right of a Nazi party to march in a pre-dominantly Jewish suburb of Skokie, Illinois.

Liberals would not likely set aside their distaste for such a group in order to preserve individual rights.

What Liu and Shure are suggesting is correct, but a strict legal definition of "due process" is not that defined by Packer's model, nor that perceived by the general public. [66] Packer states that a part of the due process perspective that is important, though often not acknowledged, is a "mood of skepticism about the morality and the utility of the criminal sanction, taken either as a whole or in some of its applications". [67] Removing the emotional and ideological content from the due process and crime control orientation is ignoring important parts of the constructs, such as the anger a crime-control individual may feel when an offender is given a light sentence or the cynicism a due-process individual may feel when hearing about an illegal search.

In their research, Liu and Shure found that strictly legal due process was not related to "due process/crime control" (as represented by 7 items from the Fitzgerald and Ellsworth scale and one new, similar item composed by the authors). [68] Interestingly, the due process/crime control ideology based attitude assessment accounted for more of the overall variance in a scale combining this measure and the legal due process measure. The authors did not report which scale was a better predictor of overall verdicts for their simulated trial.

Another problem with the previous research attempting to assess due process and crime control is the automatic assumption that the concepts represent a bipolar perspective. [69] Previous studies have used low endorsement of due process to represent a measure of crime control. Although this is the relationship as Packer had envisioned it, and the face validity of the content of the constructs may endorse such an approach, there is no direct empirical test demonstrating that they are in fact two ends of a spectrum and not separate concepts entirely. [70]

Kerlinger discusses the concept of criterial referents related to social attitudes. [71] He says that one should not automatically assume that being "for" one thing necessarily means being "against" another. A referent is simply any object or thing to which an attitude can be directed—sentences imposed on offenders would be a referent for the due process or crime control perspective—while a criterion dictates the importance of the referent. For example, believing that law-breakers should be harshly punished (referent) may be criterial for a crime control perspective. Stating that two attitudes are bipolar is not just saying they are inversely related but also suggests that both attitudes have the exact same criterial referents.[72]

If crime control respondents believe that offenders should be harshly punished, a due process respondent would necessarily have to believe that offenders should not be harshly punished. Of course due process orientation does not equal wanting to see murderers set free. The fact is, as long as the punishment is justified (e.g., the offender's legal guilt, and not just factual guilt, was duly established and the punishment is not doled out differently to different groups of people), due process endorsement does not necessarily speak to its severity unless we are discussing the death penalty, which necessarily negates any future review of a case and violates the precept of due process. Crime control and due process individuals could both believe that criminals often receive sentences that are too light for their crime. For the crime control individuals this is exactly why we need to be more concerned with justice and less with individual rights. For the due process individuals, it may not be an important concern; it is not necessarily a criterial referent.

While all of the previous studies focused on what effect crime control and due process attitudes may have on an individual juror, and the definitions of the concepts (as ideologies) across the studies are near identical, none of them have developed a reliable measure built from the theoretical constructs to examine exactly how due process and crime control perspectives are structured and how they may relate to one another. [73]

CHAPTER EIGHT

Gender Discrimination

Gender discrimination is pervasive within our society and is found in a multitude of settings. How individuals are treated in everyday life, from buying a car, hiring a mechanic, and even interacting with health care professionals is often influenced by perceived stereotypical differences between genders. [1] Within the employment arena gender stereotyping can affect decisions from recruitment, hiring, promotion, job advancement opportunities to retention. [2] Additionally, how gender-based stereotypes are perceived affects biases in evaluations. [3] Individuals are perceived and evaluated differently depending on whether their actions violate expectations of how they should act or expectations of what actions are required for a role they have assumed. [4] Both male and female gender roles can lead to discrimination when those roles are in conflict with expectations of social or work roles. Women trying to succeed in a masculine work role, such as upper management, will face obstacles based on their gender. Likewise, men taking a stereotypical feminine job, such as caring for children, are likely to find themselves the target of discrimination in hiring and performance ratings. However, research has shown that gender discrimination is generally more pervasive and has a deeper impact on women than on men. [5]

Gender disparity, although decreasing, is still a reality of the modern workplace.

Although women make up half the workforce there are very few at the top levels of corporate America. Women are chief executive officers (CEO) in a little over one percent of over 800 companies recently surveyed. [6] Across all jobs, women still earn 79% of what men do. [7] Even when adjusting for seniority, work experience, and qualifications, women make less than men for the same work. [8] Bayard, Hellerstein, Neumark, and Troske examined gender differences in pay using matched, employee-to-employee data across all industries throughout the United States using U.S. census data. [9] Experience and career choice accounted for a significant portion of gender differences in earnings, but a sizable proportion of variance in men's and women's earnings was left unexplained suggesting that discrimination or bias is a plausible explanation for wage disparities. Sexual harassment also plays a role in limiting women's advancement by creating a hostile work environment. A recent meta-analysis found 24% of women had been sexually harassed and 58% had been exposed to potentially harassing behaviors. [10] More recently, Street, Gradus, Stafford, and Kelly reported that in a sample of over 4,000 military reservists 40% of women working in such a male dominated field had been harassed in the last two years. [11] Fifty percent of men reported behaving in ways that could have been perceived by female coworkers as sexually harassing according to a New York Times / CBS News national poll. [12]

Although stereotype processes cannot account for all disparity between the genders, research has shown it plays an important role. Direct self-report measures of gender bias, like racial bias, are less likely to detect anti-woman bias as admitting to negative stereotypes about women becomes less socially acceptable. Automatic measures of bias can circumvent social desirability and are able to detect unconscious beliefs in gender stereotypes. Individuating information has been found to reduce reliance on stereotypes when evaluating women. [13] Such findings provide support for Copus's and Landy's critique of the stranger-to-stranger paradigm.[14] However, individuating information that portrays women with requisite agentic characteristics associated with management may cause backlash violating stereotypes of how women are supposed to act. [15] Stereotyped bias, both intentional and automatic, directly applies to gender discrimination in the workplace. In this chapter we will explore previous research in role congruity, gender stereotyping, and the use of explicit and implicit measures. This review will focus on expanding current research methodology to include previous experience with the targets of prejudice.

Research on gender stereotypes, social cognition, conscious and unconscious bias, along with organizational performance evaluation is all relevant to the examination of gender discrimination. Stereotypes may be either conscious or automatic. [16] Conscious stereotypes are intentional and made with awareness and can be measured with explicit direct measures. [17] In contrast, automatic stereotypes are unconscious and are often active without intention or awareness and are measured with indirect or implicit measures. [18] Additionally, stereotypes can be descriptive or prescriptive. [19] Descriptive stereotypes reflect the beliefs or expectations about how people are, whereas prescriptive stereotypes are expectations of how people ought to be. The nature and activation of stereotypes, their implicit and explicit measurement, and the use of prescriptive and descriptive stereotypes are all key elements to understanding the pervasive nature of gender discrimination. [20] Special attention needs to be placed on individual and group differences in stereotyping as well as the issue of accuracy in the day-to-day use of stereotypes to aid decision-making.

Stereotypes are social cognitions traditionally measured using explicit measures and more recently using implicit methods such as the implicit association test. [21] The use of both prescriptive and descriptive stereotypes in gender discrimination is the applied focus of this review. Gender discrimination and theories such as role congruity theory will be examined. The use of implicit measures as an indicator of gender stereotype bias will be reviewed with a focus on the implicit association test construct and external validity. Familiarity of targets in implicit and explicit stereotype studies will be examined including arguments that have been leveled against stereotyping research, such as the stranger-to-stranger paradigm, where naïve raters evaluate people they do not know (often fictitious people described on paper). [22] Finally, the literature on implicit and explicit measures of stereotypes, gender discrimination, and prescriptive, and descriptive stereotypes will combined in order to generate research propositions.

A final piece that has received little attention is the role of target familiarity on the activation of prescriptive and descriptive stereotypes and their implicit and explicit measurement. A common criticism leveled at empirical findings regarding the use of stereotypes in activating prejudicial behavior is that of the stranger-to-stranger paradigm; which refers to naive raters evaluating unknown women and or men using information provided within an experimental study. [23] Landy argued that our knowledge concerning stereotype-activated prejudice and discrimination is based on experimental participants evaluating strangers. [24] Thus, Landy suggested what is known about stereotyping cannot be generalized to situations in which perceivers or evaluators know well the potential targets of stereotype based discrimination—such as managers evaluating their subordinates, or followers evaluating their leaders. With this criticism in mind, the nature of gender discrimination will be examined with a further focus on the familiarity of the person perceived.

Gender discrimination stereotyping is not only an area of interest within social and organizational psychology it is also an area with direct applied application. There is a clear business application as well as a social justice element to defining the psychological mechanisms behind inaccurate and inappropriate biases based on stereotypes. Stereotype activations affect judgments, evaluations, and outcomes for the targets of negative stereotypes. Expanded understanding of these processes and understanding the relationships between stereotypes and target familiarity of these stereotypes can directly help address and alleviate social injustice.

Stereotypes: Explicit Measures of Bias

Stereotyping is a form of social categorization in which pre-existing beliefs are uncritically associated with social categories (a particular race or a particular gender). [25] Stereotypes can be described as a syllogism where: X's believe that Y's are especially Z. For example: "men" believe that "women" are especially "communal." Once stereotypes are formed, other characteristics of the individual tend to be ignored and characteristics attributed to the group category are emphasized. Stereotypes are a group of cognitions, beliefs and feelings towards a person based on the target's perceived social identity group membership. Stereotypes, once activated, can influence how people see others. People make assumptions about individuals based on their beliefs concerning traits they have associated with a social category of which the target individual is a member. Stereotypes also affect how individuals perceive and feel about themselves. These feelings are strengthened by their own and others' endorsement of the validity of these beliefs. Stereotypes can be activated by qualities of the person being categorized including easily determined master categories such as race or gender and also harder to determine social group memberships such as being politically conservative. Measures of stereotype bias, cognitive processing of stereotypes, the internalizing of negative stereotypes, and negative stereotype-based effects on self-esteem all impact gender discrimination.

Internalizing Negative Stereotypes

Stereotypes targeted on a social group have negative consequences on the individual stereotyped. Negative stereotypes held against an individual not only affect the evaluations of others, they also affect self-evaluations and self-defeating behaviors. When individuals become aware they are the target of a negative stereotype, their performance can be affected through behavioral confirmation processes such as self-fulfilling prophecies and stereotype threat.[26] Self-endorsement of stereotypes plays an important role in prejudice as an attitude manifesting itself as discrimination.[27] Additionally, the likelihood of individuals using stereotypical thinking increases as their level of social power also increases.[28]

Self-endorsement of negative stereotypes can contribute to a self-fulfilling prophesy, behaving in such a way to validate the negative assumptions of others.[29] Implicit endorsement of stereotypes has been found in women believing that men have stronger math skills than women, for example. The stronger this endorsement, the lower the self-identification women have with math and the poorer their standardized math scores.[30] Social dominance theory suggests that legitimizing ideologies, such as supporting male superiority in math stereotypes, predict acceptance of negative stereotypes.[31] The level of an individual's endorsement of a negative stereotype may well increase the likelihood of behaviors that could indirectly reinforce the existence of the stereotype both in the target of the stereotype and others.

Internal beliefs, the individual's endorsement of a negative stereotype, a hostile environment, and situations that prime a negative stereotype can each heighten the impact of stereotyping on discrimination.[32] Hostile environments are often studied with regard to sexual harassment and have also been shown in isolation to affect female math score performances.[33] Hostile environments not only have a negative effect on stigmatized group members but also generate a positive effect for those not stigmatized.[34] As the perception of a hostile environment increased, women's self-evaluations decreased as men's self-evaluations increased. Walton and Cohen found in a meta-analysis on stereotype threat research that majority-group members often perform better when tested in the presence of negatively stereotyped individuals.[35]

The literature on stereotypes illustrate that stereotypes held against out-group members is a source of prejudice and discrimination. However, the process of internalizing or endorsing stereotypes also plays a role in inaccurate appraisals. Stigmatized out-group individuals' behavior is affected when they endorse stereotypes of gender expectations and/or work-role expectations.[36] Stereotypes become harmful when they are used to negatively evaluate an individual, ignoring information about the individual in favor of stereotype-based assumptions. Prejudicial stereotypes

Negative Stigmatization, Group Membership, and Self-Esteem

Katz, Joiner, and Kwon examined how stereotype internalization leads to emotional distress through its effects on personal and collective self-esteem. [38] Self-esteem can be defined in many ways, but in a broad sense refers to an individual's feelings of self-worth. [39] Self-esteem can be divided into personal self-esteem and collective self-esteem in accordance with social identity theory. [40] Personal self-esteem is a person's feeling of self-worth as an individual, whereas collective self-esteem is the value placed by an individual on their own social group. [41] Katz suggested three ways that stereotype internalization increases emotional distress of members of devalued groups. [42] First, negative stereotypes can directly impact collective self-esteem of the devalued group. Second, independent of personal self-esteem, negative stereotypes can cause individuals to feel devalued due to group membership. Third, individuals may develop negative attitudes and behaviors associated by stereotypes with group membership. It is through these three pathways that negative stereotypes lead to increased risk of emotional distress. In contrast, Trafimov, Armendariz, and Madson found that people make less strong self-attributions of negative behaviors. [43] Negative behavior, although still negative, is seen as less negative in one's self as compared to how negative behavior is seen in others. [44]

Swann argued against external behavioral confirmation processes, such as self-fulfilling prophecy.[45] Swann suggested that individuals use self-verification when confronted with negative stereotypes. Self-verification states that if an individual knows he or she is not captured by a negative stereotype, when confronted by that stereotype, the individual strives to disprove that stereotype. [46] For example, if people expect a woman to be communal, and she knows she is actually aggressive, she will then behave even more aggressively when faced with the communal stereotype. This process can occur intentionally or without conscious awareness. Higgins suggested that self-verification manifests when various other factors co-occur, such as self-endorsement of the stereotype. [47] Madon found that both self-verification and self-fulfilling prophecy were present in targets and perceivers in real world situations suggesting that both stereotype-based processes can lead to underperformance. [48]

Ditto and Griffin found that the way self-esteem is used as a defense is moderated by the person's level of self-esteem. [49] People with high self-esteem perceive positive traits within themselves to be rarer in the population than those with low self-esteem. Similarly, people with high self-esteem perceived their disliked traits to be more common in the population than those with low self-esteem. Stigmatized group members attribute negative feedback to outward prejudice in order to defend their self-esteem. Stigmatized individuals will compare their personal outcomes within their ingroup while tending to ignore out-group comparisons. Additionally, they will selectively devalue dimensions on which their own group does poorly while assigning larger value to dimensions in which their group is seen as excelling. [50]

Therefore, in general, self-esteem has been shown to be used as a modulated defense against the anxiety produced by stereotype-based prejudice. Blanton, Crocker, and Miller examined in-group versus out-group comparisons when faced with a negative stereotype and the effects of these comparisons on self-esteem. [51] They found that personal self-esteem increased when there was an upward in-group comparison being made. Upward comparisons are made when individuals compare their performance to those doing better. [52] Likewise, downward comparisons are made to those doing worse. Lockwood found that when someone else who was perceived as being an in-group member does better, other underperforming members of the ingroup felt better about themselves. [53] Additionally, self-esteem also increased when someone from an out-group was seen as doing worse on a task; that is, a downward outgroup comparison occurred under these conditions. Upward in-group comparisons and downward out-group comparisons lead to higher personal self-esteem. However, upward out-group and downward in-group comparisons lead to a reduction in self-esteem. Personal self-esteem is reduced when someone seen as an out-group member is seen performing well or when someone seen as an in-group member is seen performing badly.

These results have been further refined by two studies looking at people with only low and high self-esteem. Martinot, Redersdorff, Guimond, and Dif looked at ingroup and out-group comparisons and group status within the in-group. [54] Their results suggested that the findings of Blanton et al. (2000) are limited to group members with average or low self-esteem. Martinot found group members with high self-esteem saw upward comparisons with out-group members as non-relevant. [55] When someone with high self-esteem observes an out-group member doing well, their own self-esteem is not affected. High personal self-esteem provides a defense from upward outgroup comparisons. However, high self-esteem members actually suffered a self-esteem loss from upward comparisons with others of their in-group. Although high self-esteem was shown to remove the threat of out-group upwards comparisons, it does so at the cost of increasing the threat of in-group upwards comparisons. Buunk, Collins, Taylor, Dakof, and Yperen examined groups having low self-esteem—cancer patients and people experiencing marital difficulties. [56] These groups showed negative affect from both upward and downward comparison on self-esteem regardless of whether it was to in-group or out-group comparisons. When people with low self-esteem observed anyone doing better or doing worse than their own performance, regardless of whether or not they were in the observer's in-group, their self-esteem was reduced. Individuals with neither very high nor very low self-esteem are most affected by self-esteem changes dependent on the target of comparison. [57] The findings on collective and personal self-esteem, in-group and out-group-based negative stigmatization, and stereotype-based performance decrements are all directly related to discrimination in the workplace. Prescriptive and descriptive stereotypes are formed on the basis of in-group and out-group status.[58] Stereotype-based expectations directly affect both the decisions and behavior of those using stereotypes, but also the behavior and performance of those who are stereotyped. [59] The measurement of stereotypes and self-perceptions is an important element of bias research. Both explicit and implicit measures can be used to measure the degree and the way in which individuals engage in stereotyping.

Explicit Measures: Automatic versus Controlled Cognitive Processing

Although common, explicit self-report measures examining gender discrimination have serious limitations. Explicit measures are based on a the assumptions that the participant (a) has direct access to their prejudicial attitudes, (b) can report them accurately, and (c) is willing to disclose possibly socially unacceptable attitudes.[60] Therefore, explicit measures capture known, properly interpreted prejudices, which individuals are willing to express. Implicit measures infer prejudice and bias by assessing the degree to which people automatically and unconsciously associate the target category with stereotypical or negative attributes. Implicit use such secondary measures as reaction times in a sorting task. [61] Implicit measures are not suggested as a replacement, but as an alternative to self-report (explicit) measures of prejudice. Although there is still active debate concerning the validity of using implicit measures to infer attitudes, current research indicates they may be more accurate than traditional self-report explicit measures. [62] The largest advantage of implicit measures is that they are not dependent on the assumptions of explicit measures.

Individuals taking an implicit measure do not need to be aware, understand, or even be willing to express possible prejudice in order for an implicit test to detect the potential for automatic bias. The advantages of implicit measures and questions concerning their validity will be examined later. Explicit measures measure conscious or controlled processing, whereas implicit measures infer an automatic bias. The differences between automatic and controlled cognitive processing directly pertain to measures of bias and their respective explicit or implicit measurement.

Shiffrin and Schneider suggested two types of cognitive processing; automatic and controlled. [63] Automatic processing occurs without conscious control and can occur without a person's awareness. Shiffrin and Schneider originally suggested automatic processes were produced without (a) intention, (b) awareness and (c) needing to use cognitive resources. Shiffrin and Schneider later identified that these three aspects of automatic behaviors are independent and automatic behaviors can occur in the presence or absence of intention, awareness and/or cognitive resources. [64] Shiffrin and Schneider suggested that automatic cognitions are reflexive or uncontrolled. [65] Stroop illustrated this reflexivity in his classic experiment examining participants' reaction times naming words of colors presented in incongruent colors (the word "red" typed in green ink). [66] Bargh argued that automatic cognitions are not reflexive, but contingent on individuals being in the right response mode. [67] Thus, there is a conscious decision to initiate an automatic processing mode, such as deciding to tie a shoe lace.

Automatic cognitive functions have also been tied to the amount of practice a particular activity has undergone. [68] Automatic cognitive processes are highly useful allowing complex tasks to become automatic upon repetition. Findings of automatic bias based on stereotyping builds on the literature of automatic cognitive processing. Automatic processing was originally seen as reflexive and later as a cognitive resource saving activity based on practice. [69] Implicit measures examine automatic processing that is not tied to purposeful practice, but built over a lifetime of stereotype reinforcement. Implicit stereotypes are automatic and are not dependent on intention or awareness. The bias measured by implicit measures is most likely formed through repetitive use of stereotypes to make judgments.

In contrast to automatic processing, controlled cognition requires intention, awareness, and cognitive resources. [70] As a cognitive task becomes more difficult, it becomes less likely that it can be completed automatically. Controlled cognition is more likely in situations requiring attention, such as complex tasks, novel tasks, or tasks where there is motivation for concentration. Controlled cognitive intentions are measured by explicit self-report measures. Explicit measures capture intentional attitudes; the individual is aware of, and willing to self-report. This is in contrast to implicit measures of automatic bias representing bias occurring without intention or awareness. Both controlled and automatic bias may lead to discrimination in different situations. [71] For example, a person may have a strong motivation to not engage in discrimination and in situations allowing controlled cognition, is also likely to not discriminate. However, that same person may still behave in ways that subtly discriminate when automatic processing is utilized.

The use of automatic versus controlled cognitive strategies is conditioned on the type of task, past experiences, and one's motivation to use cognitive resources. [72] Similarly, the use of explicit or implicit measures capture different conditional aspects of bias based on the type of interaction, our past experiences and motivation. Thus an individual with a strong automatic bias, who is strongly motivated to not exhibit prejudicial behavior, may well not act on biases in situations allowing controlled cognition. However, if the situation does not allow attention and/or awareness an individual's implicit bias will manifest in reflexive behavior. [73]

An example of automatic bias is found in Banaji and Greenwald's findings of gender bias against female names. [74] Participants were quicker and more successful with associating famous male names with fame than famous female names with fame. A past immediate experience, such as priming participants with famous images prior to the implicit testing, was found to influence later performance. Those participants who were exposed to the famous images before completing an automatic bias measure showed less gender bias. However, self-report sexism scores were not found to have a relationship with implicit bias. In other words, people who self-reported having no or very low scores of explicit sexism had the same level of implicit bias for male famous names than participants with high explicit sexism.

Being the target of negative stereotypes has both direct and indirect effects on performance, self-esteem, and perceptions of the target, which subsequently affect discrimination. The study of direct and indirect effects of stereotyping of individuals based on gender can be further refined. Stereotype-based discrimination differs depending on the stereotype being validated and violated. Women can either confirm or validate cultural held stereotypes of how women should act or violate these same expectations.

Prescriptive and Descriptive Gender Stereotypes

Through literature, researchers have found that bias against women is related to the social roles women occupied. [75] Openly negative or hostile views of women, in general, are not common. [76] Women are typically seen as possessing positive yet passive traits. [77] Discrimination often occurs when women are seen as occupying culturally unacceptable roles requiring "masculine" traits. [78]

Descriptive norms are beliefs about what women and men actually do, whereas prescriptive norms are expectations of what men and women ought to do. [79] As evidence of descriptive stereotyping, Schein found higher correlations for male stereotypes and leadership stereotypes than stereotypes of women and leadership. [80] The men-as-leaders bias has been found in Europe, China, and Japan. [81] This is also known as "think-manager-think-male" bias. [82] This bias states that traits associated with attributes ascribed to men correspond to traits associated with managers more so than do traits ascribed to women. [83] Schein found that women, but not men, have been moving to a more androgynous view of leadership. [84] Jackson and Engstrom found that men still supported the think manager-think male bias, but women did not. [85] Duehr and Bono found that male managers endorsing the think-manager-think-male bias has been receding, but found that it was still strong in male college students. [86] The incongruity between perceptions of women and perceptions of leadership provides an environment ripe for discrimination and prejudice.[87] Gender bias includes less favorable evaluations for potential women leaders and of actual women leaders.

Eagly and Karau suggested that when women violate descriptive and prescriptive stereotypes they are more likely to be negatively evaluated. [88] Eagly and Karau proposed role congruity theory to provide a model explaining gender differences in performance appraisals.[89] Role congruity theory is an extension of Eagly's social role theory. [90] Social role theory states that men and women behave differently, including work related choices, because of societal expectations of what roles men and women should occupy. In industrialized countries, women are still expected to assume caregiver roles and men to assume provider roles. [91] Although the focus of role congruity theory is on social roles, prescriptive and descriptive stereotypes of those roles are a key feature. Descriptive stereotypes indicate what a job or person *is* like and prescriptive stereotypes indicate what a job or person *should* be like. Rudman and Glick suggested that aggressive and instrumental behaviors (agentic) are seen as masculine whereas expressive and nurturing behaviors (communal) are seen as feminine. [92] Role congruity theory predicts gender bias when women violate descriptive and/or prescriptive stereotypes.

Stereotypes are beliefs and opinions held by and individual, compared to stereotyping that refers to a process—the extent to which stereotypes are applied and affect behavior. Descriptive stereotyping reflects the perception of certain traits or characteristics belonging to a member of a social category based only on their membership in that group. Prescriptive stereotyping is the expectation that a person belonging to a social category ought to possess expected traits or characteristics. [93]

Prejudice occurs when there is incongruity between a person's gender role and the social role an individual wants to fill. [94] Thus, a woman with generally desirable trait of kindness may be seen as less competent when assuming a role associated with assertiveness. Role congruity theory is similar to Heilman's lack-of-fit model examining bias in performance appraisals when there is inconsistency between work roles and traits associated with an individual's group membership. [95] Role congruity theory suggests that it is this lack-of-fit between the perceived traits of the individual and the perceived required traits of the social role that leads to prejudicial hiring, compensation, evaluation, and promotion decisions. [96] In certain roles women will be seen as more competent than men and vice-versa depending on the masculine or feminine nature of the roles. Women will be seen as less competent than men in a masculine role such as a manager. Likewise, men will be seen as less competent in a feminine role such as nursing.

Role congruity theory suggests how prescriptive and descriptive stereotypes and stereotyping can lead to disparate impact and disparate treatment.[97] Disparate impact can result from violations of descriptive stereotypes and results in hiring and promotion practices that are biased against individuals based on group membership. Potential role occupants are the primary target of disparate impact discrimination. Women are hired and promoted less often when a work role is seen as masculine. Disparate treatment can result from violating prescriptive stereotypes and affects performance evaluations once an incongruent work role has been assumed. For example: a woman who has become an upper level manager may receive lower performance appraisals as she violates the prescriptive stereotype of how women should behave. [98] Gender prejudice as predicted by role congruity theory has been supported by meta-analysis and field studies manipulating the gender of job applicants. [99]

Role congruity theory examines the role of social roles and stereotypes. Glick and Fiske suggest that benevolent sexism and hostile sexism are individual difference variables. [100] Glick and Fiske offered the theory of ambivalent sexism, which implies that overt hostile sexism has direct links to discrimination; however, benevolent (well meaning) sexism also plays a role in discrimination. [101] Hostile sexism includes negative opinions of women supporting male dominance, whereas benevolent sexism involves positive attitudes about women, putting them on a pedestal while simultaneously reinforcing their subordinate position compared to men. Benevolent sexism is characterized by a strong positive regard for women as long as they fulfill specific, expected roles. [102] Role congruity theory provides a situational model and ambivalent sexism provides a personal variable framework in which to examine why and how gender discrimination occurs.

Prescriptive and descriptive stereotypes are strongly tied to agentic and communal behaviors. For example, agentic women possess descriptive traits of a workplace leader, but they simultaneously violate the prescriptive stereotype of what women should be like (i.e., communal). Agentic behaviors are strongly linked to competence. [103] Thus, to be perceived as competent women need to exhibit agentic behaviors, however doing so leads to a backlash where they are viewed as less communal, and therefore less likeable. Rudman showed that agentic women are seen as socially deficient compared to agentic men. [104]

Rudman and Glick examined prescriptive gender stereotypes and how violations of these stereotypes lead to a backlash of negative evaluation towards agentic women. [105] Jobs with feminized job descriptions compared to masculine jobs lead to lower ratings for women described as agentic. Agentic women who were perceived as equally agentic to men were perceived as less likable and less capable. Discrimination based on perceived incompetence (not fitting the descriptive agentic stereotype of a job) was found along with gender stereotypes (that women should be communal). To overcome descriptive stereotypes, women needed to act agentic in order to be seen as equally suited as men. [106] However, agentic women then violated prescriptive stereotypes of what women should be like.

Agentic behavior has further been separated into competence (self-reliant, individualistic, ambitious) and social dominance (competitiveness, decisiveness, aggression, forceful). Rudman and Glick showed that women's self-ratings are similar to men's on agentic competence but lower on agentic social dominance. [107] Women are discouraged from showing social dominance and are rated lower on performance when they do. Women who exhibit competence without exhibiting social dominance do not suffer from a reduction in performance ratings. Men do not suffer a reduction in ratings for showing social dominance.

Lower-status groups regardless of gender are often stereotyped as communal and not agentic. In women this can be seen directly in examples of benevolent sexism, perceiving women in a positive but inferior light. [108] This lower-status communal stereotype is strengthened by the dominant group's need for subordinate's cooperation. [109] The dominant group benefits from perpetuating a positive but submissive social expectation for subordinate groups.

Further supporting gender biases are stable sex differences in the endorsement of self-descriptive stereotypes. Men and women strongly endorse communal stereotypes of women, but they are endorsed more strongly by men. [110] Women using an agentic style are seen as competent but are seen as insufficiently nice. Identically described men do not suffer this backlash against their perceived likability. [111] Women and men along with sexists and non-sexists all endorse women's communal nature. [112] Furthermore, sexist men exhibit backlash against agentic women rating them as less likable, but so do non-sexist men and women. [113] Additionally, communal word pairs and women along with agentic word pairs and men have strong correlations. [114] Glick and Fiske's explicit measure, the Ambivalent Sexism Inventory (ASI), has provided supporting evidence of prescriptive and descriptive stereotypes of women as communal. [115] Finally, implicit measures have also found an equally strong bias regarding women as communal in both men and women. [116]

Role behavior and culture shapes gender stereotypes, and stereotypes of women are dynamic and changing, especially due to the increase of women in leadership roles. [117] For example, Twenge recently found no gender differences in expectations of assertiveness. [118] There is a growing trend in the business world to feminize jobs by having a stronger social focus and favoring more participatory leadership styles. [119] Additionally, transformational leadership which contains a strong communal component is regarded as the most effective form of leadership. [120] Women are generally perceived to be more transformational in leadership style compared to men.[121] This feminization trend is expected to result in agentic women facing even more backlash. Phelan, Moss-Racusin, and Rudman found when deciding to hire an agentic women, social skills were more highly weighted in the hiring decision over competence.[122] Agentic women were not only seen as less friendly, but when evaluating agentic women, friendliness was the primary criteria used in the hiring decision.

Phelan suggests that the feminization trend may result in backlash for agentic women.[123] Agentic women are viewed as less likable, less socially skilled, and less hirable for feminized jobs compared to agentic men.[124] The agentic subset of social dominance seems to be linked more to backlash against agentic women. The combination of a higher demand for likeability in addition to competence in the workplace puts women in a tenuous position. Women must project competence, without showing social dominance, while remaining communal. Men, in contrast do not need to worry about a backlash against their likeability due to exhibiting competence or social-dominance-based agentic behaviors.

Men are seen as more agentic and women more communal and agentic traits are associated with leadership.[125] Leaders are associated with more task-oriented and agentic skills.[126] Agentic behaviors are often referred to in business as initiating structure and communal behaviors are termed as consideration.[127] Schriesheim examined the differences between genders on initiating structures and consideration.[128] Schriesheim supported role congruity theory by finding that initiating structure was associated with masculine traits and consideration was associated with feminine traits.[129] Additionally, they found that men were perceived as leaders more often than women. Although a small percentage of participants exclusively associated men with leadership, none of the participants exclusively associated women with of leadership roles. Scesny examined the prescriptive and descriptive fit between women and leadership roles.[130] Using an implicit measure of bias, individuals associated men more quickly with executive roles compared to women. However, women and men did not differ on task and person skills when self-assessed. Also men and women did not differ on self-reports of the importance ratings of these skills. Scesny also found that task-oriented skills were attributed more strongly to leaders and men, than women attributed such skills to themselves.

Women have a difficult road to travel in order to compete with men for leadership positions in the workplace. Men are free to use multiple paths to express agentic qualities without fear of suffering setbacks because they are perceived as being less likable. Women are limited in behaviors they can exhibit and must guard against being seen as non-communal. Prescriptive and descriptive stereotypes illustrate the differences between the genders on the path that must be followed to gain promotion and advancement. The perception and bias associated with prescriptive and descriptive stereotype violations are often automatic and therefore need to be measured using implicit methods.

Gender Stereotypes and Negotiation

Negotiation is an important skill both in managing and obtaining promotion. O'Shea and Bush found an average increase of $1,500 on final salary offers for recent graduates who used negotiation compared to those that did not. [131] Unfortunately for women, negotiation are often seen as an agentic behavior violating prescriptive stereotypes of how women should behave. Kray and Thompson reviewed over 25 years of gender differences in negotiation. [132] Their review found support for men being seen as higher performing compared to women in mixed gender discussions. However, findings were not consistent and indicated a complex relationship dependent on the outcome measured, goals of the negotiation, perceptions and stereotypical beliefs of both participants in the negotiation, and genders of the participants. In contrast Stuhlmacher and Walters used a meta-analysis of 21 studies and found that men received better distributive outcomes in negotiation compared to women even after adjusting for relative power differences in the negotiation, gender composition, and suggested modes of communication.[133] Negotiation is a highly useful skill and instrumental in obtaining higher salaries. Men have been found to have an advantage in negotiation outcomes.

Nash identified two dominant styles of negotiation: cooperative and non-cooperative. [134] Although non-cooperative negotiation is more often seen as involving masculine or agentic skills, using cooperative negotiation is also associated with agentic/masculine skills. [135] Andreoni and Vesterlund found that men used instrumental (agentic) strategies in negotiation more often than women and would be cooperative only when there was low cost associated with cooperative behavior. [136] In contrast women used communal strategies more often and cooperated even when such behavior had a large cost associated with it. Buchan, Croson, and Solnick found that men were more strategic in negotiation and women felt a stronger obligation to both trust and be trusting in negotiations. [137] Kray, Galinsky and Thompson found that when instrumental traits were associated with successful negotiation men out performed women, and likewise if communal traits were emphasized women outperformed men. [138]

Kray, Thompson, and Galinsky found evidence that stereotype threat was active in dyadic mixed gender negotiations. [139] When women thought their negotiation skills were under evaluation as a woman, they underperformed compared to men. This difference between men's and women's performance was not found when the negative stereotype that women lack masculine negotiation skills was not activated. Likewise Small, Gelfand, Babcock, and Gettman found that women were less likely than men to initiate negotiation as women reported feeling intimidated. [140] However, when the same activity was described as an "opportunity to ask" gender differences in initiating negotiation were no longer found. Stuhlmacher, Citera, and Willis examined gender differences between face-to-face versus virtual negotiations in a meta-analysis of 22 studies. [141] There was no difference in men's hostile (agentic) behavior across face-to-face and virtual studies; however, women were significantly more agentic in virtual negotiations. Unfortunately, Stuhlmacher also found that virtual negotiations were less successful compared to face-to-face negotiations. Stevens, Bavetta, and Gist found that women were less successful in salary negotiation but specific and extensive training in self-management training could remove these differences. [142]

In general men tend to set higher goals, are more willing to initiate negotiation, and feel more entitled to negotiation conforming to masculine, agentic stereotypes. [143] Likewise, women set lower goals, view negotiation apprehensively, are less certain of their worth, and tend to use more tentative speech in negotiations compared to men. [144] These behaviors conform to communal descriptive stereotypes of women. Impression management, controlling the impression an individual makes on others, is also an important skill in negotiation. Guadagno and Cialdini found that men were more likely to use instrumental techniques of impression management including self-promoting and favor rendering, whereas women used communal tactics such as modesty and opinion conformity. [145] Gender differences in negotiation and impression management tactics provide further support for Eagly and Karau's role congruity theory. [146]

Bowles, Babcock, and Lai directly examined role congruity theory and prescriptive and descriptive stereotypes in women's negotiation outcomes. [147] Women who initiated negotiations for a higher salary were viewed as less desirable to work with, less likable, and more demanding compared to the negotiating men. These findings were supported using men and women negotiations using scenarios and videos. The backlash against women negotiators was stronger in men evaluators compared to women. Prescriptive and descriptive stereotypes are clearly active when evaluating the performance of women in negotiating.

Gender Stereotype Bias: Target Familiarity and Other Criticisms

The bulk of social science findings on prejudice, discrimination, and bias are based in the stranger paradigm. [148] Both experimental and quasi-experimental findings have focused on bias against women in general compared to men in general. Copus argued findings of bias against women who are strangers to raters cannot generalize to specific women with whom the participant is familiar. [149] Landy has been the most recent to call into question the validity of both implicit and explicit measures of bias and prejudice. [150] Landy, like Copus, argued that laboratory findings cannot and do not generalize to the workplace. Landy primarily cites two factors that he suggested overcomes any bias that might be held against unknown women. [151] First, Landy stated that real world evaluators have training, experience, knowledge, and motivation not to discriminate. Second, in real world evaluations, the person under evaluation is familiar to the rater, thus individuating information is used instead of stereotypes. Fiske, Bersoff, Borgida, Deaux, and Heilman noted that gender stereotype bias research is commonly used in the court room. [152] Likewise, criticism of the "stranger paradigm" is a commonly used defense against stereotype bias as an explanation of discrimination. Landy questioned inferences taken from experimental studies using student samples arguing that these findings are not relevant to "real world" workplaces. [153] He suggested that "real world" raters are well trained, experienced, and are making decisions based on individuated knowledge of the ratee, and therefore are not impacted by stereotype bias. The task of employee evaluation is important and has consequences both for the individual rated and the success of the organization in which the ratee and rater are embedded. Landy stated that the importance of performance evaluation is sufficient motivation for real world evaluators to carefully process such decisions using only controlled cognitive processes. Using this argument, Landy suggested that stereotype findings are strongest in a stranger-to-stranger research paradigm and minimized in context-specific settings.

Landy suggested that gender stereotypes fail to explain a meaningful amount of variance in any single instance of promotion or performance evaluation. [154] However, Lyness and Heilman found statistically significant, though small, effects in such managerial decisions in the field. [155] Even small effects of gender bias present an additive "real world" scenario of discrimination. Although a particular study may not find a meaningful example of bias, small additive effects of discriminatory stereotypes may well explain gender-based pay and position inequity in the workforce. Gender bias in any one managerial decision may only account for a very small amount of the variance, but these differences accumulate over individual's careers. Martell, Lane, and Emrich demonstrated the devastating nature of small additive effects using a computer simulation within a hierarchically organized company. [156] A one percent bias favoring men over women at each level of a company's promotion decisions explained the "real world" gender disparity and glass ceiling effects present in businesses today. The glass ceiling is a common metaphor for workplace discrimination of women. Half of all workers in the United States are women, yet few hold positions in upper management. [157] Eagly and Carli acknowledged the subtle gender discrimination's incremental, additive effect. [158] More recently, Eagly and Carli suggested that the "glass ceiling" women must break to obtain upper management positions should be envisioned as a "labyrinth". [159] A "glass ceiling" implies a certain level women are unable pass. The "labyrinth" suggests a series of barriers both large and small, both explicit and implicit that limit women every step of the way. Processes such as job segregation, prescriptive and descriptive stereotype bias, and disparity in opportunities all restrict women's forward career advancement. There is not an impassable glass barrier for women. There is a different and more difficult pathway to success for women compared to men.

Ryan and Haslam further elaborated on the "glass ceiling" stating that past the ceiling lies a "glass cliff." [160] Ryan and Haslam found that once a woman succeeds in obtaining a position in top management, gender bias does not end. Women in high profile positions are more likely to find their position precarious and have qualitatively different experience than similarly-appointed men. Women are often promoted to positions with a high chance of failure compared to men. Thus, the "glass cliff" further explains differences in the amount of men and women in top management positions Fiske and Neuberg suggested that when an individual meets a new person of a particular group or thinks about a particular group, stereotypes are activated. [161] New information as it is learned is compared to the stereotype. Each piece of new information either confirms or contests the existing stereotype. When information contests the stereotype it is (a) dismissed and ignored, (b) used to create a new sub-category for the target, or (c) used to disconfirm the stereotype, replacing it with individual information about the target. Landy stated that the third process, using individual information over stereotypes, is the prevalent model. [162] Individual information as it is learned and processed overrides stereotypes and eventually eliminates stereotype bias. [163] Thus, the more a person knows a particular woman the less that person will rely on stereotypes, and the less likely they are to hold inaccurate biases. According to Landy stereotype bias is a laboratory phenomenon that rarely occurs in the workplace due to raters having familiarity with those being evaluated, eliminating stereotype bias. [164]

The evidence drawn from laboratory research, legal precedence, and real world studies suggests individuating information is not a sufficient answer to address stereotype based discrimination. [165] Hunt, Borgida, Kelly, and Burgess reported that research has consistently found that people use stereotypes over individualizing information when forming initial impressions. [166] Borgida found that stereotypes were more influential in decision making over individuating information when (a) gender is salient, (b) the situation is ambiguous, or (c) the rater is not strongly motivated to make accurate evaluations. [167] Welle and Heilman reviewed numerous studies of informal gender discrimination. Informal gender discrimination is stereotype driven and occurs in the presence of specific individual information. [168] Social exclusion, lack of mentoring, exclusion from informal communication networks, and inhospitable work environments are all found more often for high ranking women compared to men. Welle and Heilman suggested the following steps beyond individualizing information are needed to reduce bias: (a) jobs should be defined by actual requirement for performance, (b) employees should have structured evaluations, and (c) managers must be held accountable for bias free evaluation. [169] Borgida, Hunt, and Kim found that gender stereotyping is often supported in legal proceedings providing a convincing model of how stereotype activation leads to prejudicial behavior. [170] Finally, Swim, Borgida, Maruyama, and Myers used meta-analysis to find that overall there was only a slight bias against women in performance evaluation. [171] However, the size of the bias increased substantially when the job was stereotypically masculine.

Confirmation bias predicts that a rater who has a pre-existing bias against a target will better remember information that confirms their bias and forget information that does not. [172] Marks and Fraley examined gender confirmation bias in perceptions of sexual activity. [173] The sexual double standard in Western society is well known and pervasive. [174] Sexual activity is seen as a positive trait in men and a negative trait in women. Marks and Fraley had participants read a scenario that had both positive and negative comments about either a man's or woman's sexual activity. [175] Marks and Fraley found that participants remembered different information based on the gender of the person in the scenario.

Positive information about sexual activity was remembered more often for men and negative information was more often remembered when the person described was a woman. Cook and Smallman found evidence of confirmation bias being used in military promotion decisions. [176] Naval officers when first presented negative information concerning a person disproportionately attended to further confirming negative information. Confirmation bias can lead to managers attending only to information which confirms their initial beliefs and stereotypes of employees, reducing the positive effects of additional familiarity. In sum, the research indicates that although there are some situations where individual information may mitigate gender bias, it is not sufficient to address the problem of gender discrimination.

Gender disparity in compensation for similar jobs is a useful indicator of discrimination and serves as a rallying call for interventions based on social justice. The validity, interpretation, and generalization of such statistics are still under discussion. [177] However, differences between men and women in occupational segregation, pay disparity, and promotion rates are a workplace reality. Adams found that women CEOs in large Fortune 500 corporations had reduced pay rates prior to promotion to upper management compared to their male counterparts. [178] Additionally, in contradiction to this pay inequity, just promoted women had a more distinguished performance record prior to promotion than men similarly promoted. This suggests that women need stronger credentials to be promoted compared to men.

Productivity has also been suggested as a possible reason for pay inequity, regardless of gender. The argument is that men tend to gravitate to higher visibility jobs, are more devoted to work, and more willing to travel and forgo family obligations in favor of work. These traits lead men to actually be more productive, explaining pay and promotion discrepancies between the genders. These arguments ignore stereotyping research as well as real world studies. For example, Jones and Frick discredited the productivity argument in their analysis of productivity data. [179] Jones and Frick found after accounting for other explanations for gender discrepancy, that gender bias is still present in "real world" productivity evaluations. [180]

Although individual knowledge of an employee may reduce specific bias based on descriptive stereotypes, backlash against agentic women is actually dependent on individuating information. Descriptive stereotypes may weaken as individual information is gathered. However, if that information contradicts prescriptive role expectations, individuating information will lead to biased appraisals. [181] Gill found knowledge of job-relevant skills of women holding a job associated with masculine traits resulted in the women being seen as unlikable compared to men. [182] Likewise, Heilman, Wallen, Fuchs, and Tamkins found that women need to be seen as both competent and well liked to be promoted. Information about individuals may provide increased accuracy in evaluating competence, but at a cost of likability. [183] Individuating information may reduce descriptive gender bias; however, it increases prescriptive stereotyping bias. Further research needs to examine the nature of familiarity in gender bias ratings outside of the stranger paradigm.

CHAPTER NINE

Portrayal of Sex Differences in Popular Culture

The idea that women and men experience emotion in starkly different ways seems to be quite popular. The classic example is perhaps Gray's *Men Are from Mars, Women Are from Venus*. [1] This and his other books on the topic have sold over 14 million copies worldwide, and have been translated into 40 different languages. [2] Another classic in the popular literature, Tannen's *You Just Don't Understand: Women and Men in Conversation,* contrasts men's fact-based, instrumental "report talk" with women's emotion based, relational "rapport talk" approaches to communication. [3]

Many other successful books published in recent years also make extensive use of the premise that large sex differences exist in emotion. For example, two books by Pease and Pease became number one bestsellers on the International Bestsellers list. [4] The authors of these and other popular books assert that women and men exhibit significant, sex-based emotional differences. Many further argue that those differences are innate and unchangeable, citing research from evolutionary psychology, comparative psychology, and biological psychology to support those claims. [5]

The sex-differences theme can be found in other popular media, such as the theatre. The record for the longest-running solo play on Broadway is held by Rob Becker's *Defending the Caveman*, [6] which makes extensive use of the premise that women and men are psychologically very different. Becker's play has been "recommended by thousands of psychologists and counselors" and he was invited to perform at the 1999 convention of the American Association of Marriage and Family Therapists. [7]

The message that the sexes inhabit separate emotional worlds is also conveyed through television and film. For example, Seidman found pervasive sex-stereotyping on many dimensions, including affective expression, in music videos. Seidman's analysis of sixty hours of music videos shown on MTV revealed that women were portrayed as affectionate, dependent, or fearful more often than were men, whereas men were portrayed as adventuresome, aggressive, or domineering more often than were women. Similar findings have been reported for televised sports coverage and prime-time shows. [8]

The portrayal of separate emotional realms for males and females can also be seen in children's entertainment. Thompson and Zerbinos studied 175 episodes of 41 different children's cartoons, and found sex-stereotypic portrayals in numerous domains, including affective behaviors. [9] For example, males displayed pride or anger more often than did females, whereas females displayed virtually all other emotions more often than did males, especially affection. Dundes observed that Disney's animated films have been widely criticized as promoting gender stereotypes, and went on to argue that the film *Pocahontas*, although often held up as a counterexample, in fact continued the trend by reinforcing "stereotypes of girls whose identity is determined first by romantic relationships and later by their role as selfless nurturer." [10]

Sex Differences in Research

It is clear from the portrayal of his-and-hers emotional worlds in best-selling books, on stage, in movie theaters, and in television shows marketed to adults, adolescents, and young children that the idea of sex-segregated emotions is a very popular one. However, a growing body of psychological and sociological research seems to indicate that men and women are actually much more alike than different in their experience of emotion. Canary & Emmers-Sommer used an extensive review of the then-existing research literature to argue that traditional stereotypes about sex differences in emotion usually fail to predict people's behavior. [11]

They wrote that there seems to be more overlap than separation in the sexes' experience of emotion, and explicitly rejected John Gray's analogy of separate planets of origin. In a review of published literature reviews on the topic, Wester, Vogel, Pressly, and Heesacker came to a similar conclusion, stating that "sex differences are small, inconsistent, or limited to the influence of specific situational demands." [12]

In a 2005 meta-analysis of studies dealing with all types of sex differences, Janet Shibley

Hyde concluded that only a very few large differences exist; men's physical upper body strength is reliably greater than that of women, for example. [13] On most studied dimensions, however, reliable sex differences were found to be small or non-existent. Hyde found the results striking enough to entitle her article "The Gender Similarities Hypothesis," and she reiterated a theme found in Canary & Emmers-Sommer and Wester: on a given dimension, variation within each sex often eclipses the average difference between them. [14]

The sociology literature also contains the gender similarities theme. In the *American Journal of Sociology*, Simon and Nath reported that men and women in the U.S. are broadly similar in their self-report of their emotional experiences. [15] Upon review of data from the emotions module of the 1996 General Social Survey, the investigators seemed rather surprised to conclude that "there is *little* correspondence between men's and women's feelings and expressive behavior and gender-linked cultural beliefs about emotion". [16] After examining the same data using a variety of theoretical and statistical models, Lively and Heise reported that "sex accounts for less than 1% of the variance on any of these emotionality dimensions". [17]

In the cases where emotional differences between the sexes have been observed, there are often qualifying factors to be considered. For example, differences are sometimes found in the ways men and women express emotions—but this has been convincingly explained in terms of culture-bound display rules as opposed to differences in the experience of emotion. [18] Sex-stereotypical patterns of emotional expression can be elicited in men by manipulating the social context to make them emotionally vulnerable, suggesting perhaps that these behaviors represent a defensive strategy of adhering to low-risk normative expectations rather than a genuine expression of their inner experiences. [19]

Additionally, observed differences are most often small relative to the within-sex variation on the examined dimension. [20] So while studies do frequently describe statistically significant average differences in women's and men's emotional behaviors, these studies can be seen in a broader context to reveal more convergence than divergence.

Factors in Perception of Sex Differences

To summarize, much of the available research indicates that emotional experience is fundamentally similar for men and women, with most differences being small, situational, or otherwise qualified. This is clearly at odds with the position taken by Gray, Tannen, and other authors, and portrayed in various entertainment media. Nevertheless, in light of the fact that self-reported data, such as the General Social Survey, show that American men's and women's *subjective* experiences are so alike, it seems odd that *Men are from Mars, Women are from Venus* and other works from this perspective should be so widely embraced. How can this disjunction between perception and empirical findings be explained?

One potential contributing factor is that while peer-reviewed journal articles usually contain the context and qualifiers necessary to put results in the proper perspective, in the popular media this information may be jettisoned to tell a more easily understood, if somewhat misleading, story. Another potential contributing factor lies in the fact that the concept of sex differences is a pervasive one, embedded in western culture. Therefore, popular opinion may have remained at odds with scientific findings because those findings are seen as counterintuitive—just as when the concept of a spheroid Earth met with much resistance because people's senses seemed to indicate otherwise. Such a scenario can certainly be imagined.

Gestalt theories of perception argue that relatively frequent instances of similarity will provide a less attended-to background against which relatively infrequent instances of difference stand out starkly. The large similarities may therefore simply be neglected, becoming the virtually invisible background against which the relatively small differences stand out, thereby receiving the larger share of conscious consideration.

Whatever the origin of the notion that there are large sex differences in emotion, once such a belief has formed it could presumably sustain itself by biasing the person's attention, provided enough ambiguity in observed expressive displays. Ambiguous events could be interpreted within the framework of the belief, seemingly providing ongoing reinforcing evidence for the belief. So, it seems possible that even if the emotionally expressive behaviors of men and women aren't systematically different, observers might unknowingly apply a bias as they encode ambiguous expressive behaviors.

Facial Expressions as Displays of Emotion

In a variety of social contexts, facial expressions are an important source of information regarding the emotional states of the participants.

[21] Nonverbal cues about emotional states play a vital role in effective communication in day-to-day interactions as well as in more constrained and goal-directed interactions, such as teaching, sales, and psychotherapy. [22] However, emotional communication is susceptible to distortion from various sources of bias. Of particular interest is people's tendency to view certain emotions as inherently masculine or feminine, as this might lead people to interpret nonverbal emotional communications in a manner consistent with this sex-based categorization of emotions. American culture has long included a widespread belief that women are more "emotional" than men in general, and that many emotions are regarded as especially feminine, while a few are seen as at least relatively masculine. [23] More recent data show that the categorizing of emotions by gender is still alive and well. For example, in a study of the relationships between gender, job status, and the interpretation of emotional signals, Algoe, Buswell, and DeLameter found that their participants rated anger and disgust as relatively masculine emotions, and fear as relatively feminine. [24] The participants in the Algoe study also rated anger and disgust as more instrumental and fear as more expressive; traits which are themselves strongly associated with masculinity and femininity respectively. [25]

Plant, Hyde, Keltner, and Devine asked 117 undergraduates to estimate the frequency with which men and women experience and express 19 emotions—12 were regarded as being experienced and expressed significantly more often by women, and only 2 as more typical of men. [26] Plant also tested participant's ratings of facial expressions of emotions, and found that pictures depicting blends of sadness and anger (upper and lower portions of the face mismatched) were rated in a way consistent with gender stereotypes.

Other recent research has also shown that people do at times display a sex-stereotypical bias in their interpretations of facial expressions. Plant, Kling, and Smith morphed together photographs of men and women posing facial expressions of anger and sadness. [27] Male typical and female-typical haircuts and clothing were added to the resulting blends to manipulate gender. Figures in the images perceived by participants to be male were rated as more angry than those perceived to be female, and figures perceived to be female were rated as sadder than those perceived to be male.

Hess, Adams, and Kleck used a similar methodology, using drawings of facial expressions differing only by hair and clothing for one study, and photographs of people rated as androgynous in their facial appearances with different hairstyles and clothes added using a computer program in another. [28] Hess found that using this method, the sex-stereotype effect was eliminated in some instances and even reversed in others. The authors offered the rationale that certain aspects of facial appearance, such as thickness of eyebrows and width of jaw, convey dominance or affiliation cues. They posited that these aspects of appearance, rather than gender per se, yield the cues that trigger the stereotyped interpretations. However, it also seems possible that Hess were over-dichotomizing gender, and that there is a broader range of possible gender associations than they seemed to expect. Their drawings of lantern-jawed women and photos depicting slender-faced men with barely visible eyebrows may in fact have triggered mixed or ambivalent gender associations, rather than associations to only male only female construct categories.

Sex of encoder effects have been interpreted in various ways. In some older studies it was speculated that the observed effect might result from women being superior encoders relative to men. However, some studies produced results not easily explained in this way, for example that certain emotions were more easily recognized when portrayed by male encoders. In some studies, the sex of the encoder was manipulated without changing the expression of emotion, often by pasting different hair and clothes onto a photograph. In these studies also, the explanation that women were better at encoding emotion facially was inadequate to explain the differences. It is studies such as these that give rise to the hypothesis that a sex bias drives sex of encoder differences observed in studies dealing with the interpretation of visual displays of affect. Some recent studies advance the theory that at least some of the observed differences are attributable to the effects of certain facial features that people associate with personality characteristics of dominance and affiliation. These are usually confounded with sex of encoder, such that facial features associated with dominance are most often found on males and facial features associated with affiliation are most often found on females. Buck, Miller, and Caul were among the first to study the impact on interpretation of visual affect of the sex of the encoder (i.e., the person displaying an emotion). [29] Observers of both sexes were more accurate in categorizing the slides when responding to female encoders. The authors concluded that females have "greater facial responsiveness" than males. [30]

Zuckerman Lipets, Koivumaki, and Rosenthal had 40 students (termed "encoders") pose in expressions of anger, happiness, sadness, fear, disgust, surprise, bewilderment, suffering and determination. [31] Photos were made of these expressions, and later a group of 102 students, including 30 of the original encoders, viewed the slides and chose from a list of emotions the one they thought best fit each slide. It was found that people were more accurate in decoding emotions from opposite-sex faces than from same-sex faces, and that female faces were more accurately decoded on the whole than male faces.

Perhaps the first study to manipulate the apparent sex of a target person in order to detect sex bias in the interpretation of emotional expressions was Condry and Condry's seminal investigation of people's interpretations of an infant's display of emotions. In this case, apparent sex was manipulated by simply telling half the participants that the infant in the film they were watching was a boy, and telling the other half of the participants that it was a girl. [32] In the film, the 9-month-old infant is exposed repeatedly to four emotionally evocative stimuli: a teddy bear, a doll, a buzzer, and a jack-in-the-box. Participants were instructed to rate the infant's expressions by type (pleasure, anger, and fear) and intensity.

The investigators found that participants were likely to interpret the infant's emotional expression in sex-biased ways—for example the "boy" as more angry and the "girl" as more fearful—but only in some instances. They wrote that "it appears to us that the more 'ambiguous' the situation, the more of a difference subjects report between the sexes". [33] The infant's response to the buzzer, for example, was rated as relatively pure fear whether the infant was labeled a boy or a girl. On the other hand, the infant's response to the jack-in-the-box was interpreted as more angry if the infant was labeled male and more fearful if the infant was labeled female.

Eiland and Richardson created a large set of photographs depicting various expressions of emotion using male and female encoders from two age groups (adults and children) and two race groups (black and white). [34] Their participants were demographically similar to their encoders. They were male and female, black and white, second graders and college students. The participants sorted the pictures into boxes, each labeled with an emotion. The investigators found that the sex, race, and age of the participant did not affect interpretation of the emotions depicted in the photographs. However, the sex, race, and age of the encoders each impacted the interpretation. The investigators did not designate particular responses as right or wrong, so there were no accuracy data. In fact they did not characterize the differences they found at all beyond simply observing that people " . . . do not interpret 'messages' sent by black faces (whether young, old, male, or female) the same as 'messages' sent by white faces.

Similarly, we do not interpret 'messages' sent by male faces (whether white, black, young, or old) the same as 'messages' sent by female faces". [35]

In a study published in 1983, Felleman, Barden, Carlson, Rosenberg, and Masters examined children's and adults' recognition of the emotional expressions of children. [36] The researchers took photographs of children displaying happiness, sadness, anger, and neutrality.

Posed expressions as well as expressions spontaneously generated in reaction to emotion eliciting stimuli were used. Children more quickly identified the emotional content of the expressions of same-sex children. However, the sexes of the children in the photographs had more of an impact on adults' interpretations than on children's interpretations. The authors speculated that this might be caused by adults' more developed stereotyped beliefs, for example that boys are more angry or aggressive.

In another study published in 1983, Knudsen and Muzekari reported more evidence that the sex of the encoder can affect interpretations of facial affect. The investigators used four male and four female encoders to pose expressions of fear, anger, sadness, and happiness. These photographs were shown to 98 undergraduate students, along with, in some cases, verbal statements manipulating the context in which the expressions were supposed to have occurred.

Participants rated the emotions they perceived to be present by choosing from a list of six emotions (fear, anger, sadness, happiness, surprise, and disgust) and/or by writing in a response.

Female encoders were rated as sadder than males in conditions where verbal context was provided. Male encoders were interpreted as being more fearful than female encoders in conditions where verbal context was not provided. The authors refrained from trying to provide a rationale for these differences, and simply noted that the sex of the encoder appears to affect interpretation. The finding regarding interpretation of female encoders' expressions as sadder is consistent with stereotypes about masculinity and femininity of particular emotions, but the finding that male's expressions were seen as more fearful is not. As noted by Condry and Condry however, stereotyped interpretations are more likely to be observed in conditions of ambiguity, and the visual stimuli used in this investigation were unambiguous expressions of a single basic emotion. This limitation crops up in much of the literature on the subject. [37]

In a study designed to examine brain lateralization in processing faces expressing emotion, Thompson did not find differences based on whether faces were presented in the left or right visual field, but he did find differences based on whether the encoder was male or female.[38] Participants were shown pictures of faces with happy, sad, or neutral expressions for either 30 mille-seconds or 200 mille-seconds, then shown another picture and asked whether the two pictures matched. Participants were more accurate in judgments involving the male face. Thompson cautioned against drawing firm conclusions about this, however, because only one encoder of each sex was used. Small numbers of encoders, and the attendant possibility of artifacts relating to features of specific encoders, is another problem frequently encountered in the literature.

Noting that the literature on decoding facial expressions to date was concerned mostly with static images, and often with posed expressions, Wagner, MacDonald, And Manstead investigated whether dynamic, spontaneous facial expressions could be correctly interpreted.[39] The researchers filmed one set of participants' faces as the participants viewed emotionally loaded slides, and asked these participants to identify what emotions they were experiencing at different points in the film. They then showed the films to another set of participants, and asked them to identify which emotions were being expressed. They found that participants were more accurate in interpreting the expressions of females, and concluded that females are better encoders than males, particularly of neutral and surprised expressions. Males and females performed similarly as interpreters or "receivers."

Rotter and Rotter studied the encoding and decoding of facial expressions using methods similar to prior studies, but introduced hypotheses making different predictions for different emotions.[40] Specifically, Rotter and Rotter predicted that females would be better encoders and decoders of disgust, fear, and sadness, whereas males would be better encoders and decoders of anger. This prediction was based on the idea that people would best pose and detect the emotions they were most likely to express, and some prior research had suggested that women suppressed aggression but were more expressive than men regarding other emotions, whereas men tended to suppress most emotions but were more expressive of anger than women.

The researchers photographed students, staff, and faculty members in posed expressions of anger, disgust, fear, and sadness. They recruited 10 judges to select photographs that were perceived to express the target emotion particularly well, ending up with 30 pictures of each pose, with 39 different female encoders and 15 different male encoders represented. Participants were asked to categorize each photograph as representing anger, disgust, fear, or sadness.

Women performed more accurately in the categorization on the whole, and photographs of females were more accurately categorized for all emotions except anger. Male decoders were better identifiers of male-encoded anger than female decoders. These results were interpreted as supporting the concept of differentiated sex roles, caused by "socialization which encourages females to be more expressive than males," and socialization of males to be both more aggressive and more attuned to aggressiveness from other males. [41]

Walbott tested whether facial expressions carry sufficient information to categorize emotions without context, by using clips from movies. [42] Short clips in which professional actors displayed joy, sadness, fear, or anger (according to judges familiar with the films) were shown to participants, who rated the expressions for nine component emotions—happy, sad, surprised, fearful, angry, thoughtful, in despair, full of contempt, and full of guilt—on five-point scales. Participants identified joy with high accuracy for encoders of both sexes. They identified fear and sadness more accurately for female encoders and anger more accurately for male encoders. The investigators interpret these results as art imitating life, citing prior research describing socialized display rules requiring men to suppress feelings of sadness and fear, and requiring women to suppress anger. [43]

Erwin, Gur, Gur, Skolnic developed a set of facial emotion stimuli for an instrument for use with various clinical populations, and tested it initially on a non-clinical sample. [44] In the first of the two experiments sex of encoder effects were not examined. In the second experiment, pictures of male and female encoders posing expressions of happiness, expressions of sadness, or neutral expressions were shown to participants, who were asked to rate the perceived emotion on a seven-point scale from very happy to very sad. Interactions between participant sex, encoder sex, and posed emotion were observed. Female participants were more accurate with male encoders generally, and were more accurate especially in identifying happiness for male encoders than for female encoders. Male encoders identified happiness similarly for male and female encoders, but were less accurate in identifying sadness for female encoders.

These findings are difficult to rationalize in terms of sex biased interpretations, which would presumably lead people of both sexes to identify these stereotypically feminine emotions more readily in females. However, as with many studies that examine sex of encoder effects, the stimuli are limited in that they do not include ambiguous expressions, which is where bias effects would be most likely to manifest. Nor are expressions of stereotypically masculine emotions included, ratings of which could be directly compared to ratings of stereotypically feminine emotions for each stimulus face.

Keltner observed that prior research literature on facial expressions was largely focused on just 7-10 emotions, fewer than the total number identified by lay people and emotion theorists. [45] He set out to determine whether a distinct display of something like embarrassment, guilt, or shame could be identified. He theorized that this type of emotion should have a distinct display because it served a useful social function of appeasement when norms had been violated.

He further theorized that this type of emotion should be more easily recognized when displayed by individuals from low social status groups.

In a series of five experiments, Keltner set out to describe an expression of embarrassment and then test whether it could be distinguished from other expressions of emotion. In the first, he elicited embarrassment by having participants perform a task that had been identified as embarrassing in previous research. Participants' nonverbal behavior was observed, and they were asked to report on their experiences. From this information, components of a tentative expression of embarrassment were identified and differentiated from amusement, an expression that shared several components with the expression of embarrassment being described. In the next four experiments, participants viewed short films of people making expressions intended to convey embarrassment and other emotions, and tried to identify they emotions being displayed using a variety of response formats. Expressions of embarrassment were correctly identified and distinguished from other emotions. Embarrassment displays from women and African-American targets were more easily identified and judged to be more intense than embarrassment displays from male and Caucasian targets.

Keltner's study is of particular significance in that an "eye of the beholder" effect similar to that observed by Condry and Condry was considered in the interpretation of the results. [46] Keltner posited that observers' perceptions of targets' social status influenced the observers' judgments about the expressed emotion. In the majority of the literature, Condry and Condry being the notable exception, females were regarded as being better encoders of emotion, but the possibility of observers applying different standards when interpreting expressions on female faces as opposed to expressions on male faces was not considered.

Baron-Cohen, Wheelwright, and Jollife showed participants pictures of various expressions of basic and complex emotions, using whole face images, eyes-only images, and mouth-only images. [47] Pictures made with a female encoder and pictures made with a male encoder were used in separate studies. The same pattern of results was found with female and male encoders, namely that whole-face pictures yielded the most accurate judgments for basic emotions, that accuracy was as good for the eyes-only pictures as for the whole-face pictures for complex emotions, and that whole-face and eyes-only pictures yielded better accuracy than mouth-only pictures. No direct comparison was made between ratings for the male and female faces.

The use of computer morphing programs to manipulate facial expression stimuli was introduced in a study by Hess, Blairy, and Kleck. [48] Morphing is a process in which one image is gradually deformed until it matches another. Intermediate images can thereby be created that combine aspects of the two endpoint images. The investigators chose neutral and emotional expressions from a pre-existing set of stimulus faces and used a morphing program to create varying levels of intensity for each expression. The target emotions were anger, disgust, sadness, and happiness. Photographs of two Caucasian male encoders and two Caucasian female encoders were used. Participants viewed each stimulus picture on a computer screen and rated the perceived intensity of anger, contempt, disgust, fear, happiness, sadness, and surprise along a continuous scale. For each rated emotion, participants used a computer mouse to click a point along a line, anchored at one end with the phrase "not at all," and at the other end with the phrase "very intensely." Accuracy in identifying the portrayed emotion and rated intensity of that emotion varied linearly with portrayed intensity for most images, which was interpreted as a validation of the manipulation technique.

The investigators observed main effects of sex of encoder, qualified by some interactions.

For happy and sad expressions, low-intensity expressions were more accurately identified for images of male encoders than for images of female encoders. At higher intensities, ratings of these emotions were similar for male and female encoders. Also, male raters were more accurate in evaluating male encoders' expressions of disgust than female raters' expressions of disgust.

After reanalyzing the data by including the perceived intensity of the expression as a covariate, and thereby controlling for actual differences in intensity between the expressions made by the four encoders, sex of encoder effects remained. Female encoders' expressions of joy were more accurately rated, and male encoders' expressions of sadness were more accurately rated. The authors interpreted this finding as evidence for "a decoding bias suggesting that observers decode women's and men's low to mid-intensity emotional facial expressions differently". [49] They refrained from speculation regarding the source or exact nature of this bias.

Algoe, Buswell, and DeLamater showed participants slides of male and female encoders, or "focal people" as they put it, posing one of three expressions: anger, disgust, or fear. [50]

The investigators put forth two competing hypotheses. Theorizing from the "universality" perspective they first hypothesized that the expressions being posed by the focal people should be correctly identified regardless of any contextual cues. Theorizing from the "context-specific" perspective, their second hypothesis was that participants would adjust their interpretation of the focal person's expression based on contextual information such as the focal person's gender and job status.

The researchers found that the gender of the focal person did influence participants' interpretations in some circumstances. Males posed in expressions of anger were seen as angrier as and less fearful than women posed in expressions of anger. Across posed expressions, men were seen on average as expressing more contempt than women, and women were seen on average as expressing more fear than men. These results are consistent with sex-stereotyped interpretation of the expressions.

Dimitrovsky, Spector, and Levy-Shiff studied the ability of learning-disabled and non-disabled children to recognize facial expressions of emotion that varied in their ease of identification. [51] Photographs from a preexisting stimulus set were chosen for relatively high and relatively low inter-rater agreement. Portrayals of happiness, sadness, anger, surprise, fear, disgust, and neutral expressions were used, with four male and four female encoders.

Participants from both the learning-disabled and non—learning-disabled groups more accurately identified emotions from the female faces. This effect increased with difficulty of identification. That is, for emotions with lower inter-rater agreement, there was a larger difference between the accuracy rating for female faces and the accuracy rating for male faces than for emotions with higher inter-rater agreement. This was interpreted by the authors as evidence of women's superior facial emotional expressivity as compared with men. The authors concluded that "the present results can be viewed within the wider context of women's greater emotionality". [52] The authors did not appear to entertain the possibility of sex bias in their interpretation.

Hess, Blairy, and Kleck conducted a study to investigate the impact of facial expressions of emotion, sex of encoder, and ethnicity of encoder on participants' perceptions of the encoders' levels of dominance and affiliation. [53] Images of male and female Caucasian and Japanese people displaying high and low intensities of happiness, anger, disgust, sadness, and fear were presented to participants.

A main effect of sex of encoder was observed. However, sex of encoder interacted in complex ways with the other independent variables, and the magnitude of the effect of facial expression of emotion dwarfed the effects of the other variables. All this led the authors to conclude that "observers interpret the information regarding behavioral intentions provided by affect displays in similar ways regardless of the ethnic group membership or the sex of the expressor," but that sex of the expressor has subtle effects on the observer's interpretations. [54]

Plant, Hyde, Keltner and Devine addressed the connection between gender stereotypes and facial expressions of emotion in this series of three studies. [55] The first study established which emotions are currently considered to be stereotypically masculine or feminine in the U.S. In the other two studies, participants' interpretations of emotional expressions were solicited and discussed in light of the stereotype information garnered in the first study.

In the first study, participants responded to two questionnaires. The first questionnaire required participants to indicate the frequency with which men and women experience and express 19 emotions according to U.S. cultural stereotypes as the participants perceived them. The second required them to rate the frequencies according to their personal beliefs, regardless of what they perceived the cultural stereotypes to be. Eleven of the 19 emotions were rated as being experienced and expressed more by women than men on both questionnaires. Two emotions, anger and pride, were rated as being experienced and expressed more by men than by women on both questionnaires.

In the second study, the investigators created photographs of two men and two women posing facial expressions of anger, sadness, and blends of the two, using Ekman and Friesen's Facial Action Coding System to pose the expressions. [56] The blended expressions were created by posing the upper half of the face in one expression and the lower half in the other expression. Participants viewed the photographs and rated the degree to which they perceived each to express four emotions. The investigators found that participants rated the blended expressions in a stereotype-consistent manner. That is, they rated men's blended expressions as angrier than women's, and they rated women's blended expressions as sadder than men's.

In the third study, participants interpreted an infant's display of emotion in a methodology similar to that of Condry and Condry. [57] Participants, who were tested regarding their own endorsement of sex stereotypes, viewed a videotape of an infant and rated the infants' behavior on several emotions. Half were told that the child was a boy half were told that the child was a girl. The participants' beliefs about the sex of the baby did not influence their interpretations of emotion except in the case of high-stereotyped men rating anger. In this case, the men rated ostensibly male infants as angrier than ostensibly female infants.

The majority of the literature available in English dealing with the effects of encoder sex on interpretations of facial expressions of emotion describes experiments done in English speaking countries. A study performed by Thayer and Johnsen in Norway provides an exception. [58] In this case participants rated their own experience of happiness, sadness, anger, fear, disgust, surprise, interest, pleasantness, activation, calmness, arousal, and liking for the stimulus in response to viewing slides showing facial expressions of emotion. The slides depicted one male encoder and one female encoder displaying expressions of neutrality, disgust, fear, happiness, surprise, sadness, and anger. Responses were considered to be correct classifications when the participant reported an elicited emotion that matched the emotion displayed. Female participants' responses included more correct classifications and fewer misclassifications than male participants' responses, and did not vary as a function of encoder sex. Male participants performed at chance levels in differentiating female encoders' expressions of anger and fear. In the discussion, the authors framed this difference in terms of females' presumed superiority in decoding emotion and greater sensitivity in experiencing elicited emotions. However, it seems possible that emotions elicited through viewing the emotional display of another might not always be congruent with that emotional display, and that this might have played a role in males' reactions to seeing the female encoder displaying negative emotions.

In an effort to develop stimuli for future use in evaluating populations of neurologically impaired people, Pell created facial and vocal stimuli depicting six target emotions: neutrality, happiness, pleasant surprise, disgust, anger, and sadness. [59] The facial stimuli consisted of pictures of 4 male and 4 female encoders posing facial expressions of each target emotion.

The investigator tested the stimuli with non-impaired participants in order to establish baseline parameters for the stimulus set. In doing so, he found that the sex of the encoder influenced the interpretation of the displayed emotion in some cases. Specifically, participants correctly identified expressions of neutrality on male faces more accurately than on female faces, and correctly identified disgust on female faces more accurately than on male faces. In the discussion of this finding, Pell did not provide a rationale as to why this specific pattern may have been manifested. Rather, he wrote that the observed effect of encoder gender might reflect "systematic properties of how these emotions are decoded and labeled," or it might reflect an artifact of specific properties of some or all of the eight encoders used in this particular case. [60] The apparent tendency not to label female faces as neutral seems consistent with stereotypes regarding women's emotionality, but the author did not engage in this level of speculation.

Widen and Russell examined the effect of the apparent sex of the encoder on preschoolers' interpretations of facial expressions of emotion. [61] Participants, who were 4 or 5 years of age, were shown pictures of what appeared to be a male and a female child of around 12 or 13 years of age displaying facial expressions of happiness, sadness, anger, fear, and disgust. In reality, these pictures were created from photographs of a 13-year-old girl and a 12-year-old boy in posed expressions. Pictures of the boy and the girl displaying the same expression were morphed together using computer software, and hairstyles typical of boys and girls were electronically placed onto the resulting blended-sex faces to create a set of apparent males and apparent females. Pairs displaying each emotion had exactly the same face—only the hair differed.

The apparent sex of the encoder impacted participants' ratings of emotions. Male participants labeled the male figure as disgusted more often than they labeled the female figure as disgusted, and female participants labeled the female figure as fearful marginally more often than they labeled the male figure as fearful. The authors discussed the results in terms of the presumed influence of gender stereotypes of emotion. They noted, however, that participants' ratings of anger were the same for apparently male and apparently female encoders, whereas the theory of gender stereotyping of emotions would lead one to predict that ratings of anger in particular should yield stereotypical interpretations.

Mignault and Chaudhuri used high-resolution 3-D models of stimulus faces in an examination of the impact of head tilt on participants' interpretations of perceived dominance and emotional content. [62]

Apparently male and apparently female stimulus faces displaying neutral expressions were presented on a computer screen at different angles. In addition to rating the perceived dominance, participants were asked to give a one-word answer to the question "what is the main emotion expressed in this picture?" [63] Responses were categorized as anger, fear, happiness, sadness, neutral, and other.

Participants rated apparently male faces as angry more often than they rated apparently female faces as angry. Apparently female faces were more often rated as happy compared with apparently male faces. Apparent sex had no detectable effect on ratings of fear, sadness, or neutrality. The authors interpret these results as being consistent both with theories of "social stereotyping based on women's unequal status" and with "an evolutionary explanation based on greater innate aggressiveness in males". [64]

Hess, Adams and Kleck tested the theory that facial features conveying dominance and affiliativeness actually drive effects identified elsewhere in the literature as evidence of sex bias.[65] Because the features that they assert are cues for dominance or affiliativeness—eyebrow thickness, height of forehead, jaw form, and facial rounding—are confounded with sex, they reasoned that effects of these features may easily be misinterpreted as effects of encoder sex. They employed two studies with different types of stimuli to test this theory.

In their first study, black-and-white drawings of the center of faces (as opposed to the outer edge of faces) displaying anger, sadness, happiness, disgust, and a neutral expression were created. (Interiors of faces convey relatively little information about the sex of the person, but a lot of emotional information, whereas the outer edge of faces conveys relatively little emotional information, but a lot of sex-cue information.) Various levels of intensity were generated by morphing emotional expressions with the neutral expression, and apparent encoder sex was manipulated by adding masculine and feminine hairstyles to the drawings. Participants rated the perceived intensity of anger, contempt, disgust, fear, happiness, sadness, and surprise for each stimulus face. The investigators hypothesized that because apparently male and apparently female faces were exactly the same except for hairstyle, and therefore shared all identified dominance and affiliativeness cues, the often-observed effect of encoder sex should not be observed.

Results of the first study were mixed. Ratings of disgust were, as predicted, equivalent for apparently male and apparently female faces. Ratings of sadness were higher for apparent females than for apparent males, consistent with a theory of sex bias and inconsistent with the hypothesis. Interestingly, the typical effect of encoder sex was reversed for expressions of anger and happiness—apparent females were perceived as angrier than apparent males, and apparent males were perceived as happier than apparent females. The investigators tentatively conclude that facial features rather than perceived sex of the encoder may be responsible for effects commonly attributed to sex bias in interpreting facial expressions of emotion, but caution that it is possible that the drawings used introduced an artifact.

In the second study, a largely similar methodology was employed using photos of androgynous faces for the interior parts of stimulus faces, and once again using different hairstyles to manipulate apparent sex. Intensity of expressions was not manipulated in the second study. Similar results to those from the first study were obtained for ratings of anger and happiness, again reversing the pattern predicted by the sex bias hypothesis.

Hess was faced with trying to explain the fact that they seemed to have observed a sex bias in the opposite of the usual direction for expressions of anger and happiness. To do so, they ended up invoking a version of the sex bias theory, by speculating that participants carried expectations that women should appear less angry and men less happy, and when those expectations were violated the female faces' anger and the male faces' happiness stood out all the more starkly.

Palermo and Coltheart observed that much of the prior research on facial expressions relied on a few databases of stimulus faces. [66] In an effort to expand the available pool of facial expressions of emotion stimuli, they gathered photographs of 50 individuals displaying expressions of happiness, sadness, anger, fear, disgust, surprise, and neutrality. To test the utility of these photographs, the researchers asked a group of 24 participants to view the images and select which of the seven target expressions they perceived each image to portray. They found a main effect of encoder sex in that expressions posed by females were more often accurately identified than expressions posed by males. Anger and sadness especially were correctly recognized more often when posed by female encoders as opposed to male encoders. The investigators observed that other studies have yielded similar findings, i.e. that expressions posed by female encoders are often recognized at higher rates than corresponding expressions posed by male encoders. The authors did not speculate as to why that might be. In this case, the finding that anger was more often identified when displayed by female encoders does not seem to be consistent with sex bias theory. The finding that sadness was more readily recognized on female faces than male faces, however, does seem consistent with sex bias theory.

Plant, Kling, and Smith used stimuli similar to those used by Hess to investigate the effect of encoder sex on the interpretation of facial expressions, but produced different results.[67] Here, Plant created stimulus faces by morphing together photos of males and females posing expressions, then adding gender-typical hairstyles to manipulate apparent sex. The expressions were ambiguous, being constructed either from an anger expression in the upper half of the face and a sadness expression in the lower half of the face, or vice-versa. Participants were asked to rate the perceived intensity of two stereotypically feminine emotions, sadness and sympathy, and two stereotypically masculine emotions, anger and contempt.

Apparently female encoders' expressions were rated as sadder than those of apparently male encoders, and apparently male encoders' expressions were rated as angrier than those of apparently female encoders. Apparently female encoders' expressions were also rated as more sympathetic than those of apparent males. As in Hess faces that were exactly the same except in hairstyle and clothing were interpreted in different ways. [68] However, whereas Hess et al. observed a partial reversal of stereotype-consistent interpretations using this approach, the findings of Plant et al. were consistent with a sex bias in the interpretation of facial expressions.

Rahman, Wilson, and Abrahams measured accuracy and reaction time as participants categorized happy, sad, and neutral facial expressions. [69] The stimuli were pictures of four male and four female encoders posing the expressions, presented on a computer. Sex of encoder interacted with sex of participant in that female participants were more accurate in categorizing male faces, whereas sex of encoder did not impact accuracy for male participants. Sex of encoder interacted with facial expression in that sadness was more accurately identified on male faces than on female faces, and responses were faster to happy and sad male faces than to happy and sad female faces. The authors conclude that males' facial expressions may be easier to read.

The finding that sadness was more accurately identified on male faces than on female faces runs counter to what theories of sex bias in interpreting facial expression would appear to predict. Recognition of stereotypically feminine emotions such as sadness on male faces should be hampered by the bias. However, given that there were no stereotypically male emotions as response options, the methodology used does not lend itself well to examination of sex bias questions.

In a study designed to examine the impact of encoder sex on emotion classification, as well as the impact of displayed emotion on judgments of encoder sex, Atkinson, Tipples, Burt, and Young found evidence that variations in sex of encoder significantly influenced decisions about what emotion is being portrayed. [70] First, the researchers showed participants pictures depicting facial affect in blocks with all male encoders, all female encoders, or mixed, and asked participants to make a rapid judgment as to whether fear or happiness was being portrayed. In the mixed sex-of-encoder blocks, performance was significantly slower than in blocks with all male or all female encoders. Next, participants completed a similar task requiring them to judge quickly the sex of the person in the picture while expression of emotion was held constant or varied. The speed with which the participants made judgments about sex was not significantly different in the varying conditions.

The results of the Atkinson study do not directly indicate evidence for or against a sex bias in interpreting emotional expressions. The authors of this study did not report on the reaction times for male encoders versus female encoders, but only for blocks of homogeneous encoder sex versus blocks of heterogeneous encoder sexes. However, the results of this study do help establish the stage of processing at which such a bias would take place, as they interpret their results as supporting a model in which information about the sex of a face is processed faster than information about affect. Therefore, any interpretation of affect is conducted within a context where information about sex has already been processed.

A series of three studies by Hess, Adams, and Kleck continued their investigation of perceived dominance and affiliation as mediators of the sex-stereotypical processing of facial affect that is frequently observed. [71] In the first, photographs of male and female faces displaying neutral affect were shown to three groups of participants. One group rated how likely they thought the people in the pictures were to show anger, fear, contempt, sadness, disgust, happiness, and surprise. Another group rated each picture for how dominant the people appeared to be, and a third group rated each picture for how affiliative each person appeared to be.

A mediational analysis showed that the sex of the encoder contributed strongly to his or her perceived dominance and affiliation, and to predictions about what emotions the encoders were likely to show. Additionally, dominance and affiliation contributed to predictions regarding shown emotion after controlling for sex of the encoder. Males were judged to be more likely to show the stereotypically masculine emotions of anger, contempt, and disgust, and less likely to show the stereotypically feminine emotions of fear, sadness, happiness, and surprise. This pattern was reversed for females. After factoring out the effect of sex of the encoder, perceived dominance was positively correlated with the stereotypically masculine emotions studied, and negatively correlated with two of the four stereotypically feminine emotions, fear and sadness.

Affiliation, after factoring out sex, was negatively correlated with the masculine emotions and positively correlated with three of the four stereotypically feminine emotions, namely fear, happiness, and surprise.

In the other two studies, participants viewed pictures of encoders previously rated as high or low dominance (Study 2) and affiliation (Study 3), along with vignettes describing the encoders in situations likely to evoke a variety of emotions. Participants were asked to indicate which of a series of schematic drawings depicting facial expressions of emotion they believed the encoder would show in response to the situation described. In the dominance study, male encoders and high dominance encoders of both sexes were judged more likely to display angry facial expressions, and female encoders were judged more likely to display expressions of sadness. In the affiliation study, high affiliation encoders were judged more likely to display happiness in the happy vignette condition than were low affiliation encoders, and the effect was stronger for male encoders than for female encoders. In the angry and neutral vignette conditions, male encoders were rated as more likely to show anger regardless of affiliation level, and female encoders were rated as less likely to show anger regardless of affiliation level.

The authors interpret these results as supporting both an effect of sex bias and effects of perceived dominance and affiliation. They observed that these variables were confounded, because facial features associated with dominance are more typical of males and facial features associated with affiliation are more typical of females. However, the authors concluded that their findings "show that sex-based stereotypical expectations can be partially overruled by expectations based on our perceptions of the dominance and affiliativeness of a person". [72]

Hugenberg and Sczesny examined the impact of the sex of the encoder on the happy face advantage, which refers to the fact that happy expressions are categorized more quickly than other expressions in speeded response studies. [73] Participants viewed images on a computer monitor of encoders displaying a negative emotion—anger in one version, sadness in another—or happiness, and were asked to categorize the emotion as quickly as possible.

The authors presented two rationales, both of which lead to predictions that the happy face advantage would be stronger for female encoders than for male encoders. One rationale was sex bias in interpreting expressions. Because happiness is stereotypically more closely associated with women than with men, it was argued that the expectation of seeing happiness on female faces would lead to a stronger happy face advantage for women. The second rationale was based on the valence of women compared with men as a stimulus category, and effects of emotional congruence. The authors cited evidence of the so-called "women are wonderful" effect, i.e. that women are generally regarded more positively than are men, and argued that valence-congruent processing would lead to a stronger happy face advantage for women. In the happiness versus sadness trials, it was argued that these two rationales lead to different predictions. They stated that the stereotype-based expectancies should not lead to a stronger happy face advantage for women because sadness and happiness should be equally expected on female faces. On the other hand, they argued that the congruent valence rationale would still predict a stronger happy face advantage.

As predicted, on the whole the happy face advantage was present for all encoders but more pronounced for female encoders. In the happiness versus sadness trials, a larger happy face advantage for female encoders was observed, which the authors interpreted as stronger support for the valence-congruence model than for the stereotype-based expectancy model. They commented that this finding doesn't detract from the utility of sex-stereotyped interpretations of affect in explaining effects other than the happy face advantage, particularly because this and other happy face advantage studies use unambiguous expression stimuli, and stereotypes are more likely to affect interpretations of ambiguous stimuli.

The most recently published investigation uncovered in this review that addressed the effects of encoder sex on interpretations of emotion expressions provides an in-depth, multifaceted examination of perceptions of happiness and anger as a function of the perceived sex of the encoder. Becker, Kenrick, Neuberg, Blackwell, and Smith considered the related phenomena of (a) anger being more quickly and accurately identified on male faces and (b) happiness being more quickly and accurately identified on female faces. [74] They conducted a series of seven studies to compare the utility of two theoretical explanations for these effects: the theory of bias arising from sex stereotypes rooted in social learning, and the theory of bias arising from evolved tuning of human perceptual systems to avoid threats and approach opportunities. The authors started with a hypothesis that could be formed from either theoretical perspective: "judgments and speeded decisions about expression would be dependent on the sex of the displayer of the emotion, revealing correlations of maleness with anger and femaleness with happiness". [75] They then went on to examine the issue using multiple methodologies and tried to evaluate the hypothesis and also to search for factors supporting or undermining each of the theoretical perspectives under consideration.

In the first study, participants were asked to imagine a face. Half the participants were instructed to imagine a happy face, and half were instructed to imagine an angry face. They then provided details pertaining to the face they imagined by responding to items on a questionnaire.

Among other things, they were asked whether they had imagined a male or female face. Most participants of both sexes who were asked to imagine an angry face imagined the face to be male. A significant majority of males who imagined a happy face imagined it to be female.

Marginally more females also imagined happy faces as female. The authors noted that this procedure tapped participants' associations of these emotions to sex, and was able to do so without cuing sex explicitly, but that it revealed little about the source of those associations.

In the second study, participants viewed a series of photos of encoders displaying angry and happy expressions on a computer and were instructed to categorize each as quickly as possible. Afterwards, they completed an implicit association task to assess any automatic associations of male or female names with synonyms for happiness or anger. Happy faces were judged more quickly than angry faces, and the quicker reaction to happy faces was more pronounced for female faces than for male faces. Angry male faces were categorized more quickly than angry female faces, and happy female faces were categorized more quickly than happy male faces. Accuracy for categorization of angry expressions was better for male encoders than for female encoders, and accuracy for happy expressions was better for female faces than for male faces. On the implicit association's measure, the overall pattern was for participants to associate males with anger and females with happiness.

Categorization and reaction time data were reanalyzed for a subset of participants whose associations were in the opposite directions from the overall averages. This was done to investigate the possibility that the previously observed patterns would be reversed in this subset, as one might expect if the observed effects were caused by automatic associations between the sexes and the emotions in question. However, some aspects of the patterns persisted. This subset of participants was also faster and more accurate in categorizing angry male faces as compared with happy male faces, and they were faster in categorizing happy female faces compared with angry female faces. The authors conclude that the overall results for the categorization and response time task support the initial hypothesis and are consistent with both the social learning rational and the perceptual mechanism rationale, and the results for the subset of participants with the less common pattern of associations is somewhat more compatible with the perceptual mechanism rationale.

In the third study participants viewed the same images as were used in the second study, but were asked to determine quickly the sex of the encoder instead of the emotion being displayed. Participants categorized male faces more accurately when they had an angry expression, and they categorized female faces more accurately and quickly when they had a happy expression.

The stimuli for study four consisted of computer-generated faces created to simulate men and women expressing anger and happiness. This was done in order to control for the possibility that men actually portray expressions of anger better than do women, and the possibility that women actually portray expressions of happiness better than do men. The methodology of the second study was repeated with the computer-generated faces. Anger was categorized more quickly on apparently male faces than on apparently female faces, and happiness was categorized more quickly on apparently female faces apparently male faces. Participants were more accurate in identifying anger on apparently male faces than on apparently female faces, and more accurate in identifying happiness on apparently female faces than on apparently male faces. The authors interpreted the results as supporting the primary hypothesis.

For the fifth study, photographs of angry, happy, neutral and fearful faces were presented for very short time intervals. Participants were asked to identify the emotions they saw. Neutral male faces were misidentified as angry more often than were neutral female faces. Happy female faces were correctly identified more often than were happy male faces. Accuracy rates were the same for angry male faces and angry female faces. These results were considered partially supportive of the original hypothesis, regarding the association of maleness with anger and femaleness with happiness. In addition, fearful female faces were more accurately categorized than fearful male faces.

For the sixth study, computer graphics software was again used, this time to generate nine androgynous faces with neutral expressions. From these, nine pairs of faces were created by making a slightly feminized and a slightly masculinized version of each. Four of these pairs were used with the neutral expressions. The remaining five pairs were given emotional expressions of happiness or anger. Each member of a pair had an almost identical expression, with the feminized version being slightly modified to be either less happy or angrier than the masculinized version.

Participants viewed each pair, and made judgments either as to which one of the two was more masculine, or which one appeared angrier. Participants' judgments of masculinity and femininity aligned with the ways the investigators made the faces, i.e. faces that were masculinized were judged to be male, and faces that were feminized were judged to be female.

Despite the fact that the emotional expressions of the pairs had in every case either been left neutral or changed to make the feminized face angrier or less happy, the masculinized faces were always rated the angrier of the two on average. The authors interpreted this as a "natural confound between sex and facial expression". [76]

In the seventh study, six androgynous faces were generated using computer software, then modified in each of six ways: a body with traditionally masculine or feminine clothing was added, the jaw was made squarer or was made rounder and narrower, and the brow ridge was raised or lowered. Each original face and its six variants were presented as a stimulus. Half the participants were told the stimuli had been modified to look slightly angry or slightly happy.

These participants rated each stimulus on a nine-point scale from "slightly angry" to "slightly happy." The other half were told the stimuli had been modified to look slightly masculine or slightly feminine, and asked to rate each stimulus on a nine-point scale from "slightly masculine" to "slightly feminine."

Masculine clothing caused the faces to be rated as more masculine compared with the original versions, but did not cause them to be rated as angrier, as would be predicted from sex stereotype theory. Feminine clothing caused faces to be rated as more feminine compared with originals, but did not cause them to be rated as happier. Faces with lower brow ridges were seen as more masculine and angrier. Faces with higher brow ridges were seen as more feminine, but higher brow ridges did not cause faces to be rated as happier. Making the jaw more square did not result in higher ratings of masculinity as expected by the investigators, but did cause faces to be rated as more angry. Similarly, the rounding and narrowing of the jaw did not result in higher ratings of femininity, but did result in higher ratings of happiness. The investigators regarded these results as being inconsistent with the social learning hypothesis.

Becker interpreted their results as a whole to be more consistent with the theory that human perceptual mechanisms are tuned to associate anger with males and happiness with females, rather than with the theory that social learning leads to stereotyped beliefs about gender and emotion that in turn bias the interpretation of affect. They speculated that certain facial features that are associated with human sexual dimorphism, but that are not always or necessarily associated with *concepts* of masculinity or femininity may be perceived as conveying anger and happiness. They did not dismiss social learning as a factor, however, emphasizing that both sources of variance may be at play in a given situation. Situations involving ambiguous and complex emotional expressions might give stereotypical interpretations the opportunity to emerge, as Condry and Condry observed three decades earlier. Such expressions were not studied in the Becker et al. investigation. [77]

Conclusion

The impact of encoder sex on the interpretation of emotion expressions has been observed several times in the scientific literature. The exact nature (or natures) of this effect has not been firmly established. The theory that females are more skilled at encoding emotions has been offered and may be correct. However, this theory fails to explain findings that certain emotions may ascribed to males more quickly and/or accurately, or at a higher level of intensity as compared with females. Studies in which faces are kept constant across conditions while sex of encoder is manipulated using peripheral cues like clothing and hairstyle also reveal the inadequacy of such an explanation. An interpretive bias based on the sex-stereotyping of emotions has been offered and may also be correct. Many of the studies designed with the intention of studying sex of encoder effects, as opposed to those revealing such effects more or less incidentally, support this theory. But not every study's results fit readily into such a model, and interesting alternative or complementary models are beginning to arise, such as those tying observed effects to particular facial features, for example Hess and Becker. [78]

Lingering questions in this area may soon be answered, though doubtlessly new questions will arise in the process. New techniques are being developed, such as the use of computers to perform tasks such as combining images, adding or removing cues such as hairstyle and clothing, and even generating very realistic, highly manipulable synthetic encoders. The literature already reflects some of the innovative methodologies and superior controls these techniques make possible, and more will surely come. These better investigative tools challenge researchers to examine old issues in new ways, and to ask new questions that require shifts in one's assumptions, similar to Condry and Condry's innovative manipulation of the apparent sex of the encoder—something that was conventionally assumed to be fixed. The interplay between the application of developing technologies and the creative formulation of research questions will likely soon shed considerable light on the interpretation of emotional states and on all the processes by which we humans understand each other.

CHAPTER TEN

Conflict

For most people, hardly a day goes by without some type of disagreement or conflict rearing its ugly head. It could be a husband and wife disagreeing about who's turn it is to take out the trash, two co-workers arguing over who contributed more to the team project, or political partisans exchanging barbs over some valued social issue. On a larger scale, it could be two nations going to war, not only resulting in high monetary, resource, and infrastructure costs, but also resulting in the loss of many lives. While these are only a few examples of the ways conflict can appear in our lives, they illustrate the extent to which disagreement and conflict can impact (often negatively) one's day-to-day experience.

Due to the significance of conflict in our world, there is value to asking questions such as, "Why does conflict develop?" and "What causes conflict to escalate?" These are questions that this thesis attempts to address by seeking a greater understanding of the mechanisms underlying conflict. In particular, this research focuses on the role of interpersonal perceptions of bias in the context of a disagreement by suggesting a *bias-perception conflict spiral*. Examples of these bias perceptions would be suspecting that others are unable to see a situation or an issue in an objective manner, due to some motivational factor such as liking, self-interest, or group membership. The perception of another individual as biased may also result from concerns about cognitive biases, such as anchoring and adjustment, availability, or accessibility of certain judgments or beliefs. It is hoped that this greater understanding of conflict, by acknowledging and assessing the prevalence of bias perceptions in disagreements, might allow for recommendations of interventions—ways to limit or prevent conflict from spiraling out of control.

The Conflict Spiral

It is important to review and understand the traditional model of conflict spirals before attempting to expand upon this model by including perceptions of bias. The "conflict spiral" model is often discussed in analyses of persistent conflicts on the global scale. Pruitt and Kim offer a description of the model.[1] The basic idea is intuitively satisfying and captures the tendency for disagreements to turn into conflicts and then into yet worse conflicts—i.e., for conflict to "spiral" forward. This model is typically used as a way to *describe* social conflict and has lacked some of the psychological underpinnings that make it more useful as a way to *understand* social conflict. This chapter will discuss the structure of the conflict spiral and the past thinking about this spiral.

Structure of the Spiral

A disagreement, dispute, or tension between two parties serves as a trigger for the conflict spiral. The dispute can be based on any number of things, including real or imagined disagreement, disputes over resources, or intergroup differences, and it can be initially small or large. From this starting point, the structure of the spiral is quite simple.

Trigger → Party A behaves aggressively/conflictually Towards Party B → Party B behaves aggressively/conflictually towards Party A

Party A acts, and then Party B reacts to those behaviors (causing Party A to react back, etc.). The model elaborates on the idea that, in a conflict, there is a "mirroring" taking place where, if Party A sees Party B as aggressive and greedy, then Party B sees a similar (or mirror) image of that in Party A. Essentially, both sides share the same suspicion of, and inclination towards defensiveness against, the other in an interactive dynamic involving both sides perceiving and acting according to the other's perceptions and actions.[2]

For example, if two individuals both believe that a piece of land is their rightful property, then that could trigger the first cycle of the conflict spiral (in which, for example, one individual might put up a hedge to keep the other off the property, and the other might respond by driving a tractor through the hedge). Once the conflict spiral has been triggered, the model progresses in a relatively orderly manner. One side takes action against the other and then the other responds, in a cyclic fashion.

Conflict spirals often occur in cases of similar power as this allows the back and forth responding to occur.[3] If either side is especially strong, the weaker side may have difficulty "fighting back" in response to a competitive or aggressive move by the other. The model does not represent as well cases in which a dominant side exerts its will over another. Nevertheless, conflict spirals between adversaries of unequal power do occur as seemingly weak adversaries can find novel methods of accruing power (e.g., engaging in terrorist attacks). Generally, in a conflict spiral, what both sides share is an interest in the conflict issue, as well as the capacity to work to protect that interest.

The spiral model is appealing because it describes how initially small, or even imagined, conflicts can become larger and more violent, occasionally to the point that the parties involved cannot even remember the reason for the original disagreement and are no longer are driven by concern for it.[4] The conflict between the Hatfields and McCoys (which, according to American lore, began over a dispute about the rightful ownership of a pig and resulted in the deaths of over a dozen members of the two families) is a classic example of how things can spiral from an originally small incident into a much larger one involving reciprocation of violence on both sides.

Potential Mechanisms of the Conflict Spiral

The spiral model has been discussed by psychologists when reviewing theories of conflict and conflict escalation.[5] Despite its frequent mention and description in the social conflict literature, little research has examined the psychological mechanisms underlying the conflict spiral. Research on the conflict spiral model has generally been focused on international conflict and war, a much larger scale than most of the conflicts that individuals face in everyday life, and one more often examined by political scientists and historians than psychologists. Political scientists have argued for a mechanism that explains the spiral in terms of fear.[6] Other theorists have suggested that entrapment is what causes the spiral to occur, and yet others have argued that it is the perception of the other side as the "villain" (or as a less than human adversary) that fosters the continued escalation of conflict. We now discuss these different ways in which the conflict spiral model has previously been conceptualized. Although each of these accounts is useful, each falls short of offering a explanation for the conflict spiral in terms of accounting for both the development and the escalation of conflict.

Fear

Most research focused on conflict spirals can be found in political science's work on international relations. This research is compelling because it is based on real-world events—it examines conflicts that people are familiar with and about which people are seriously concerned. Using this approach, researchers adopt a strategy that could be described as imputing "minds" to nations, groups, and states, suggesting that these entities perceive and react to each other much the same way that one individual perceives and reacts to other individuals. Using this approach, researchers present analyses that attribute the conflict spiral pattern to opposing nations' fears and concerns about the other's motivations and potential to do them harm. Looking back at conflicts after they have occurred, these analyses offer rich historical explorations and nicely illustrate the escalating nature of the conflict spiral. However, they lack a careful psychological theorizing (and evidence) for their propositions.

The Cold War between the United States and the former Soviet Union is one of the most common targets of political science analyses of conflict spirals.[7] Both sides were powerful players on the international stage and, not surprisingly, did not always see eye to eye. Different, at times opposing, interests suggest that both states had reason to fear the other. According to the analysis, each side recognized that any inferiority to the other would be potentially dangerous, and so both attempted to increase their power so that they would be able to defend themselves. If one side increased its stores or added new weaponry, the other side responded in kind and the situation became a "race" to gain superiority. The conflict grew larger and larger (and could have ended in mutual destruction between two states that were theoretically capable of mutual cooperation).

Arms races, like this one, illustrate the potential for fear to escalate conflict and fuel the spiral, as each side believes the other is aggressive and malicious and therefore builds up its own capabilities in order to defend itself. This building up of weapons, even when the motivation for doing it is defensive, can signal aggression to the other side—this then leads that side to respond by increasing its own weaponry (and therefore sending the same signal). The result is a back and forth in which each side becomes continually more invested and more powerful, until at last one side becomes fearful enough of the other that it strikes an initial blow in the hopes of displaying its resolve and inflicting damage to the opposing side's ability to retaliate (thankfully this preemptive strike was avoided in the case of the Cold War).

While this explanation that fear fuels conflict spirals is intuitively compelling, it falls short in several respects. First, it is focused on international and large-scale intergroup conflict, and may not apply as well to smaller-scale conflicts in which "fear" is likely to be less of a driver of conflict escalation. For example, it seems less likely that fear is the mechanism underlying a husband and wife's fight over who should do the laundry or a hostile exchange between a Republican and a Democrat over the latest welfare reform bill. Second, the model is based on the idea that nations and states are entities that possess "minds" and "feelings." Given that this is a metaphor rather than a reality, it provides a somewhat tenuous basis for theorizing. Members of nations can have collective goals and concerns, but nations themselves do not have minds or emotions. In conflicts at the intergroup level, it is the individuals who make up those groups that possess psychological states such as impressions of the "other side." Therefore, it is likely more useful to focus on the psychology of those individuals than to look at the bigger picture interaction between groups.

Entrapment

Another potential mechanism of conflict spirals is that of "entrapment", though it has not been explicitly study in this context. [8] One type of entrapment, escalation of commitment, seems particularly relevant to conflict spirals. This phenomena is discussed in organizational psychology, most frequently with reference to investments and sunk costs. [9] These researchers argue that people can descend into a spiral of losses due to the psychological difficulty of exiting from a losing plan of action.

For example, people may fail to abandon, and may even invest more money in, a venture that is losing money. [10] In the realm of conflict, escalating commitment has been used to describe the back and forth interactions of the U.S. and Japan in a dispute over apples. [11] Even though the total potential value for either nation was small ($10-15 million dollars), both felt compelled to continue promoting their side of the dispute, pursuing it to the highest levels of government and international politics. This pursuit itself incurred high costs in both time and money. In the end, *any* earlier bargain would have benefited both sides more, but each became more entrenched in their strategy the more they pursued it. In an interpersonal dispute, one can imagine a similar scenario—if a man has already spent several days refusing to give into his wife's argument, accepting high costs such as sleeping on the couch, he may become even more trapped in his course of action, because his own commitment is evidence of just how right he is (and just how unreasonable his wife must be).

Related to people's propensity for escalating commitment is work on social traps. Platt described these traps as similar to fish traps, which tend to be difficult to back out of, and are often deadly. [12] Social traps typically describe situations where each individual behaves in a manner that is beneficial for their self, without consideration of the greater good or the needs of others, leading to a collective dilemma. As the social conflict develops, each individual is reluctant to take action to solve the problem for the group, simply because such action would be personally costly. When individuals observe that others are not accepting such costs, they may feel that it would be foolish for them to do so, and thus the negative behavior persists on all sides. Thus, social traps may characterize the conflict spiral in the sense that those involved behave in self-interested ways that perpetuate the conflict, and discourage acts of cooperation and problem solving.

Both escalation of commitment and social traps illustrate the tendency for people to become "caught" in self-destructive (and even group-destructive) paths of action. [13] Such paths, once adopted, may be difficult to abandon because of cognitive dissonance over past behavior. [14] Although these approaches contribute to our understanding of conflict spirals, they fall somewhat short. Theories of escalation of commitment are largely descriptive rather than mechanistic.

Dehumanization

Moral and social norms dictate that we should treat others in a respectful and cooperative manner—this seems counter to the reality of conflicts developing between individuals, groups, and nations. While one of the factors that researchers have identified as a potential fuel of the conflict spiral is a simple need to respond in kind (to reciprocate aggression with aggression), this does not explain why the conflict spiral is able to begin in the first place. One suggested mechanism for why the competitive or aggressive behaviors in conflict spirals are allowed (and even *likely*) to be used is dehumanization or infra-humanization. [15] Essentially, if one sees the other side as "less human", then it would be easier to behave in a conflictual way.

Mere ingroup/outgroup differences (real or imagined) have been shown to foster negative evaluations of others, and people have a tendency to de-individuate and even dehumanize those who are in a different group. [16] If one sees a member of another group as different, less good, and less human, then competition and aggression are more easily justified. Those who have moral or ethical objections to violence against other human beings may not have those same objections to using violence or aggression against a less-human target. [17] Dehumanizing one's opponent can thereby allow for a moral disengagement that facilitates the development and escalation of conflict. [18]

The idea that people dehumanize their opponents, thereby making aggressive and conflictual against those opponents more likely, helps to account for the pattern of aggression and violence that can occur in some conflict spirals. [19] However, the model does not offer (nor does it aim to offer) a full account of the conflict spiral. The dehumanization framework offers an account for how people become comfortable with using violent, aggressive, and competitive methods for dealing with adversaries, but it does not explain why people first come to prefer those methods over other options. A dehumanized individual may be met with a number of different reactions, including pity and disgust, which likely would not elicit conflictual behaviors, but rather alternative ones such as avoidance (in the case of disgust) or assistance (in the case of pity). [20] Second, dehumanization does not seem as relevant in accounting for innocent or minor conflicts that nevertheless can erupt into spiral-like situations—such as when a disagreement over whose turn it is to do the dishes can spiral into the throwing of those dishes. In such cases, the spiral of conflict is unlikely to be primarily driven by the two sides' perceptions of the other as something less than human.

Disagreement and Perceptions of Bias

While people generally tend to see more bias in others than in themselves, past research supports the notion that disagreement makes it especially likely that people will show this tendency. [21] According to the tenets of naïve realism, people believe that they see the world as it "really is"—that they see things as they are in "objective reality." [22] Moreover, this perception leads people to assume that others will share their views and that, if others fail to do so, they must be either uninformed or incompetent, or they must be allowing some sort of biasing or non-normative influence to cloud their perception. Individuals are often able to discount the notion that they themselves have been susceptible to biases by performing a quick analysis of their internal processing and "discovering" no evidence of bias.

Because bias generally occurs non-consciously, introspective evidence of it is typically absent. [23] However, people tend not to value such "evidence" when it comes from others. In the case of others, people generally look to those others' behavior for assessing bias. [24] In the case of disagreement, then, people are likely to be internally assured of their own objectivity, but they are likely to focus on their adversaries' expressed views (which seem to ignore or deny reality) when assessing those others' bias.

Interpersonal Conflicts

Mounting evidence from a variety of experiments supports the notion that disagreements induce perceptions of bias in one's adversaries. A number of these studies have focused on people's perceptions of the biasing effects of group membership. Vivian and Berkowitz showed that people anticipate members of an outgroup to be biased by their group membership in assessing their group's relative contribution to a task—that is, they expect outgroup members to be group-serving in their assessments. [25] Similarly, Kruger and Gilovich found that people expect others to make biased and self-interested responsibility allocations regarding their work contributions when they are from opposing groups rather than when they are teammates.[26] In another example, researchers have shown that people believe others' public policy opinions are biased by self-interest (such as a belief that the only reason one opposes a smoking ban is because she is a smoker), but view their own opinions on the same issues as relatively unaffected by self-interest. [27] And, Cohen showed that when it comes to domestic policy issues such as welfare, people tend to see those on the other side (i.e., with an opposing partisan affiliation) as merely following or being influenced by the "party line." [28]

Other researchers have demonstrated the tendency for people who disagree on political or social issues to see their adversaries as biased by their commitments to extreme ideology. [29] In a more general sense, people have been shown to view their own group memberships as a source of enlightenment about issues, while viewing outgroup members' group memberships as a source of bias about those same issues. For example, one experiment showed that minority students viewed their group identity as enlightening their perspective on affirmative action, whereas they viewed their outgroup (i.e., White) peers' group membership as biasing their view of the issue; White students felt the reverse. [30] Nesselroade, Williams, Nam, and McBride found that people's perceptions of the gap between their own and another's objectivity was greatest when parties not only disagreed about the issue but when the issue was also especially important to them. [31] Consistent with this finding, another study showed that participants saw their disagreements as larger when the disputed issue was more central to them and that, regarding such central issues, they saw the other side as irrationally opposing them. [32] And, looking at a different bias entirely, Frantz found that people believed that those who disagreed with their view about a social dilemma (i.e., involving a roommate conflict) were biased by their like or dislike of the parties involved in the dilemma. [33]

One experiment sought to directly investigate the link between disagreement and perceptions of bias. [34] Participants provided their opinion on 10 political issues and public figures (e.g., capital punishment, abortion rights, Hillary Clinton) and then read through the positions of another anonymous participant. They rated the similarity of their opinions compared with the other student's, and then rated the degree to which they believed the other student was influenced by normative (objective) or non-normative (biasing) factors. Consistent with the relationship between disagreement and bias perception, participants saw a peer as more influenced by non-normative, relative to normative, concerns the more that peer's position differed from their own.

Large Scale Conflicts

Studies in the context of large-scale political conflicts suggest that disagreement induces perceptions of bias in those cases. Pronin, Lin, and Ross describe an experiment conducted among Unionists and Nationalists in Northern Ireland, in the wake of the Good Friday Agreement (that established the conditions for peace in that region). [35] They found that political activists involved in the conflict perceived the leaders who took the opposing point of view from their own as especially affected by biases (e.g., being ruled by emotions rather than reason, distorting the nature of past events in a manner that serves the interests of one's own side, etc.). Those biases, and the perceptions of those biases in the opposition, tend to act as barriers to fruitful negotiation. This example demonstrates how disagreement leads to potentially problematic imputations of bias in a serious, real world disagreement.

A number of other studies provide related evidence, in the context of conflicts involving U.S. foreign policy. In one study reported by Pronin et al., college students indicated how they believed the U.S. should respond to the attacks of September 11, 2001, from a spectrum of response options that ranged from extremely hawkish (all-out war with any potential enemy) to extremely doveish (taking all the blame and making amends). [36] They then rated the degree of bias that they associated with people who held each of the other points of view. The result was that the further those points of view were from the participants' own preferred response, the more bias participants imputed to those who took those points of view. In a related study, Reeder, Pryor, Wohl, and Griswell found that the more their participants disagreed with President George W. Bush's decision to invade Iraq, the more they perceived him as having been motivated by the biasing effects of self-interest. [37] A correlational study of perceptions of suicide terrorists demonstrated that the more individuals disagreed with the terrorists' political goals and motivations, the more biased and irrational they perceived them to be. [38]

These studies provide evidence that disagreement between parties leads them to perceive each other as biased. The research shows that not only does disagreement lead to bias perceptions, but that there is a measurable relationship between the two such that the more intense people's disagreement is with each other, the more biased they perceive each other to be. Having thus provided evidence for the first step of our model, we now present suggestive evidence for the second component, i.e., that bias perceptions lead to competitive and aggressive responding.

Perceptions of Bias and Conflictual Action

The bias-perception conflict spiral begins when two parties disagree. In response to the disagreement, each party comes to see the other as influenced by bias. The next stage of the spiral, we suggest, is that each party responds to the other side by acting aggressively and competitively rather than peacefully and cooperatively. Conflict researchers have characterized these different classes of responses as the two key ways people react to conflict and disagreement: i.e., they either adopt conflict-escalating *competitive* behavior, or conflict-deescalating *cooperative* behavior. [39] Examples of cooperative behavior include talking, negotiation, bargaining, compromise, concessions, and exchanging information. These tactics make peaceful conflict resolution most likely.

Competitive behavior can include hostile language, threats, coercion, and violence. These aggressive tactics tend to block conflict resolution and escalate the conflict. The use of conflictual behavior is often motivated by a desire to push through one's own goals and needs, regardless of the costs to the other party, whereas cooperation is characterized by a concern for both sides. [40]

It has been suggested that people's inclination to choose conflict-escalating approaches over de-escalating ones reflects people's perceptions, generated by disagreement, that their opponents are biased. When an opponent is seen as incapable of seeing things objectively (or unwilling to do so), one may conclude that cooperative efforts (such as sitting down to talk things out or providing relevant facts and arguments) will not be effective. For example, if a person believes that the judgments of his opponent are distorted by self-serving motives and the need to cling to long-held ideologies, one might infer that efforts to reason with that person would be a waste of time. In this case, an individual might instead turn to more aggressive means that would forcefully prevent that opponent from expressing or advancing her opposition. In short, people are likely to choose responses to their adversaries that fit their quick assessment of the other side's capacity for objectivity versus an inclination towards bias.

Theorists have pointed out that cooperation often begets cooperation and competition often begets competition. [41] Therefore, in the traditional conflict spiral, one aggressive act leads to reciprocation of aggression. Perceptions of bias could help explain this effect, as parties are likely to view the other side's aggressive actions towards them as a signal of the other side's bias (e.g., "What reasonable and objective person would have done *that*?"), thus encouraging them to respond with their own aggression. We now present evidence suggesting that bias perceptions will lead to conflictual action and will contribute to the spiraling nature of conflict.

Large Scale Conflict

A set of studies investigated whether perceptions of bias would lead to conflictual responding in large scale conflict, specifically, in responding to the serious real-world issue of suicide terrorism. [42] In two experiments, participants read a description of suicide terrorists that portrayed them as either driven by irrational biases (e.g., such as extreme hatred, ideology) or by rational and objective analysis (e.g., such as a thorough analysis of the relevant history, the overall situation, and available options). In one study, the description of suicide terrorists was presented as a news analysis piece from the *New York Times,* entitled "Mind of the Terrorist." The article consisted of portions of (and quotations from) real scholarship (largely from political science) about terrorists' motives and behaviors. [43] The second experiment also presented participants with a description of suicide terrorists as objective or as irrational but, in this study, descriptions written by the researchers themselves were employed in order to control for possible confounds.

In both cases, after reading one of the two descriptions of suicide terrorists, participants were asked to respond to standard public opinion questions about how terrorism should be combated. In particular, they were asked about their endorsement of aggressive and militaristic options (e.g., air strikes or ground attacks) and diplomatic and negotiatory ones (e.g., talks and negotiation). In both experiments, participants who read that terrorists were biased, rather than objective, advocated more aggressive and conflict escalating responses than cooperative and conflict de-escalating actions (see Figure 2.2).

Those differences could not be attributed to differences in people's dislike for suicide terrorists—rather, they were statistically driven by their beliefs regarding whether terrorists could or could not be persuaded by reasonable arguments. These studies provided evidence that people's perceptions of the other side's susceptibility to biasing influences can lead them to prefer conflict-escalatory behavior, even when that behavior has dire consequences involving high costs, death, and destruction. [44]

The Bias-Perception Conflict Spiral in Negotiation

Thus far, we have discussed how people perceive their adversaries and how those perceptions might influence their preferences for responding. In negotiations, parties agree (implicitly or explicitly) to have a discussion about the disputed issue. Therefore, *opting* for a negotiation might be considered a move toward cooperation, as it suggests a desire to work with the other side to reach an agreement. However, there are many situations where the default reaction to a disagreement is negotiation (e.g., many legal and business disputes) and despite the fact that the stated purpose of negotiations typically is to resolve conflicts of interest through discussion, some negotiations are better than others, both in terms of the time it takes to reach a decision and in terms of the outcomes for each side. [45] Many of the same problems that plague conflicts more generally also exert influences on parties involved in negotiation (including perceptions of the situation as "fixed-pie", fears of the other side, defensiveness, and concerns that the other side is being unfair and mistaken assumptions about the transparency of one's motives.[46] It has been suggested that the same bias perceptions that affect conflicts more generally can occur in the special case of negotiation, leading to a spiral of competitive tactics that can prevent conflict resolution.

The role of bias perceptions in negotiation has been directly examined in a series of studies by Kugler and Pronin. One study revealed that, in a negotiation, individuals tend to see their negotiation partners as more biased than themselves. [47] Students in a negotiation course were asked to rate both their own and their fellow students' tendencies to display various biases (e.g., "being more influenced by feelings and emotions than by pure logic") during the process of negotiating. They perceived their fellow students as showing more negotiation biases than themselves.

Following these results, Kugler and Pronin conducted an experiment manipulating bias perceptions. [48] Participants were told that they were participating in a paired negotiation exercise, but that they would not meet or interact with their partner during the exercise. As part of the cover story, they filled out a personality questionnaire, the results of which would be shared with their partner. In fact, there was no partner. They negotiated with a computer algorithm and were presented with the personality test results of a fictitious person. Those results informed them that their partner was either particularly rational or particularly biased (e.g., susceptible to biases such as giving "special consideration to the ideas of people who are physically attractive and/or socially skilled"). They then participated in a labor-management negotiation exercise (adapted from Raiffa), in which the participants took the role of management and were negotiating with labor (the computer algorithm) about a new contract salary. In this negotiation, when participants believed that their partner (labor) was biased, they made smaller initial wage offers (i.e., raises of 8 cents on the dollar vs. 19 cents in the objective condition). [49] As a result, their negotiations took significantly longer, leading to more lost value due to the high costs of the strike (i.e., costs of $6.99 million vs. 4.60 million). This research tells a story about negotiation that resembles the bias-perception conflict spiral. Here, the manipulated perceptions of bias resulted in adversaries making more competitive initial offers, moving them away from efficient dispute resolution.

The forgoing evidence supports the notion that while negotiation is a special case of disagreement and conflict, there is still room for competition rather than cooperation, and at least some of the variance in terms of which path is taken depends on the parties' perceptions of each other's bias. Understanding how bias perceptions may affect negotiation is important, as there are often cases where negotiation is viewed as the default response, rather than one of several options for responding. In these cases, the parties still may opt to behave cooperatively versus competitively, and which of those responses is more likely may depend on their perceptions of those adversaries' bias. The bias-perception conflict spiral model and the understanding that comes with it thus can help us to make recommendations about how to improve negotiation situations and outcomes.

Support for the Role of Bias Perceptions in Conflict

The preceding pages have presented a theoretical base for the assertion that bias perceptions are relevant, and indeed important, in cases of disagreement and developing conflict. In many instances, individuals attribute specific cognitive and motivational biases to those who disagree with them on a specific issue or who belong to opposing groups. These interpersonal perceptions of bias can then induce people to behave in a more aggressive, competitive, and fixed-pie manner, reducing the possibility of amicable resolution.

Bias-Perception Conflict Spiral for Conflict Intervention and Prevention

A theoretical approach to conflict development and escalation that focuses on bias perceptions and conflictual behaviors has advantages. Whereas other approaches may only allow for a description of what is happening from an outside perspective, a psychologically-enriched model will provide an understanding of *why* the parties involved in the disagreement see and respond to their opponents as they do. Without this understanding, attempting to develop interventions for conflict will be more haphazard and less likely to succeed, because they may not address the entire conflict situation (by neglecting imputations of bias).

As the above review suggests, the time is ripe for developing and testing new strategies for intervening in bias perceptions and the conflicts they escalate. The bias perception conflict spiral suggests a direct point of attack—reducing or eliminating the imputations of bias between adversaries. An intervention that could achieve this should result in more cooperative approaches to the disagreement in question, leading to better resolutions and avoiding spiraling conflict. Here what is presented is two potential new strategies of intervention: 1) directing people to listen in a non-counter arguing way, and 2) increasing temporal distance from the dispute.

Non-Counter-arguing Listening

When people encounter adversaries, who see the world, or even just a single issue, differently from them, they generally listen to those adversaries in a way that involves actively counter-arguing their reasoning rather than listening with an open ear and mind. [50] Such *counter-arguing listening* might involve making online judgments of the problems and weaknesses in the person's position as she is stating it, thinking about ways that one's own position is superior, and preparing counterarguments to be leveled against the opposition when it is one's turn to reply. Indeed, this type of counter-arguing is bolstered by the structure of the legal system in many countries, including the United States. These systems are explicitly set up as adversarial, with those directly involved in the dispute (plaintiffs, defendants, and lawyers) told to represent "opposing" sides and trained to mount convincing counter-arguments against their opposition. This is in contrast to third parties, such as judges and jurors, who are typically tasked with listening with an open ear and mind.

Given the inclination of people, and especially of adversaries, to listen by counter-arguing, it is not surprising that adversaries tend to conclude that their opponent is biased. This type of listening not only focuses adversaries on the flaws and biases in their opponents' thinking, but it also may prevent them from *hearing* what their opponents have to say. An alternative to this listening approach would allow individuals to truly hear the other person, by suppressing impulses for online counter-arguing, so that individuals might reach a better understanding of their opponent's actual position and of its underlying subtleties. Thus, we predict that a non-counter-arguing approach to listening will reduce the amount of bias individuals impute to their opponent.

Temporal Distance

Manipulating adversaries' temporal distance from a conflict situation may work to alleviate the bias-perception conflict spiral. Temporal distance (how far into the future an event is), as well as physical and social distance (how geographically distant or socially removed an event is), can increase the extent to which individuals see events in more global, indirect, or abstract terms. [51] Researchers have shown that those various forms of *psychological distance* can have dramatic effects on decision-making, evaluations of actions, self-control, and trait inferences. [52]

In circumstances involving disagreement, increasing psychological distance might allow adversaries to adopt a "cooler" perspective toward the situation, including toward the disagreement itself and the opposing party. A more abstract perspective might lead individuals to perceive that the other side is not so different, and might lead them to be more open to acknowledging both their own biases and their adversaries' objectivity. Resulting reductions in the perceived size of their disagreement or the extent to which they view their adversary as especially biased could interrupt or prevent the bias perception conflict spiral.

Psychological distance may allow individuals to step away from the conflict for a moment, presenting them with a fairer picture of the situation. That could have practical implications in a number of ways. First, it suggests that people who mediate conflicts might, in some cases, want to encourage conflicting parties to commit to future rather than present compromises. Second, when the luxury of time is not available, mediators might at least emphasize the relative temporal distance (rather than closeness) of parties' commitments, so that the parties involved can be encouraged to feel as though the disagreement is subjectively further away. When mediators are not available or practical, individuals might attempt to implement a distant time perspective on their own, for example by reducing demand for immediate results and by considering commitments on a longer time horizon.

The bias-perception conflict spiral is a psychologically-enriched model of developing and escalating conflict. This model asserts that bias perceptions are especially likely in the case of a disagreement and conflictual responding is especially likely to result from those negative perceptions. This structure is supported by previous research that alludes to the connection between disagreement, conflict development, and bias perceptions. An additional benefit of this bias-perception conflict spiral is the potential to use it for developing interventions. By targeting the interpersonal imputations of bias, it may be possible to shape individuals' responses to be more cooperative and constructive, rather than aggressive or competitive.

Non-Counter-arguing Listening as an Intervention in the Bias-Perception Conflict Spiral

The bias-perception conflict spiral allows for the development of conflict interventions that target the imputations of bias between adversaries. If these bias perceptions can be reduced or eliminated, it should follow that parties would respond to their disagreements in a more cooperative and conflict de-escalatory manner. This approach for intervention is based on the idea that some styles of listening are better than others. Most examples of research involving active listening come from papers recommending how health care professionals or teachers should respond to their patients or students so that the target "feels good" about the person listening to them. [53]

Negotiation researchers recommend that one important way to improve negotiations is to employ active listening, whereby individuals repeat back what the other person has said and ask for clarifications. [54] This technique, which may have been derived from Rogers' recommendations for providing counsel and therapy, has potential benefits to the speaker and the listener. [55] Speakers may feel that they are being heard and understood, listeners may benefit by actually gaining a better understanding. However, while many conflict and negotiation researchers emphasize how important *good* communication is for the successful resolution of disputes, they often do not provide clear prescriptions for what better listening entails. [56]

In a disagreement or dispute, one of the common listening styles people employ is to "mentally critique" what the other person is saying. [57]

Individuals actively prepare counterarguments and criticisms in response to what the other person is saying, rather than simply listening to and processing the other person's argument. This process may inflate perceptions of bias, if one is constantly in a state of countering and criticizing the other party. The hope with this intervention is to temper the imputations of bias that individuals make to their opposition. It is hoped that improving the way individuals listen may allow them to see opponents as more objective, leading people to behave in a less conflictual way.

Why Listening?

In many disagreements, the opposing sides communicate their positions verbally (e.g., a screaming match between two siblings or a debate in a political forum). At this point in a dispute, when one is presenting one's own arguments and listening to what the other side has to say, there is room for a number of things to go wrong. We have already demonstrated that, in the context of a disagreement, people are likely to impute bias to their adversaries. It seems especially likely that these imputations will develop online, as one is finding out about the other side's position. As one learns that another individual (a) has a position different from one's own and (b) has reasons for that position that one disagrees with, then the "logical" conclusion is that this other person is biased. Opponents discover much as they are listening to each other (although some of these discoveries, such as conclusions about how biased the other is, may be inaccurate). For these reasons, listening is an important part of interpersonal interactions, but even more so in the case of potential conflict, where the stakes are high.

It is suggested that people do not hear their adversary's arguments as a mere sensory input, free from the influence of the listener's own motivations and assumptions. Rather, it has been argued that the perception of the adversary's argument is highly subjective, and is especially susceptible to coloring by one's own tendency towards a counter-arguing listening style (i.e., making online judgments and preparing rebuttals). Sensation and perception are not identical, and a large body of research in physiological psychology has established ways that perception, in many different modalities, can be "constructed" by the perceiver or the environment. [58] More relevant to the bias-perception conflict spiral, research has established ways that perceptions of social situations (individuals, behavior, and events) can be subjective.

Perceiving Social Situations

A constructivist approach to sensation and perception helps to account for why people often perceive the same social situation as very different. [59] The individual supplies an additional input (motivation, past experiences, expectations, etc.) that will influence the perception above and beyond any objective sensory input. One classic example of social perception is a case study.[60] This study demonstrated how fans on opposite sides of a Princeton-Dartmouth football game perceived the rough (and potentially foul) play very differently, depending on who they were rooting for. Though they all watched the same sporting contest, the individual accounts of whether the game was fair or dirty varied greatly. A similar effect is found in today's society when viewing news media reports. People often view the same news feed, but draw very different conclusions about how fair or accurate the report was with respect to their side of the issue. In this hostile media effect, a common occurrence is that members of both sides of an argument believe the news story was biased in favor of the other side. [61]

When perceiving social situations or other people, individuals bring their own baggage with them, including expectations. A great deal of work has been conducted in psychology to address the problem of confirmation biases and expectancy confirmation (similar to self-fulfilling prophesies). "Confirmation bias" is a term used to describe what is happening when people seek or interpret information to confirm an existing belief or expectation. [62] This could be a case where people ignore information that would counter their initial hypothesis and only attend to the evidence supporting their own claims. What is more relevant to this thesis, however, is that a confirmation bias can color an individual's perception of any one piece of information so that it is suited to support his or her own argument—people's desires and motivations actually lead them to evaluate an objective piece of information as meaning something very different than what others perceive it to mean.

Expectancy confirmation expands the idea of confirmation bias into the realm of interpersonal perception. [63] According to the theory, one party (the perceiver) begins with a preexisting conception about the other party (the target). The perceiver acts towards the target in a way that accords with that preconception. The target, in turn, considers how the perceiver has acted, and responds accordingly—in a way that confirms the perceiver's preconception, thereby creating a self-fulfilling prophecy. This pattern can continue indefinitely, perpetuating an initial misunderstanding.

The larger idea of self-fulfilling prophecies also addresses motivated cognitions. [64] The notion, consistent with expectancy confirmation, is that people are motivated and cognitively predisposed, to perceive information in ways that align with their prior beliefs. For example, in the context of a conflict between Democrats and Republicans over a welfare reform bill, each side might expect the other to be intransigent and ideologically-driven, and therefore might view the other side's questions and concerns as evidence of that (rather than of an interest in the facts or in finding common ground).

In a classic experiment, Lord, Ross, and Lepper showed that political partisans perceive evidence that supports their views as persuasive and evidence that opposes their views as unconvincing; as a result, they come to hold yet stronger views in the face of mixed evidence. [65] This suggests that once people are committed to a certain notion of the other side, they may evaluate evidence in a way that makes them continually more convinced of their initial perceptions. Others have directly demonstrated the effects of expectancy on the preference for cooperation and competition. [66]

In an example of how one can attempt to prevent expectancy effects, Babcock, Loewenstein, Issacharoff, and Camerer showed that lack of knowledge about which side of a negotiation one would be on (e.g., with naïve participants in a study) led to more successful settlements. [67] This is a case where, because individuals did not know which side of a disagreement they would be on, they were less biased in their processing of the information and likely less extreme in their attribution of bias to the other side (the confirmation bias was blocked). They were able to better agree upon what was a fair and objective outcome. In a way, this forced perspective taking and bias-free evaluation took the disagreement out of the issue, allowing for more positive perceptions of the other party and less competition.

Even small "changes" to how information is presented can have large impacts on the way it is perceived. This provides additional evidence that social perception is not merely the result of objective processing of sensory input. Labeling an individual as warm or cold can alter perceptions of a lecturer's performance. [68] People report very different reactions to the same quote, depending on whether it is attributed to Lenin or Lincoln and attributing a quote to an expert, rather than a novice, influences the perceived validity of the statement. [69]

Collectively, this evidence supports the general notion that social perceptions (perceptions of people, information, and situations) are not immune to influence by the perceiver himself. In the context of a disagreement, one especially likely assumption about the other side is that their positions are wrong and their reasoning has been biased. Therefore, when listening to an adversary, people will naturally be inclined to judge as they listen, to find evidence of the other side's bias. This effect can then have serious consequences for the course of a disagreement—if I become even more certain of my opponent's bias, I will be inclined to behave in a more competitive and aggressive manner, thus escalating the situation into a conflict. Finding a way to prevent these confirmations of expectations of bias might then be a useful way to intervene in the bias perception conflict spiral.

Why Temporal Distance?

The bias-perception conflict spiral suggests points for intervention in the development from disagreement into conflict: by either reducing the perceived size of the disagreement or by directly impacting how biased (vs. objective) people perceive their adversaries to be. The hypothesized result would be a decrease in conflictual responding and a more cooperative approach for dealing with those adversaries. This chapter aims to demonstrate that temporal distance (thinking about or making a decision for the future self in a disagreement) can serve as an intervention in the bias-perception conflict spiral.

Given that we see and treat the future self like another person, disagreement between the future self and another person may be more like a disagreement between two other people. [70] This could be beneficial in the context of the bias-perception conflict spiral in two ways: first, by "closing the gap" between how the self and others are perceived (either by reducing the imputations of bias to one's opposition or leading individuals to admit a greater susceptibility to cognitive and motivational biases in their own, future self), or secondly, by having individuals make decisions about how they will respond to a disagreement from a more distant perspective. Any reductions in the perceived size of the disagreement that result from having a more psychologically distant perspective should also translate into seeing the opposition as less biased.

If any, or all, of these effects on people's *perceptions* result from a more temporally distant perspective, we would expect greater cooperative responding and less conflictual *behavior* (thus weakening the bias-perception conflict spiral's potential to grow and spiral out of control). Indeed, Henderson, Trope, and Carnevale have shown that people behave differently in a negotiation when they take a temporally distant perspective (they behave more in line with their abstract, big-picture goals). [71] Using hypothetical negotiation tasks, the authors are able to show that a distant, rather than an impending or urgent negotiation, leads to superior outcomes and behaviors. Specifically, when the negotiation is occurring in (or is about) the hypothetical future, participants express a desire for simultaneous bargaining (rather than piecemeal), are more willing to concede on their lower priority issues and make more multi-issue offers, and they reach better individual and joint outcomes. The authors attribute the findings to the abstract perspective of the negotiation when it is distant, and do not investigate interpersonal perceptions.

Effects of Time on Judgments, Decisions, and Behavior

Within the decision-making literature, a good deal of attention has been paid to how decisions are affected by or vary across time. For example, research has suggested that people prefer to have rewards and positive things now (or in the near future), but they prefer to put off pain or negative things until later in the future. [72] This can lead to difficulty with delaying gratification and procrastination, problems that most people are familiar with. Researchers have demonstrated that there are many inconsistencies with how people choose across time. The classic temporal discounting finding suggests that people will forfeit a greater reward (in favor of a smaller, more immediate one) if they have to wait for it. [73] So, if an individual is offered a choice of $10 today or $11 in a week, the tendency is to choose the immediate, though smaller, $10 (the de-valuing of future rewards creates a hyperbolic discounting function).

However, people generally make a different choice if both options are delayed into the future. For example, if offered $10 in a year or $11 in a year and a week, people will revert to choosing the larger, though technically more distant, option. [74] Another inconsistency related to decision-making and time is that individuals often make different choices if they are all made together vs. spread out over time. [75] So, if asked to choose 10 different candies all at once, people generally choose a variety of options. However, if the choices are made separately, at 10 different points of time, people will generally pick the same option at each point: their favorite.

It should come as no surprise that people often fail to fulfill the decisions that they make for their future self. [76] This could be due to a failure of self-control (such as, "I said I wasn't going to have dessert, but now that it is right in front of me, I am going to eat it.") or it could be because one realizes the decision that was made was simply the wrong one (such as, "I know I said I would go visit my friends this weekend, but I simply have too much work to do and cannot go"). People's ability to renege or back-out of decisions that they make for their future selves will, of course, vary as a function of how binding and irreversible the decisions were themselves. Time pressure (such as impending deadlines or a perceived need to "rush") can have effects on individuals' information processing and decision-making. Work in negotiation has demonstrated that time pressure leads negotiators to stereotype more, to use heuristic processing, and to fail to move away from a fixed-pie perception of the dispute. [77] These effects of salient time pressures led to less integrative agreements. Others have demonstrated that longer time horizons in a negotiation can result in better outcomes and greater efficiency. [78] In these examples, the perception of being rushed or of being free from time pressures has important consequences for the way individuals view their disagreements and how they choose to respond to their adversaries.

Multiple Selves

Often in our daily lives, we make decisions in the present about what we will do in the future. One classic example of this is deciding what time to wake up in the morning by setting the alarm clock. In the evening we set the alarm and in the morning we are jolted awake when the alarm goes off. Some mornings (if not all), we might feel quite irritated at having been forced to awake so early and we might wish that the evening before we had set the alarm for just 30 minutes later so that we could get more sleep. What is particularly interesting about this situation is that the self that decides what time to set the alarm for and the self that experiences the consequences of that decision seem like they are almost two different people—two people who cannot agree about the appropriate time to wake up. The "evening self" thinks that it is perfectly reasonable (indeed, advisable) to get up at 5am so that we have plenty of time to get ready, while the "morning self" thinks it would have been fine to get up at 6am even though that would mean rushing out the door to avoid being late for work. In reality, of course, these two selves are the same person at two different points in time.

There have been many philosophers and psychologists who have asked questions about the possibility of multiple selves. Ainslie engages in a discussion of multiple selves as he considers issues like addiction, immediate gratification, and lack of willpower. [79] He sees these situations as a battle between two competing selves, one with short-range interests and one with long-range interests—essentially, two minds in one person. Similarly, Thaler and Shefrin describe the self as an organization of selves, some who are "far-sighted planners," others who are "myopic doers." [80] Shelling provides colorful examples of instances when the self seems to be in conflict, particularly when it comes to inter-temporal decision making, and he poses difficult questions about which self should be obeyed. [81] For example, a woman who is about to give birth might insist that she does not want anesthesia (and that if she should ask for it, it should be denied her), but she may later scream at the doctor to give her the drugs—which patient should the doctor obey? Shelling acknowledges that this is a difficult question and that, even though they may have opposite goals, our multiple selves are all "authentic." In many of Schelling's examples, the present-self is able to anticipate the misbehavior of the future-self, and can take steps to block that bad behavior—for example, giving your car keys to the host if you anticipate that you will be too drunk to drive home at the end of the night and you worry that your later judgment will be too clouded to make the right decision. These ideas of pre-commitment have been pursued by others in psychology as a way to bind the future self to do what the present self deems best. [82]

A slightly different tact has been taken by those who consider multiple selves in the framework of a should-self and a want-self, which focuses on individual's motivations and goals, or between actual, ideal, and ought selves. [83] Still others have constructed the idea of multiple selves as the multiple possibilities of what we might be in the future. [84] These stories convey the sense that we cannot simply think of the self as one, fixed, stable creature. Instead, we must be conscious of the changes that occur in the self across time and when thinking into the past or the future.

Psychological Distance

Trope and Liberman, along with their colleagues, have done a great deal of work examining different types of psychological distance. [85] These include social distance, temporal distance, physical distance, and hypotheticality. [86] A sense of psychological distance may apply to events, objects, and people (including the self).

One basic assertion of the psychological distance literature is that *increases* in psychological distance will lead to a more abstract focus. [87] This can be articulated as a more integrated, superordinate, or higher level focus. This abstract, rather than concrete, way of thinking about something that is psychologically far away may lead to an emphasis on goals and end results, rather than the piecemeal steps of implementation. Related to the idea of multiple selves, these researchers have suggested that there may be parallels between temporal and social distance (in terms of the effects they have on individuals' perceptions and judgments. [87] This suggests that the future-self may be, in some respects, like another person, different from the current, experienced self.

There has been some recent work to suggest that interpersonal distance and inter-temporal distance may share some similarities. Howard Rachlin and colleagues have demonstrated that, when making decisions regarding other people, social distance (that is, how far a person is from you in terms of your relationship to them) creates a similar hyperbolic discount function to temporal distance (that is, how far the event is in the future) when making decisions for the self.[88] These similarities suggest that social and temporal distance have similar properties in terms of their effects on the decisions people make. Neuroimaging has been used to address the question of parallels between social and temporal distance. Social neuroscience has asserted that there are different levels of activation in the rostral anterior cingulate (rACC) when thinking about the self-relative to thinking about others. Ersner-Hershfield, Wimmer, & Knutson showed that similar patterns of differential activation are found when thinking about the future self-relative to the present self. [89]

There are parallels in terms of the way future selves, past selves, and others are perceived. People are more likely to make dispositional explanations for other people's behavior (while more prone to make situational explanations for the present self), but we are also likely to make dispositional explanations for the distant past or future self. [90] While we are hesitant to assign fixed traits to the present self (instead, we err on the side of "it depends"), we are willing to assign traits to both other people and temporally distant versions of the self. Not surprisingly, we tend to view others from an outside, observer perspective, but the self from an inside, actor perspective. What is less obvious, however, is that we also view our past and future selves from an outside perspective (like watching oneself in a video, rather than seeing the situation through one's own eyes. [91]

Decision-making research supports the notion that there are differences between the future self and the present self. [92] That is, when making a decision for the immediate, present self, the internal subjective experience of that decision will be stronger and more heavily weighted, but it will be neglected when choosing for someone else or for the future. [93] Internal subjective experience refers to the combination of thoughts, emotions, moods, introspections, or other arousals experienced as a result of the decision that one is presented with. The different use of these internal subjective experiences when deciding for the present and future selves leads to different decisions, presenting the paradox of which self should be obeyed.

Conclusion

It is not uncommon to view those on the other side of a disagreement as being extreme, blinded by their position or group allegiances, and unable to see the issue in a fair-minded, objective way. These beliefs about the opposition may lead one to forsake response options such as engaging in a calm discussion or exchanging information, because they would seem like futile acts—what is the point of giving this other person good information about the reality of the situation if she is hopelessly biased? So, rather than attempting cooperation, one may resort to more aggressive means of dealing with the opposition, such as anger, violence, or attempts to eliminate her ability to stand in the way of one's own ends. The resulting conflict may cost time, energy, and resources that could have otherwise been saved or directed towards more constructive efforts.

CHAPTER ELEVEN

Bias: Extreme Prejudice

Horrific incidents of violence motivated by bias against particular groups of individuals mar the history of modern society. Some of the more severe examples of these events include post-civil war lynching's of African-Americans in the United States; the rise of the Nazi state in Germany; the ethnic cleansings in the Balkans, Rwanda, and the Sudan; the rising tide of Anti-Semitism in Europe at the end of the twentieth century; and, the September Eleventh terrorist attacks. [1] There also have been innumerable, more confined incidents ranging in severity from simple harassment on school playgrounds to the deaths of an African-American man dragged by a truck and a twenty-one year old gay college student severely beaten and left to die crucified on a fence. Research suggests that there are both psychological and sociological variables involved in the formation and expression of the biases involved in all of these types of incidents; however, questions still remain about why some individuals choose to violently express their biases and whether the same behavioral dynamics are involved in the expression of different kinds of bias. [2]

Despite bias-motivated events occurring throughout all of history, it was not until 1991, following the Hate Crime Statistics Act of 1990, that the United States government officially designated all of these events as bias-motivated crimes. While the Hate Crime Statistics Act and almost all subsequent discussions of these behaviors use the term hate crime, this chapter will refer to such incidents more accurately as bias crimes or bias-motivated crimes to avoid the myriad of issues and criticism that are associated with the more recent use of hate. Various political, social, and academic groups have questioned the need for or even the existence of a special group of crimes known as hate crimes because they feel that many crimes, at their cores, involve hate. The reasoning being who would assault, rob from, or more specifically kill someone they liked. This often purposeful confusion of the issue is minimized when bias is used to describe these events. The term bias conveys the more accurate idea that the offender was motivated in part or in whole by a bias towards who or what the victim was known or believed to represent. It is this random, faultless on the part of the victim, motivation which legitimizes the recognition of these incidents and crimes as unique events.

With the passage of the Hate Crime Statistics Act, the United States government officially began collecting national data on these events. Since its first days of collection, bias crime data, perhaps due to various issues with its collection (e.g., victims hesitant to report, law enforcement non-participation/mistakes, legal definitions), has varied greatly from year to year, and has left researchers wondering how much goes unreported or misclassified. [4] The data that has been collected, however, has allowed the formation of general ideas about bias crime and its place in the larger context of all crime. Uniform Crime Report (UCR) data reveal that during the end of the 1990s and the early part of the next decade, crime, and especially violent crime, dropped precipitously in the United States. [5] At the same time, bias crime, once a mostly race-related issue, was increasing, diversifying, and intensifying. There were more incidents—including more homicides—and more were reported as anti-homosexual, anti-Asian, and following September 11th, anti—Arab/Muslim. [6] It is not yet known how much of this increase was due to changes in reporting practices, increased awareness, increased sensitivity, or actual increases in the incidence of bias crime. The most recent data available indicate that there were 7,163 bias crimes reported to police agencies participating in the UCR program in 2005, just under two-thirds of which were crimes against a person, including 6 bias-motivated homicides. [7]

Given that official data collection for bias crimes did not begin until 1991, it is not surprising that there has been limited research on the issue. There has been a plethora of research on bias, but little on how bias manifests itself in criminal acts, particularly the act of murder. On average, fourteen bias homicides were reported in each of the past five years. An analysis of bias-motivated homicide intent on developing a better understanding of the situational dynamics—behaviors of the individuals involved, the bias motivating the incident, and the physical setting of the act—of bias homicides, therefore would require an in-depth examination (i.e., not just the limited information recorded in the UCR) of bias homicides over several years. [8]

The fact that the United States has over 15,000 homicides a year has prompted a tremendous amount of research—both psychological and sociological—on the dynamics of homicide. The techniques and approaches employed by homicide investigators have improved dramatically as a result of the combination of this research. Similar advances could be achieved in understanding the dynamics of bias-motivated homicides, which could assist criminal justice professionals in both investigating and perhaps even preventing/reducing such incidents. These advances will require much more to be learned about bias homicide. General descriptions of the phenomenon, which have not been compiled specifically for bias homicide, need to be determined. The actions of offenders at bias homicide crime scenes need to be examined, as do the behavioral backgrounds of these offenders. Ultimately, the connections between the victims, the offenders, the physical setting, and the biases involved, need to be understood.

Bias Crime Data and Trends

Official collection of data on bias crimes in the United States began in 1991, following the passing of the Hate Crime Statistics Act in 1990. The Federal Bureau of Investigation (FBI) took on the responsibility of collecting and disseminating this data and incorporated the process into the preexisting Uniform Crime Report. The collection of this data is based on the legal definition outlined in the Hate Crime Statistics Act, which states that a bias crime is any criminal offense that is "motivated, in part or in full, by prejudice based on race, religion, sexual orientation, disability, or ethnicity" [10] This new source of data, along with increasing interest in bias crimes following several high-profile incidents, gave rise to a growing number of data collection efforts and the existing body of research. Uniform Crime Report data were collected by and for police, and, therefore, were not initially rich in research-oriented data. Early studies predominantly focused on describing, or categorizing, the types of bias crimes that were reported to police. [11] Similar to researchers working with non-bias-motivated Uniform Crime Report data, bias crime researchers were very aware of the data quality issues inherent in a collection system that is voluntary. In response to these problems, researchers began to take advantage of data collected by various advocacy groups, despite the criticism that these groups often record incidents that do not meet legal standards to be considered bias crimes. [12] Research found that the two sources of data often provided the same picture of the problem, which allowed the development of initial, but still incomplete, snapshots of the problem. [13]

Considering the well-known problem of the underreporting of crime, specifically in the Uniform Crime Report, many of the early studies on bias crime attempted to ascertain how well the official programs were measuring bias crime. [14] Several studies administered victimization surveys to college students and, generally, found that up to seventy percent of bias crimes go unreported. [15] As is the case with non-bias homicides, bias homicides have, nevertheless, consistently had the highest solved and reported rates of bias-motivated crimes. [16] This information, compared to data indicating that over ninety percent of homosexuals—one of the top three groups affected by bias crime—report some victimization, with over one-third experiencing violent victimization, highlights the many gaps that exist in the collection process. [17] Despite the problems with official and advocacy data, researchers found that the methods used at least reliably measured the problem. [18] This consistency has allowed researchers to develop the following general profiles of bias crime offenders, victims, and incidents based on conglomerations of official and advocacy data.

Offender Characteristics

More attention has been paid to collecting data on bias crime offenders because, while victim characteristics are an important factor in understanding the dynamics of bias crimes, it would be unfair—and generally impossible—to ask victims, who usually were doing nothing illegal, to change anything about themselves to avoid this kind of victimization.

Almost the entire body of research devoted to the investigation of who commits bias crimes has found that the offenders tend to be young males, acting as part of a group—but not as parts of organized hate groups—who come from middle class families, have no criminal record, victimize targets of convenience, and are complete strangers to the individuals they victimize. [19] Specifically, research indicates that bias crime perpetrators are young men in their late teens to early twenties. [20] According to Bufkin, up to 90% of all bias crime perpetrators are males, and in the small percentage

(6%) of instances when offenders are female, the females are almost never the instigators; rather, they are usually dating the perpetrator. [21]

The New York City Police Department reported that 80% of the bias crime offenders handled by the department were adolescents. [22] Another study based on data collected in New York City found that individuals under the age of 21 committed more bias crimes than those individuals over 21, and that up to 71% of the crimes included in the study sample were committed by individuals under the age of 20. [22] It is important to consider the average age of offenders given that research has found that when adolescents—the most common offenders—engage in bias crimes, they tend to physically victimize their targets. [23]

Group dynamics, including the number of offenders and the ratio of offenders to victims, are central components of the process of bias crimes. [24] Bufkin's research found that multiple perpetrators are involved in 48% of bias crimes, and in only 22% of non-bias crimes. [25] Craig and Franklin assert that bias crimes are very much a group activity, citing official data as indicating that up to two-thirds of reported bias crimes were committed by 2 or more people. [26] In their study examining bias crime data collected in New York City, Maxwell and Maxwell found that the average number of offenders was usually higher than one for all types of bias incidents/crimes. [27] The fact that research has revealed that most bias crimes involve multiple offenders is important because research has found that the higher number of perpetrators involved in a violent crime, the more severe the crime. [28]

A majority of the research indicates groups of bias crime offenders are typically complete strangers to their victims, particularly incidents involving youth offenders and youth victims. [29] Specifically, Reasons and Hughson found that around 41% of offenders were complete strangers.[30] With 67% of offenders under the age of 30 known to the victim and only 21% of offenders under the age of 18 known, it appears that the younger the offender the more likely they are to victimize a stranger. [31] Franklin found that 63% of self-reported bias crime offenders were strangers to the victims, 10% were friends of friends, and 3% were relatives. [32] It also has been found that when assailants are known to the victim (e.g., friends, relatives, and lovers) bias crimes are less likely to be reported, but more likely to be extremely violent. [33] Given the apparent differences in bias crimes depending on the characteristics of the offender(s) and their relationship with the victim, the fact that there has been no detailed study of the characteristics of offenders involved in bias homicides represents a new avenue for understanding their dynamics.

Victim Characteristics

Despite the focus on offenders, with over seventy-percent of bias crimes classified as crimes against a person there still has been a decent amount of bias crime research focused on understanding the characteristics of the victims through examinations of official data and surveys. [34] As part of a survey on the self-reported responses of non-criminal bias crime offenders, Franklin found that a majority (two-thirds) of victims were alone, 15% were in pairs, and 18% were in groups of three. [35] About two-thirds of victims were Caucasian and 12% were African—American. [36] Comstock, who produced one of the first seminal studies in the area, examined bias crimes on college campuses and found that homosexual college students are four times more likely to suffer some form of victimization than other college students. [37] Taken together these data provide a description of who is at risk to be the victim of a bias crime and how the risks for such individuals compare to individuals who are not targets of bias crime. With the work that has been done to examine the victims of bias crime, there is no specific information on the victims of bias homicides, perhaps due to the difficulty of obtaining the very limited data on such incidents.

Bias Crime Incidents Characteristics

The main body of research on bias crime incidents—in an effort to legitimize the study of bias crime as a unique type of event—has focused on how such incidents are different from non-bias crimes. Studies on bias crimes have found that up to three-fourths of bias motivated assaults involve physical injury, while only twenty-nine percent of non-bias assaults do. [38] Thirty-percent of bias-motivated assaults are so severe that the victim requires hospitalization, while only seven percent of non-bias ones are that severe. [39]

Bias homicides also have been found to be more severe than non-bias homicides, with over seventy-percent of bias homicides classified as involving overkill. [40] Overall, researchers have concluded that bias crimes are different on almost every factor. [41] The differences that have been examined, however, are descriptive at best, and lacking when it comes to bias homicide. Determining if the situational and behavioral dynamics of bias homicides differ based on the motivation and the location could significantly increase the understanding of what occurs in different scenarios.

Bias Crime Trends

With data on bias crime having been collected for over twelve years, trends in bias crime are beginning to be discussed. These trends, however, are seen generally as tenuous given that it is a relatively new field and many researchers are unsure if the changes represent actual variation in bias crime or if they are results of ever increasing attention to the problem. One consistent trend in the bias crime data is that racially motivated incidents and crimes are the most common.[41] Interestingly, during the mid to late 1990s official data indicated that bias crimes were increasing and that they specifically were increasing for incidents not motivated by racial bias.[42] Groups particularly being victimized more included Asians, Hispanics, and Homosexuals. Overall, the end of the twentieth century was marked by a three percent decrease in bias crimes; however, at the same time anti-homosexual bias crimes rose an outstanding eighty-one percent.[43] Following the September 11th terrorist attacks, bias crimes significantly increased, mostly attributable to the spike in anti-Arab/Muslim bias crimes following the attacks, but have leveled off in the years after. One of the more startling trends recently uncovered is that while bias crimes have been generally leveling off or decreasing, they have been increasing in intensity.[44] Other than research indicating that bias crimes are becoming more severe, which is based primarily on basic official data, patterns of severe bias violence have not been addressed. With studies showing that bias crimes are changing—both intensifying and diversifying—it is becoming increasingly important to understand how the dynamics of the most violent form of bias differ for various bias motivations.

Summary of Data and Trends

Researchers, despite finding that up to seventy-percent of bias crime may go unreported, have developed a descriptive picture of the factors involved in their occurrence. Studies routinely have found that most bias crimes are crimes committed against a person, who is most likely to be a young male alone at the time of the incident. Offenders have been found to be young males who are acting in a non-organized group, from middle class families, lacking a criminal record, and who victimize individuals who are complete strangers. The combination of these factors—young, in a group, and an unknown victim—has also been found to be associated with an increased severity of the associated crimes.

In general, bias crimes have been found to be more physically severe than non-bias crimes and to differ in situational and behavioral dynamics based on the event location. Research, however, has not been able to develop detailed profiles of the victims, offenders, and situations involved in bias homicides. [45] More specifically, given that the research suggests that situational and behavioral dynamics of bias crimes differ significantly based on who is involved and where they occur, the situational and behavioral dynamics of bias homicides need to be examined to determine how this severe form of bias differs based on the victim(s), offender(s), situation, and bias involved. [46]

Bias Crime Motivation

Despite the abundance of demographic information that has been collected on bias crimes, limited information exists in regards to what is involved in the motivations that lead the perpetrators to act. [47] Developing an understanding of how different bias motivations manifest themselves in violent physical acts could assist law enforcement officials, who currently rely mostly on eye witness accounts in determining if, and what kind of, bias was involved. Being able to recognize what type of bias is involved in an homicide not only allows investigators to approach the event as a bias crime, but also, based on research linking motivation to type of offender, could allow them to investigate the crime more efficiently. [48]

A significant amount of psychological and sociological research has focused on understanding the processes involved in the formation and expression of bias and prejudice. Such research has found that bias is an almost automatic process, which supports the contention that in social situations individuals rely on categorization to help them navigate interpersonal interactions.[49] Developmental psychology research has determined that common bias and/or prejudice concepts and habits are communicated within the parental family structure. [50] This style of research, however, has been general in nature and has not explored the question of whether different forms of bias and/or prejudice are expressed differently. [51] Generally, the research has not made specific connections between specific criminal elements and specific motivations.

Psychologists, who have studied violence much more intensely than specifically bias motivated violence, have found, based on interviews with offenders, that the motivation to perform a bias crime can be representative of both reactive (expressive) and instrumental violence. The perpetrators can be seen as defending a set of social values or economic opportunities against attack from an out group when they act reactively, or they can be viewed as hoping to maintain or achieve social dominance when they perform instrumental bias violence. [52] This vein of psychological research has found some connections between the degree of motivation and the situational aspects of bias crimes. Offenders who enter a bias incident highly motivated to perform the act are more likely to be doing so for instrumental reasons, and they are more likely than other bias offenders to be strangers with their victims and have prior criminal convictions for violent acts. [53] Homicide researchers have recently focused on the differences between instrumental and reactive violence, and bias-motivated violence researchers believe that examining the differences between bias-motivated aggression that is a response to a perceived provocation (reactive) and aggression that is planned, voluntary, and intended to achieve a specific goal (instrumental) can provide insight into the motivations and behaviors of violent bias crime offenders. [54]

Other researchers, who were specifically interested in the psychology involved in different biases, have found that there are considerably different psychological processes behind moderate and extreme forms of bias. [55] More severe forms of bias involve negative self-attitudes, self-rejection, a need to conform, and an extremely high authoritarian personality. [56] The intensity of the bias has been found to affect the type of aggression that is expressed in a violent bias crime. [57] While information has been discovered regarding connections between motivations and bias violence, there has been no effort to determine if the aggression displayed in a crime scene can be used to identify the bias involved, and, perhaps, some of the characteristics of the offender(s) and their relationship with the victim(s).

Classification

Despite all the information that has been collected about the characteristics of bias crimes and the research into the causes and forms of bias and prejudice, one of the main hurdles that prevents more in-depth research from being conducted about the connections between the two areas is the difficulty law enforcement professionals have in determining if a crime should be classified as a bias crime, and, if it should, what bias was involved. There is an ongoing debate about how reliably an offender's bias motivation can be discerned from a crime scene, especially when the crime is homicide and there are likely to be few, if any, surviving eye witnesses. [58] For a bias crime to be investigated and prosecuted successfully, investigators must be able to identify behavioral and situational components that can reliably be used to prove that the crime was motivated in part or completely by bias.

Generally, law enforcement personnel rely on reports of bias speech when investigating whether a crime involved bias. This approach results in an impossibly narrow avenue of discovering the inner dynamics of the incident. [59] In some instances law enforcement personnel can rely on other details such as bias graffiti, the crime occurring in conjunction with cultural/ethnic holidays and/or events, or the crime taking place at a location/neighborhood known for a concentration of a specific group. [60] Improving this kind of investigation depends on conducting a systematic analysis of bias crime offenders' attitudes and behaviors so that an examination of the co-occurrences of offender and victim demographics and behaviors can help identify the presence of bias in a homicide.

The idea of classifying bias crimes has not been completely overlooked. Some of the first researchers of bias crime realized that a classification system of the types of bias crime could greatly assist in understanding and even investigating such crimes. Levin and McDevitt are responsible for a significant portion of the research that seeks to explain why some individuals act out their negative attitudes. [61] Their work has focused on developing the main classification of bias crimes, which primarily has focused on understanding offender motivations including: thrill-seeking, mission, defensive, and retaliatory. While this classification system is broad enough that it most likely captures all bias crime offenders, it is not mutually exclusive and still paints the typical bias crime offender as someone who is not part of normal, everyday culture. [62] While this sort of system does explain, at least at the general individual level, what gives rise to bias crimes, it does not provide any sort of framework or information that could help investigators. Law enforcement personnel unfortunately do not have the luxury of access to the offender's mind when they are investigating a case with an unknown offender; therefore, making connections between psychological motivations and crime scene behaviors would become guesswork instead of an empirically-based process.

Summary of Motivations and Classifications

Social scientists have made great strides in helping society comprehend the psychological and social processes that are responsible for the formation and expression of bias and prejudice. Armed with a more advanced knowledge of bias, researchers have begun to examine and understand the connections that exist between the type and intensity of the bias motivation and the manner in which it is expressed. Research suggests that the most extreme expressions of bias tend to be performed by individuals with a specific set of personality characteristics, who tend to act out in certain situations. All of this information, however, has still produced only offender motivation classifications, which while helpful in understanding the general dynamics of bias, do not provide help to those responsible for investigating bias homicides. A classification framework must be developed that is grounded in an analysis of the behaviors, demographics and situational characteristics that make up bias-motivated homicides. Recent studies conducted to develop a more advanced classification system for homicides have focused on the Expressive/Instrumental dichotomy. Research also has suggested that the same split exists for violent bias-motivated behavior. [63] The work that has been done on non-bias-motivated homicide presents a validated methodology for taking the next step in analyzing violent bias-motivated behavior. That work has focused on the role that aggression plays in violent and homicidal interactions. Examining this area of research provides the theoretical basis for distinguishing the types of behaviors offenders engage in at bias-motivated homicide crime scenes.

Brief Discussion of Aggression

Before approaching the relevant homicide research, briefly summarizing the literature on aggressive behavior is an important step in comprehending how crime scene behaviors can be used to distinguish between offenders. Psychologists have generally concluded that aggression is very similar to assertiveness; in that, the two characteristics are very similar early in development, but later evolve into distinct traits. [64] Both of these traits, depending on the situation, can be either positive or negative; however, when discussing homicide, one usually views employing such an aggressive approach during the interpersonal interaction as a bad behavior.

Specific the study of homicide, aggression is viewed not as a general psychological trait, but as a strategy for dealing with specific types of situations. Studies of non-bias homicide have found that these strategies are learned behaviors, which are called upon by the offender(s) in similar types of situations, and that they can be observed and connected between homicides and the responsible offenders. [65] This connection is believed possible because these researchers view homicide as an interpersonal interaction which exhibits many of the same interpersonal behaviors seen in the way that the offender has interacted with others in the past. In these specific types of situations, aggressive offenders have learned to use aggression as a strategy to maintain their reputation or to control the behavior of others they view as objects to be used for a purpose or even just for entertainment. [66] After multiple instances of the aggressive strategy working successfully the behavior transforms into a habitual one. The habit of aggression may be limited to the instinctual level, where the perpetrator only engages in such behavior when certain stimuli provoke the response without any thought from the perpetrator. [67]

Expressive and Instrumental Forms of Aggression

A short discussion of the psychology behind the expressive/instrumental aggression dichotomy, which has become so central to the investigative psychology approach to understanding homicide, also is a germane topic before moving on to the specific field of homicide. The Expressive/Instrumental dichotomy originates in the work of Fesbach who viewed aggression as an action meant to accomplish one of two goals or rewards for the offender. [68] Fesbach described expressive aggression as acts meant to inflict pain on the target in response to events (e.g., fights, insults, personal failures, etc.), which made the offender angry. Instrumental aggressive acts are committed to satisfy a desire for the possessions or status of another person, regardless of the costs and consequences. Toch's work, mentioned earlier, named these two forms of aggression differently (self-preserving and needs-promoting), but conceptualized them very similarly. [69] Aggression research has consistently found that this division is evident across all offender age groups. [70]

Complicating the discussion is the fact that individuals, be they criminal offenders or not, rarely limit their aggressive behaviors to either expressive or instrumental. An offender with a record of instrumental aggressive crimes could very easily have a bad day, lose their temper, and engage in expressive aggressive behavior. [71] Furthermore, an offender who was committing what would have been a strictly instrumental act could become upset by something the victim says and respond with expressive aggressive behavior. Cornell et al. specifically examined this issue of mixed aggression and found that most criminal aggression is expressive. [72] Salfati and Canter suggested that instrumental violence may be an indicator of a pathological ability to use aggression to achieve a goal. [73]

Homicide Research

Understanding the evolution of homicide classification frameworks into the current system that is based on the Expressive/Instrumental dichotomy is a necessary step in comprehending how to apply the same methodology in examining bias-motivated homicide. According to the FBI's Uniform Crime Report, violent crime has dropped precipitously in the United States over the past few years, declining 3.2 percent in 2003 alone. [74] This reduction of violent crime, however, has been marred by an increase in homicide and by a continuing decline in homicide clearance rates.[75] In recognition of these facts researchers have continued working to improve the understanding of the interrelations between offender, victim, and situational variables and how that information can assist homicide investigators. These efforts have included developing more sound methods of connecting offender crime scene behaviors and offender characteristics expressed at crime scenes with offender background characteristics.

Wolfgang, Pokorny, and Block—recognizing that murder is an interpersonal event that is influenced by the individuals involved and their relationship to each other—were some of the first social scientists to conduct studies on homicides and those who are involved in them. [76] These early explorations of this extreme expression of aggression primarily focused on offender demographics, the relationship between the offender(s) and the victim(s), and the method of killing. Psychiatrists, often using convenience samples or other methodologically questionable techniques, have attempted to develop typologies of murderers, but these classifications often have lacked a theoretical underpinning or have been either too exhaustive or too general. [77] The FBI expanded the scope of homicide research by focusing on the behavioral aspects of homicide that had been ignored by earlier researchers. The FBI developed a classification system where crime scene behaviors were used to categorize the homicide scene as organized or disorganized. Researchers who have evaluated the

FBI's system have found that its various methodological issues—lacking details helpful to investigators, relying on volunteers, and using extreme, often mentally disturbed participants—restricts its contribution to the field mainly to the concept of treating crime-scene behaviors as a unit of analysis. [78] These issues resulted in classification systems with questionable reliability. Overall, these previous classification systems, while helpful in adding to what is known about the behavior of these offenders, they do not connect crime scene behaviors to different types of offenders or to the background characteristics of offenders.

Crime scene behaviors form the basis of the investigative psychology approach to understanding and classifying homicide crime scenes. Advocates of this approach have attempted to develop an understanding of homicide through examinations of the psychological and behavioral dynamics that play a role in incidents of extreme aggression, which would be more systematic and empirical than approaches employed by other researchers, including the FBI. [79]

These efforts to better understand homicide have two stages: developing a description of the main characteristics of homicide crime scenes and connecting these crime-scene characteristics to offender characteristics. [80] The key concept in this approach to homicide research is the idea that an offender's actions or general themes of criminal behavior, at a crime scene can assist researchers and law enforcement personnel in identifying the offender's specific background characteristics (i.e., aspects of the offender's background that could help identify a type of person who would share those characteristics). [81] The relationship between the offender and victim also is important. Since aggression, and therefore homicide/murder, is understood to be an interpersonal interaction, the relationship between the actors is a significant factor in the dynamics of the incident. [82] This contention finds support in homicide data, which consistently shows that stranger homicides are much less frequent than homicides between individuals who know each other. The degree of the relationship also has been found to impact the incident, with better known offenders engaging in homicides expressing higher levels of emotion. [83]

In a study clearly showing this type of approach is possible, Salfati and Canter established three distinct themes of single victim—single offender stranger homicides: Expressive (Impulsive), Instrumental (Opportunistic), and Instrumental (Cognitive).[84] Expressive homicides included random, varied violent offender behaviors, with offenders who had a history of violence. Instrumental (Opportunistic) homicides had offenders who viewed their victims as means to an end. The Opportunistic offender picks victims who will make it easy to achieve their goal of obtaining property or even sex. Such offenders were found to be unemployed usually, with previous burglary/theft convictions, knew their victims, and lived close to where the crime occurred. Cognitive homicides were characterized as highly forensic, with the offender frequently trying to hide evidence of the crime. Such offenders are routinely violent in their lives because they view other people only as obstacles preventing them from reaching their goals.

Relationship with the victim is not a factor, as who they are does not matter to these offenders. This approach to research is grounded in facet theory. Facet theory holds that in research, observations are not isolated, discrete phenomenon. Under facet theory every observed variable is a point in the physical space occupied by the investigated concept. The concept, in this case bias homicide, is then examined and understood through the use of Smallest Space Analysis (SSA), which holds, based on facet theory, that the system of behavior is best understood if the relationship between every variable and every other variable is examined. [85]

Previous research in this paradigm by advocates of investigative psychology supports the concept that because individuals consistently behave the same way in similar contexts, behaviors displayed in crime scenes can be used to predict offender background characteristics, including offender-victim relationships. [86] Farrington's study, along with Huesmann work, even found that individuals who were identified as the most aggressive delinquents remained the most aggressive throughout their lives. [87] The links between crime scene behaviors and offender characteristics become investigative tools. It is also possible to differentiate between offenders engaged in the same offense by actions during the crime and their background characteristics. [88]

Homicide researchers have dramatically advanced this new method of analyzing homicides, finding that there are specific themes of behavior at crime scenes that are mirrored in past behaviors, which allow investigators to use the crime scene to identify potential suspects. Other research has found that this approach works cross-nationally and for other types of violent crime such as serial rape and serial homicide, while ongoing work is evaluating its utility cross-culturally. [89] Bias homicide, lacking such a systematic analysis of the behavioral and situational dynamics involved needs to be examined in a similar manner.

Situational Variables

As they continue to develop different and more advanced understandings of the relationships between homicide crime scenes and offender characteristics, investigative psychologists have found that one of the biggest questions facing them involves cases where there are mixed characteristics evident in a crime scene. [90] Cases where there is both evidence of expressive and instrumental violence in a homicide scene raise the question of how much of the scene is a result of the individual and how much is a result of the situation. Researchers have reached the conclusion that situational stimuli affect the actions that occur in a specific setting. [91] This research, however, did not seek to understand how specific situational characteristics could be used to differentiate types or styles of homicide; instead, it was interested in establishing if people behave differently, both criminally and non-criminally, in different situations. The evidence that situational variables affected criminal behavior on some levels lead bias crime researchers to study the situations in which bias crimes occur. It is critical to determine what situational factors tend to be present when individuals decide to express their various biases through violent behavior. [92] Understanding the effect that situational factors have on the behaviors associated with the homicide can help researchers and investigators to focus on the behaviors that connect specifically to the offender and not just the situation.

Situational factors are not just about the setting, there is a dynamic interaction of the actors involved and the setting. D'Augelli found that sixty-one percent of bias crimes directed at youth—the age group most likely to experience violent victimization—occur at home. [93] Other studies have found that crimes motivated by different biases occur amongst different situational factors. Gay males are most likely to be victimized in gay areas (i.e., neighborhoods known to be predominantly gay, gay cruising areas, and areas outside of gay business and) and schools, while lesbians were at highest risk near their homes, or in predominantly heterosexual, domestic, or higher education locations. [94] Perpetrators also differ by location of the incident, with young offenders carrying out their acts in their neighborhoods or on the street, and older offenders tending to offend in the workplace. [95] One situational factor that may concretely explain why certain individuals decide to behave violently in certain situations is the use of substances before or at the time of the event. Offenders generally report, or are found to have been, using drugs or alcohol prior to the commission of bias crimes. [96] Again, understanding and being aware of these situational factors could help to narrow down the crime scene behaviors that are specific to a particular offender and not mainly related to outside forces.

While an accurate description of the most likely scenarios for bias crime to occur is an important step in the process of understanding the phenomenon, the failure to integrate this information into a behavioral and situational framework limits its ability to assist researchers and investigators. The investigative psychology paradigm, which asserts that context is poorly understood in relation to homicide, focuses on the context—behavioral, social and situational—of homicide. [97] At the center of this work is the concept of the consistency of individual behavior. That is, using crime scene characteristics to develop a theme of the types of behaviors that occurred there to connect those behaviors at the scene with behaviors in the offender's past based on the assumption that individuals interact with others in a consistent manner. [98] The question of whether certain behaviors are part of an individual's style or a result of situational factors remains unanswered. The research has determined that situational factors, such as behaviors and scene characteristics, are a useful unit of analysis in distinguishing offenses and offenders. An examination of the context of bias homicides, with a particular emphasis on using situational factors to distinguish offenses and offenders, has not yet been attempted.

Multiple Offenders/Victims Literature

Aside from psychological, sociological and anthropological research centered on understanding general group dynamics across a multitude of behavioral and situational scenarios, limited research on violent behavior or bias-motivated behavior has included multiple offenders or victims in the theories or analyses. As highlighted previously, bias crime literature suggests, and has found in certain circumstances, that bias-motivated crimes often involve multiple offenders. Therefore, it was essential that the current research included homicides with both multiple offenders and/or multiple victims. Excluding such cases would have greatly reduced the number of available cases in an already limited population, as well as the types, and therefore number, of homicides to which the findings of this work could have been applied. As a result, it is important to understand the issues inherent in analyzing multiple offender/victim homicides as best as possible based on the available research.

Research focused on themes of behavior and their potential role in understanding homicide has centered on single-offender homicides. [99] Limited research on violent offending has considered the potential relevance of behavioral themes to multiple-offender and/or multiple-victim incidents; instead, most has excluded multiple-offender homicides because of the difficulties they present. [100] Some researchers, however, are addressing this lack of information. Porter and Alison have concentrated on co-offending in multiple-offender rapes and robberies, and Cheatwood has conducted research on multiple-offender/multiple-victim homicide. Their work, and that of others, outlines the major theoretical and analytical issues that must be addressed when studying multiple-offender violence.

Research focused on the interaction between offenders and victims, which highlights the necessity of determining which individuals are involved in the various stages of the incident, has found that there generally is one primary offender who engages in a character or business dispute with one primary victim, and the others involved know why the dispute is taking place, that violence is likely to occur, and that the primary offender's intent may be to kill the victim. [101] Some instances may involve two or more offenders who are directly involved in the violence, but most are interactions among multiple individuals where one offender kills the victim with enough involvement by others for them to be charged with the homicide as well, but not enough for their interpersonal styles to significantly impact the homicide dynamics. [102] Warr refers to these leaders as instigators in his research on hierarchies in delinquent groups, which generally finds that the instigators come up with the idea for the crime, and through incident role-stability remain the de facto leader throughout the commission of the crime. [103]

Researchers have examined is this concept of scale of influence. The idea behind scale of influence is that the leader of a group can be determined by examining who influences the members of the group throughout the stages of the offense. Examinations of violent group offending have found evidence that the leader of the group usually initiates the attack and plans the post-incident activities. [104] Research into the influence of group leaders suggests that the influential leader may be the most important group member in terms of understanding the evolution of the incident; therefore, identifying this individual and recording their actions and characteristics is vital in analyzing multiple-offender bias homicides. It could be argued, that after identification of the leader it may be possible to identify the interpersonal style of the offender group as a whole, absent some information about the other offenders.

Research into multiple-offender violence suggests that the interpersonal dynamics of the events are essential to developing an understanding of the evolution of multiple-offender bias homicides. Cheatwood's work on multiple-offender homicide has found that a majority of these crimes start out as arguments or character disputes and evolve into unforeseen lethal encounters.[105] Descriptions of bias crimes suggest that these crimes also rarely begin as severely as they end. Holstrom's and Burgess' research on rape suggests that multiple offenders often perform for the other members of the group throughout the incident.[106] Sociological research suggests that bias crimes, particularly for males, are almost strictly about performing a social role for peers observing the incident.[107] The findings that the evolution and final outcome of multiple-offender violent incidents are highly dependent on the interactions of the offenders, not only with the victim(s), but with each other, highlights the need for developing a strategy for coding data in a way that allows for the analysis of these interactions.[108]

Porter and Alison, with their work on multiple-offender rape, are attempting to develop a methodological and analytical approach for incorporating multiple-offender violence into single-offender/single-victim research that examines the possible connections between themes of behavior and co-offending multiple-offender violent crimes.[109] Porter and Alison hypothesized that the thematic behaviors of individuals involved in a gang rape actually would be quite similar and form distinct themes. The multidimensional scaling analysis of gang rapes revealed that there is a "structural coherence among members of the same group," such that when acting together individual behaviors are uniform and "structurally coherent".[110] Porter and Alison have found, as generally suggested in criminal justice literature, that similar individuals offend together just as they tend to socialize together; more so, however, their work has shown that in relation to themes of interpersonal behavior displayed both in past instances, and at crime scenes, groups of offenders often exhibit similar behavioral patterns.

Multiple-offender homicide research has sought to understand if there are distinct similarities or differences between single and multiple incidents. This research consistently has found that individual behavior does differ from group behavior in relation to decision-making factors.[111] Considering these findings and descriptive bias crime research, which suggests that a majority of bias crimes are committed by individuals acting as a group, the examination of multiple-offender bias-motivated homicides needs to be carefully considered. That is, these multiple-offender homicides can be included and analyzed as part of the entire study sample, provided that no significant differences are discovered between the single and multiple offender groups of homicides. This matter will be examined in one of the first analyses conducted in this study, which will focus on establishing whether it is acceptable to follow the conclusion that there are no systematic behavioral differences between multiple—and single-offender incidents. There also will be continued comparisons of the two groups throughout the overall study. Primarily, this is an exploratory study of bias-motivated homicides, which have never been studied specifically, and complex issues such as similarities and differences between multiple and single-offender bias homicides need to be considered, even though they warrant their own specific studies.

Summary

Despite the multitude of issues that have been raised about the quality of bias crime data, researchers have been able to develop rather detailed descriptions of the many aspects that are involved in the occurrence of a bias crime. These studies paint a picture of bias crime as one that is predominantly committed by young males, acting in non-organized groups, victimizing other, unknown, young males who are alone at the time of the incident. Bias crimes tend to be more severe than similar crimes not motivated by bias. Connections have been found between who is involved, how severe the incident is, and the situational and behavioral dynamics of the event. Official statistics have revealed that the most common motivation for bias crime is a racial bias, followed by an ethnic-bias, and a sexual-orientation bias. Research has found that the type of bias involved affects the aggression that is displayed in a bias crime. Disturbingly, bias crime data show that it is a crime that is both intensifying in severity and diversifying in motivation.

Efforts to combine these simple connections into a more complex classification of bias crime have stalled, with researchers formulating a classification system based solely on the offender's motivation. Homicide research, however, has advanced to a point where researchers are developing thematic profiles of offender behaviors at the crime scene, based on behavioral and situational factors, and connecting them to offender background information. These connections allow evidence at a homicide scene to assist investigators in determining what occurred and who was most likely to be involved.

Limited available information has forestalled the discovery of such connections in the study of bias homicides. Examinations of the characteristics of specifically bias motivated homicide victims, offenders, and crime scenes have not taken place, thus creating a significant void in the research that would need to be filled if a framework for bias homicide similar to the ones being created of non-bias homicides is to be developed. What is particularly distressing, given the intensification and diversification of bias crime, is the lack of analysis of how bias homicides might differ when motivated by different biases.

Homicide classification systems, evolving from the limited early systems, are now based on the concept that crime scene behaviors do not randomly co-occur and, therefore, there must be information that can be gained from analyzing those variables that tend to do so. [112] This research has found that the co-occurrences of crime scene behaviors have an interpretable structure based on theory. [113] Previous classification systems often analyzed the occurrence of individual behaviors against each other, leading to constructed classification themes. Discovering the behaviors and characteristics that coincide based on theory—the main goal of the most recent research—prevents certain behaviors from being taken singularly and out of context with other behaviors. Instead, the meanings of behaviors are interpreted in relation to each other, allowing the frequencies of the co-occurrences of all the behaviors with each other to reveal more subtle differentiations.

These differentiations may even reveal the underlying meanings of the crime scene behaviors. This finding allows offender characteristics to be deduced from the behaviors evident in the crime scene, potentially allowing the prioritization of homicide suspects. Differentiation is most useful when it is based on investigations of particular subsets of actions that can be identified from the crime scene. [114] Such subsets include examining the relationships between the offender(s) and victim(s), the activities of the perpetrator, including actions not directly related to the actual act of killing, and any other observable behaviors. One of the most important aspects of this process of classification is that the thematic splits must be very specific. Past classification schemes have suffered from not being mutually exclusive, and this new process focuses on insuring that characteristics in one type or theme are not repeated in others. The existing bias crime classification schemes are not mutually exclusive, which lessons their ability to help law enforcement officials narrow down the type of offender potentially involved.

Bias crimes have been analyzed with traditional research and statistical methodologies.

As has been discussed previously, studies have investigated both who most frequently commits and who most frequently experiences these crimes. In the best scenarios, research has tried to connect the most frequent offender and victim characteristics with particular aspects of bias crime. All of this work, however, only paints a picture of what bias crime looks like. There has been no systematic attempt to address bias crime, especially bias homicide, from a classification approach. If observable behaviors at a crime scene could reliably differentiate different styles of bias homicides and the people who commit them, the crime could be both understood and investigated better.

Ultimately, to better understand bias homicide, a classification framework similar to the ones being developed in the study of homicide, needs to be created for bias-motivated homicide. To do this questions about whether crime scene behaviors and characteristics can be used to identify the bias and offender(s) involved need to be answered. Considering that research into bias-motivated violent behaviors has found evidence of an Expressive/Instrumental dichotomy, adopting the methodological approach of recent homicide classification research that has looked at the occurrences and co-occurrences of the behaviors and characteristics associated with homicide crimes scenes, represents an opportunity for moving bias, and specifically bias-motivated homicide, research forward.

AFTERWORD

From ethnic cleansing in Nazi Germany to contemporary terrorist attacks, many of the most tragic instances of social conflict across human history plausibly can be linked in some way to group identity and bias. In recognition of this relationship, one of the most vibrant and enduring research traditions in social psychology has focused on investigating the fundamental processes and consequences of social categorization. A critical finding from this domain is that categorization per se is sufficient to elicit intergroup prejudice and discrimination. That is, group membership, even when it is based on some arbitrary pretext, can lead people to favor those in their ingroup over those in the outgroup. Importantly, social psychologists generally believe that this bias is fueled by ingroup favoritism and not outgroup derogation, unless other hostility instigating factors are present, such as competition for resources.

The purpose of this book was to shed light on the nature of bias. We first explored intergroup bias by various means in order to reveal prejudice against the outgroup even if outgroup attitudes were not negative in an absolute sense. This allowed us to make the type of comparisons necessary to decompose the relative intergroup bias and measure the effect as a function of *both* ingroup favoritism and outgroup derogation.

Of the two types of bias, ingroup favoritism seems to carry more weight in driving the effect, which fits with current theories regarding the underlying motivations and consequences of social categorization. But the fact that outgroup derogation also contributes to the bias suggests that the seeds of group-based conflict can take shape as soon as groups are formed—and without the influence of other factors known to incite outgroup prejudice.

Social identity theory states that individuals are inherently motivated to elevate and protect the status of the ingroup. Devaluing the outgroup (at least a little) would seem to be one effective way of pursuing these goals. The fact that outgroup derogation has been evident on both explicit and implicit measures points to the fundamental nature of outgroup bias. That is, when two groups are in competition for scarce resources, the potential success of one group threatens the well-being of the other, resulting in negative outgroup attitudes.

REFERENCES

CHAPTER ONE

1. Gardner, W. L., Pickett, C. L., & Brewer, M. B. (2000). Social exclusion and selective memory: How the need to belong influences memory for social events. *Personality & Social Psychology Bulletin, 26*, 486-496.
2. Sherif, M., Harvey, O. J. White, B. J., Hood, W. R., & Sherif, C. W. (1961). *Intergroup conflict and cooperation: The Robbers Cave experiment.* Norman, OK: University of Oklahoma Book Exchange.
3. Tajfel, H. (1969). Cognitive aspects of prejudice. *Journal of Social Issues, 25,* 79-97.
4. Suls, J., & Wan, C. (1987). In search of the false-uniqueness phenomenon: Fear and estimates of social consensus. *Journal of Personality and Social Psychology, 52*, 211-217.
5. Myers, D. (1992). *The pursuit of happiness.* New York: Morrow.
6. Hewstone, M., Rubin, M. & Willis, H. (2002). Intergroup bias. *Annual Review of Psychology, 53,* 575-604.
7. Allport, G. A. (1954). The Nature of Prejudice. Cambridge, MA: Addison-Wesley.
8. Brewer, M. B., & Pickett, C. L. (1999). Distinctiveness motives as a source of the social self. In T. R. Tyler, K. L. V. Allen & O. John (Eds.), *The Psychology of the Social Self* (pp. 71-87). New Jersey: Erlbaum.
9. Brewer, M. B. (1979). In-group bias in the minimal intergroup situation: A cognitive motivational analysis. *Psychological Bulletin, 86,* 307-324.
10. Sidanius, J., & Pratto, F. (1999). *Social dominance: An intergroup theory of social hierarchy and oppression.* Cambridge: University Press.

11. Allport, G. A. (1954). The Nature of Prejudice. Cambridge, MA: Addison-Wesley.
12. Brewer, M. B. (1979). In-group bias in the minimal intergroup situation: A cognitive motivational analysis. *Psychological Bulletin, 86*, 307-324.
13. Brewer, M. B. (1979). In-group bias in the minimal intergroup situation: A cognitive motivational analysis. *Psychological Bulletin, 86*, 307-324.
14. Tajfel, H., Flament, C., Billig, M., & Bundy, R. F. (1971). Social categorization and intergroup behavior. *European Journal of Social Psychology, 1*, 149-178.
15. Tajfel, H., & Turner, J. C. (1986). The social identity theory of intergroup behaviour. In S. Worchel & W. G. Austin (Eds.), *Psychology of intergroup relations* (pp. 7-24). Chicago: Nelson-Hall.
16. Tajfel, H., Billig, M. G., Bundy, R. F., & Flament, C. (1971). Social categorization and intergroup behavior. *European Journal of Social Psychology, 1*, 149-177.
17. Brown, R. J., Tajfel, H., & Turner, J. C. (1980). Minimal group situations and intergroup discrimination: Comments on the paper by Aschenbrenner and Schaefer. *European Journal of Social Psychology, 10*, 399-414.
18. Gaertner, L., & Insko, C. A. (2000). Intergroup discrimination in the minimal group paradigm: Categorization, reciprocation, or fear? *Journal of Personality & Social Psychology, 79*, 77-94.
19. Tajfel, H., & Turner, J. C. (1986). The social identity theory of intergroup behaviour. In S. Worchel & W. G. Austin (Eds.), *Psychology of intergroup relations* (pp. 7-24). Chicago: Nelson-Hall.
20. Fiske, A. P. (1992). The four elementary forms of sociality: Framework for a unified theory of social relations. *Psychological Review, 99*, 689-723.
21. Allport, G. A. (1954). The Nature of Prejudice. Cambridge, MA: Addison-Wesley.
22. Tajfel, H., Billig, M. G., Bundy, R. F., & Flament, C. (1971). Social categorization and intergroup behavior. *European Journal of Social Psychology, 1*, 149-177.
23. Bourhis, R.Y., Sachdev, I., & Gagnon, A. (1994). Conducting intergroup research with the Tajfel matrices: Some methodological issues. In M. Zanna & S. Olson (eds.) *The psychology of prejudice: the Ontario Symposium on personality and social psychology (pp. 209-232).* Hilldale, NJ: Erlbaum Publishers.

24. Tajfel, H., Billig, M. G., Bundy, R. F., & Flament, C. (1971). Social categorization and intergroup behavior. *European Journal of Social Psychology, 1,* 149-177.
25. Bornstein, G., Crum, L., Wittenbraker, J., Harrig, K., Insko, C. A., & Thibaut, J. (1983). On the measurement of social orientations in the minimal group paradigm. *European Journal of Social Psychology, 13,* 321-350.
26. Bourhis, R.Y., Sachdev, I., & Gagnon, A. (1994). Conducting intergroup research with the Tajfel matrices: Some methodological issues. In M. Zanna & S. Olson (eds.) *The psychology of prejudice: the Ontario Symposium on personality and social psychology (pp. 209-232).* Hilldale, NJ: Erlbaum Publishers.
27. Otten, S., & Wentura, D. (1999). About the impact of automaticity in the minimal group paradigm: Evidence from affective priming tasks. *European Journal of Social Psychology, 29,* 1049-1071.
28. Brauer, M. (2001). *Intergroup perception in the social context: The effects of social status and group membership on perceived out-group homogeneity and ethnocentrism.* Journal of Experimental Social Psychology, 37(1), 15-31.
29. Brewer, M. B., & Pickett, C. L. (1999). Distinctiveness motives as a source of the social self. In T. R. Tyler, K. L. V. Allen & O. John (Eds.), *The Psychology of the Social Self* (pp. 71-87). New Jersey: Erlbaum.
30. Pettigrew, T. F. (1998). Intergroup contact theory. Annual Review of Psychology, 49, 65-85.
31. Otten, S., & Wentura, D. (1999). About the impact of automaticity in the minimal group paradigm: Evidence from affective priming tasks. *European Journal of Social Psychology, 29,* 1049-1071.
32. Otten, S., & Wentura, D. (1999). About the impact of automaticity in the minimal group paradigm: Evidence from affective priming tasks. *European Journal of Social Psychology, 29,* 1049-1071.
33. Otten, S., & Moskowitz, G. B. (2000). Evidence for implicit evaluative ingroup bias: Affect biased spontaneous trait inference in a minimal group paradigm. *Journal of Experimental Social Psychology, 36,* 77-89.
34. Fiske, S. T. (2003). Five core social motives, plus or minus five. In S. J. Spencer, S. Fein, M. P. Zanna & J. Olson (Eds.), *Motivated social perception: The Ontario symposium, Ontario symposium on personality and social psychology* (Vol. 9, pp. 233-246). Mahwah, NJ: Lawrence Erlbaum Associates.
35. Tajfel, H., Billig, M. G., Bundy, R. F., & Flament, C. (1971). Social categorization and intergroup behavior. *European Journal of Social Psychology, 1,* 149-177.

36. Brewer, M. B. (1979). In-group bias in the minimal intergroup situation: A cognitive motivational analysis. *Psychological Bulletin, 86,* 307-324.
37. Hertel, G., & Kerr, N. L. (2001). Priming ingroup favoritism: The impact of normative scripts in the minimal group paradigm. *Journal of Experimental Social Psychology, 37,* 316-324.
38. Tajfel, H., & Turner, J. C. (1986). The social identity theory of intergroup behaviour. In S. Worchel & W. G. Austin (Eds.), *Psychology of intergroup relations* (pp. 7-24). Chicago: Nelson-Hall.
39. Otten, S., & Wentura, D. (1999). About the impact of automaticity in the minimal group paradigm: Evidence from affective priming tasks. *European Journal of Social Psychology, 29,* 1049-1071.
40. Gaertner, L., & Insko, C. A. (2000). Intergroup discrimination in the minimal group paradigm: Categorization, reciprocation, or fear? *Journal of Personality & Social Psychology, 79,* 77-94.
41. Brewer, M. B. (1979). In-group bias in the minimal intergroup situation: A cognitive motivational analysis. *Psychological Bulletin, 86,* 307-324.
42. Otten, S., & Moskowitz, G. B. (2000). Evidence for implicit evaluative ingroup bias: Affect biased spontaneous trait inference in a minimal group paradigm. *Journal of Experimental Social Psychology, 36,* 77-89.
43. Zanna, M. P., Haddock, G., & Esses, V. M. (1990). *On the nature of prejudice.* Paper presented at the Nags Head Conference on Stereotypes and Intergroup Relations, Nags Head Conference Center, Kill Devil Hills, N. C.

CHAPTER TWO

1. Maslow, A. H. (1968). *Toward a psychology of being.* New York: Van Nostrand.
2. Baumeister, R. F., & Leary, M. R. (1995). The need to belong: Desire for interpersonal attachments as a fundamental human motivation. *Psychological Bulletin, 117*(3), 497-529.
3. Caporael, L. R., & Brewer, M. B. (1995). Hierarchical evolutionary theory: There is an alternative, and it's not creationism. *Psychological Inquiry, 6*(1), 31-34.
4. Caporael, L. R., & Brewer, M. B. (1995). Hierarchical evolutionary theory: There is an alternative, and it's not creationism. *Psychological Inquiry, 6*(1), 31-34.
5. Shaver, P., Hazan, C., & Bradshaw, D. (1988). Love as attachment: The integration of three behavioral systems. In R. J. Steinberg & M. L. Barnes (Eds.), *The psychology of love* (pp. 68-99). New Haven, CT: Yale University Press.
6. Stevens, L. E., & Fiske, S. T. (1995). Motivation and cognition in social life: A social survival perspective. *Social Cognition, 13*(3), 189-214.
7. Baumeister, R. F., & Tice, D. M. (1990). Anxiety and social exclusion. *Journal of Social & Clinical Psychology, 9*, 165-195.
8. Gardner, W. L., Pickett, C. L., & Brewer, M. B. (2000). Social exclusion and selective memory: How the need to belong influences memory for social events. *Personality & Social Psychology Bulletin, 26*, 486-496.
9. Leary, M. R., Tambor, E. S., Terdal, S. K., & Downs, D. L. (1995). Self-esteem as an interpersonal monitor: The sociometer hypothesis. *Journal of Personality & Social Psychology, 68*, 518-530.
10. Baumeister, R. F., & Leary, M. R. (1995). The need to belong: Desire for interpersonal attachments as a fundamental human motivation. *Psychological Bulletin, 117*(3), 497-529.
11. Warburton, W. A., & Williams, K. D. (2005). Ostracism: When competing motivations collide. In J. P. Forgas, K. D. Williams & S. M. Laham (Eds.), *Social motivation: Conscious and unconscious processes.* (pp. 294-313). New York, NY: Cambridge University Press.
12. Williams, K. D., Cheung, C. K. T., & Choi, W. (2000). Cyberostracism: Effects of being ignored over the internet. *Journal of Personality & Social Psychology, 79*, 748-762.

13. Baumeister, R. F., & Leary, M. R. (1995). The need to belong: Desire for interpersonal attachments as a fundamental human motivation. *Psychological Bulletin, 117*(3), 497-529.
14. Strube, M. J. (1988). The decision to leave an abusive relationship: Empirical evidence and theoretical issues. *Psychological Bulletin, 104*, 236-250.
15. Hazan, C., & Shaver, P. R. (1994). Attachment as an organizational framework for research on close relationships. *Psychological Inquiry, 5*, 1-22.
16. Baumeister, R. F., & Leary, M. R. (1995). The need to belong: Desire for interpersonal attachments as a fundamental human motivation. *Psychological Bulletin, 117*(3), 497-529.
17. Beach, S. R., & Tesser, A. (1988). Love in marriage: A cognitive account. In *The psychology of Love* (pp. 330-355). New Haven, CT: Yale University Press.
18. Monson, T. C., Keel, R., Stephens, D., & Genung, V. (1982). Trait attributions: Relative validity, covariation with behavior, and prospect of future interaction. *Journal of Personality and Social Psychology, 42*, 1014-1024.
19. Baumeister, R. F., & Leary, M. R. (1995). The need to belong: Desire for interpersonal attachments as a fundamental human motivation. *Psychological Bulletin, 117*(3), 497-529.
20. Jetten, J., Spears, R., & Manstead, A. S. (1996). Intergroup norms and intergroup discrimination: Distinctive self-categorization and social identity effects. *Journal of Personality and Social Psychology, 71*, 1222-1233.
21. Baumeister, R. F., & Twenge, J. M. (2003). The social self. In T. Millon & M. J. Lerner (Eds.), *Handbook of psychology: Personality and Social Psychology* (Vol. 5, pp. 327-352). New York, NY: John Wiley & Sons.
22. McAdams, D. P. (1986). Motivation and friendship. In S. Duck & D. Perlman (Eds.), *Understanding personal relationships: An interdisciplinary approach* (pp. 85-105). Thousand Oaks, CA: Sage Publications.
23. Baumeister, R. F., & Leary, M. R. (1995). The need to belong: Desire for interpersonal attachments as a fundamental human motivation. *Psychological Bulletin, 117*(3), 497-529.
24. Twenge, J. M., & Campbell, W. (2003). "isn't it fun to get the respect that we're going to deserve?" narcissism, social rejection, and aggression. *Personality & Social Psychology Bulletin, 29*, 261-272.

25. Twenge, J. M., Catanese, K. R., & Baumeister, R. F. (2002). Social exclusion causes self—defeating behavior. *Journal of Personality and Social Psychology, 83*, 606-615.
26. Leary, M. R., Tambor, E. S., Terdal, S. K., & Downs, D. L. (1995). Self-esteem as an interpersonal monitor: The sociometer hypothesis. *Journal of Personality & Social Psychology, 68*, 518-530.
27. Fiske, A. P. (1992). The four elementary forms of sociality: Framework for a unified theory of social relations. *Psychological Review, 99*, 689-723.
28. Fiske, S. T. (2003). Five core social motives, plus or minus five. In S. J. Spencer, S. Fein, M. P. Zanna & J. Olson (Eds.), *Motivated social perception: The ontario symposium, Ontario symposium on personality and social psychology* (Vol. 9, pp. 233-246). Mahwah, NJ: Lawrence Erlbaum Associates.
29. Goffman, E. (1959). *The presentation of self in everyday life*. New York: Academic.
30. Eagly, A. H., Wood, W., & Diekman, A. B. (2000). Social role theory of sex differences and similarities: A current appraisal. In T. Eckes & H. M. Trautner (Eds.), *The developmental social psychology of gender* (pp. 123-174). Mahwah, NJ: Lawrence Erlbaum Associates.
31. Breckler, S. J., & Greenwald, A. G. (1986). Motivational facets of the self. In R. M. Sorrentino & E. T. Higgins (Eds.), *Handbook of Motivation and Cognition: Foundations of Social Behavior* (Vol. 1, pp. 145-164). New York: The Guilford Press.
32. Fiske, S. T. (2003). Five core social motives, plus or minus five. In S. J. Spencer, S. Fein, M. P. Zanna & J. Olson (Eds.), *Motivated social perception: The Ontario symposium, Ontario symposium on personality and social psychology* (Vol. 9, pp. 233-246). Mahwah, NJ: Lawrence Erlbaum Associates.
33. Jost, J. T., & Banaji, M. R. (1994). The role of stereotyping in system-justification and the production of false consciousness. *British Journal of Social Psychology, 33*(1), 1-27.
34. Janis, I. L. (1997). Groupthink. In R. P. Vecchio (Ed.), *Leadership: Understanding the dynamics of power and influence in organizations* (pp. 163-176). Notre Dame, IN: University of Notre Dame Press.
35. Cialdini, R. B. (1993). *Influence: Science and Practice (3rd ed.)*. New York, NY: HarperCollins College Publishers.
36. Miller, R. S., & Leary, M. R. (1992). Social sources and interactive functions of emotion: The case of embarrassment. In M. S. Clark (Ed.), *Emotion and social behavior* (pp. 202-221). Newbury Park, CA: Sage.

37. Jones, E. E., & Pittman, T. S. (1982). Toward a general theory of strategic self-presentation. In J. M. Suls (Ed.), *The self in social perspective psychological perspectives on the self* (Vol. 1, pp. 231-262). Hillsdale, NJ, England: Lawrence Erlbaum Associates.
38. Leary, M. R., Kelly, K. M., Cottrell, C. A., & Schreindorfer, L. S. (2001). *Individual differences in the need to belong.* Unpublished manuscript, Wake Forest University, Winston-Salem, NC.
39. Downey, G., Mougios, V., Ayduk, O., London, B. E., & Shoda, Y. (2004). Rejection sensitivity and the defensive motivational system: Insights from the startle response to rejection cues. *Psychological Science, 15,* 668-673.
40. Gangestad, S. W., & Snyder, M. (2000). Self-monitoring: Appraisal and reappraisal. *Psychological Bulletin, 126,* 530-555.
41. Buckley, K. E., Winkel, R. E., & Leary, M. R. (2004). Reactions to acceptance and rejection: Effects of level and sequence of relational evaluation. *Journal of Experimental Social Psychology, 40,* 14-28.
42. Williams, K. D., & Sommer, K. L. (1997). Social ostracism by coworkers: Does rejection lead to loafing or compensation? *Personality & Social Psychology Bulletin, 23,* 693-706.
43. Williams, K. D., Cheung, C. K. T., & Choi, W. (2000). Cyberostracism: Effects of being ignored over the internet. *Journal of Personality & Social Psychology, 79,* 748-762.
44. Gardner, W. L., Pickett, C. L., & Brewer, M. B. (2000). Social exclusion and selective memory: How the need to belong influences memory for social events. *Personality & Social Psychology Bulletin, 26,* 486-496.
45. Carvallo, M., & Pelham, B. W. (2006). When fiends become friends: The need to belong and perceptions of personal and group discrimination. *Journal of Personality and Social Psychology, 90,* 94-105.
46. Carvallo, M., & Pelham, B. W. (2006). When fiends become friends: The need to belong and perceptions of personal and group discrimination. *Journal of Personality and Social Psychology, 90,* 94-105.
47. Williams, K. D., & Sommer, K. L. (1997). Social ostracism by coworkers: Does rejection lead to loafing or compensation? *Personality & Social Psychology Bulletin, 23,* 693-706.
48. Leary, M. R. (2001). Toward a conceptualization of interpersonal rejection. In M. R. Leary (Ed.), *Interpersonal rejection* (pp. 3-20). London: Oxford University Press.
49. Fiske, S. T. (2003). Five core social motives, plus or minus five. In S. J. Spencer, S. Fein, M. P. Zanna & J. Olson (Eds.), *Motivated social*

perception: The Ontario symposium, Ontario symposium on personality and social psychology (Vol. 9, pp. 233-246). Mahwah, NJ: Lawrence Erlbaum Associates.

50. Ross, L., Greene, D., & House, P. (1977). The false consensus effect: An egocentric bias in social perception and attribution processes. *Journal of Experimental Social Psychology, 13,* 279-301.
51. Marks, G., & Miller, N. (1987). Ten years of research on the false-consensus effect: An empirical and theoretical review. *Psychological Bulletin, 102,* 72-90.
52. Mullen, B., Atkins, J. L., Champion, D. S., Edwards, C., Hardy, D., Story, J. E., et al. (1985). The false consensus effect: A meta-analysis of 115 hypothesis tests. *Journal of Experimental Social Psychology, 21,* 262-283.
53. Mullen, B., Atkins, J. L., Champion, D. S., Edwards, C., Hardy, D., Story, J. E., et al. (1985). The false consensus effect: A meta-analysis of 115 hypothesis tests. *Journal of Experimental Social Psychology, 21,* 262-283.
54. Ross, L., Greene, D., & House, P. (1977). The false consensus effect: An egocentric bias in social perception and attribution processes. *Journal of Experimental Social Psychology, 13,* 279-301.
55. Shaw, M. E. (1981). *Group dynamics: The psychology of small group behavior* (3rd ed.). New York: McGraw-Hill.
56. Marks, G., & Miller, N. (1987). Ten years of research on the false-consensus effect: An empirical and theoretical review. *Psychological Bulletin, 102,* 72-90.
57. Marks, G., & Duval, S. (1991). Availability of alternative positions and estimates of consensus. *British Journal of Social Psychology, 30,* 179-183.
58. Gilovich, T., Jennings, D. L., & Jennings, S. (1983). Causal focus and estimates of consensus: An examination of the false-consensus effect. *Journal of Personality and Social Psychology, 45,* 550-559.
59. Suls, J., & Wan, C. (1987). In search of the false-uniqueness phenomenon: Fear and estimates of social consensus. *Journal of Personality and Social Psychology, 52,* 211-217.
60. Holtz, R., & Miller, N. (1985). Assumed similarity and opinion certainty. *Journal of Personality and Social Psychology, 48,* 890-898.
61. Holtz, R., & Miller, N. (1985). Assumed similarity and opinion certainty. *Journal of Personality and Social Psychology, 48,* 890-898.
62. Crano, W. D. (1983). Assumed consensus of attitudes: The effect of vested interest. *Personality and Social Psychology Bulletin, 9,* 597-608.

63. Sherman, S. J., Chassin, L., Presson, C. C., & Agostinelli, G. (1984). The role of the evaluation and similarity principles in the false consensus effect. *Journal of Personality and Social Psychology, 47,* 1244-1262.
64. Allen, V. L., & Wilder, D. A. (1979). Group categorization and attribution of belief similarity. *Small Group Behavior, 10,* 73-80.
65. Marks, G., & Miller, N. (1982). Target attractiveness as a mediator of assumed attitude similarity. *Personality and Social Psychology Bulletin, 8,* 728-735.
66. Breckler, S. J., & Greenwald, A. G. (1986). Motivational facets of the self. In R. M. Sorrentino & E. T. Higgins (Eds.), *Handbook of Motivation and Cognition: Foundations of Social Behavior* (Vol. 1, pp. 145-164). New York: The Guilford Press.
67. Messick, D. M., & Mackie, D. M. (1989). Intergroup relations. *Annual Review of Psychology, 40,* 45-81.
68. Brown, R. J., Tajfel, H., & Turner, J. C. (1980). Minimal group situations and intergroup discrimination: Comments on the paper by Aschenbrenner and Schaefer. *European Journal of Social Psychology, 10,* 399-414.
69. Tajfel, H. (1969). Cognitive aspects of prejudice. *Journal of Social Issues, 25,* 79-97.
70. Cadinu, M. R., & Rothbart, M. (1996). Self-anchoring and differentiation processes in the minimal group setting. *Journal of Personality and Social Psychology, 70,* 661-677.
71. Tajfel, H., & Turner, J. C. (1986). The social identity theory of intergroup behaviour. In Worchel, S., and Austin, W. G. (Eds.), *Psychology of Intergroup Relations.* Chicago: Nelson-Hall.
72. DeSteno, D., Dasgupta, N., Bartlett, M. Y., & Cajdric, A. (2004). Prejudice from thin air: The effect of emotion on automatic intergroup attitudes. *Psychological Science, 15,* 319-324.
73. Cadinu, M. R., & Rothbart, M. (1996). Self-anchoring and differentiation processes in the minimal group setting. *Journal of Personality and Social Psychology, 70,* 661-677.
74. Hertel, G., & Kerr, N. L. (2001). Priming ingroup favoritism: The impact of normative scripts in the minimal group paradigm. *Journal of Experimental Social Psychology, 37,* 316-324.
75. Hertel, G., & Kerr, N. L. (2001). Priming ingroup favoritism: The impact of normative scripts in the minimal group paradigm. *Journal of Experimental Social Psychology, 37,* 317.

76. Hertel, G., & Kerr, N. L. (2001). Priming ingroup favoritism: The impact of normative scripts in the minimal group paradigm. *Journal of Experimental Social Psychology, 37*, 316-324.
77. Messick, D. M., & Schell, T. (1992). Evidence for an equality heuristic in social decision making. *Acta Psychologica, 80*, 311-323.
78. Gaertner, L., & Insko, C. A. (2000). Intergroup discrimination in the minimal group paradigm: Categorization, reciprocation, or fear? *Journal of Personality & Social Psychology, 79*, 77-94.
79. Gaertner, L., & Insko, C. A. (2000). Intergroup discrimination in the minimal group paradigm: Categorization, reciprocation, or fear? *Journal of Personality & Social Psychology, 79*, 77-94.
80. Jetten, J., Spears, R., & Manstead, A. S. R. (1997). Strength of identification and intergroup differentiation: The influence of group norms. *European Journal of Social Psychology, 27*, 603-609.
81. Blanz, M., Mummendey, A., & Otten, S. (1997). Normative evaluations and frequency expectations regarding positive versus negative outcome allocations between groups. *European Journal of Social Psychology, 27*, 165-176.
82. Berscheid, E., & Walster, E. (1978). *Interpersonal Attraction* (2nd ed.). Reading, MA: Addison-Wesley.
83. Byrne, D. (1997). An overview (and underview) of research and theory within the attraction paradigm. *Journal of Social & Personal Relationships, 14*, 417-431.
84. Pilkington, N. W., & Lydon, J. E. (1997). The relative effect of attitude similarity and attitude dissimilarity on interpersonal attraction: Investigating the moderating roles of prejudice and group membership. *Personality and Social Psychology Bulletin, 23*, 107-122.
85. Stevens, G., Owens, D., & Schaefer, E. C. (1990). Education and attractiveness in marriage choices. *Social Psychology Quarterly, 53*, 62-70.
86. Condon, J. W., & Crano, W. D. (1988). Inferred evaluation and the relation between attitude similarity and interpersonal attraction. *Journal of Personality and Social Psychology, 54*, 789-797.
87. Byrne, D., London, O., & Griffitt, W. (1968). The effect of topic importance and attitude similarity-dissimilarity on attraction in an intrastranger design. *Psychonomic Science, 11*, 303-304.
88. Kaplan, M. F., & Anderson, N. H. (1973). Information integration theory and reinforcement theory as approaches to interpersonal attraction. *Journal of Personality and Social Psychology. 28*, 301-312.

89. Ajzen, I. (1974). Effects of information on interpersonal attraction: Similarity versus affective value. *Journal of Personality and Social Psychology. 29*, 374-380.
90. Montoya, R., & Horton, R. S. (2004). On the importance of cognitive evaluation as a determinant of interpersonal attraction. *Journal of Personality and Social Psychology, 86*, 696-712.
91. Kaplan, M. F., & Anderson, N. H. (1973). Information integration theory and reinforcement theory as approaches to interpersonal attraction. *Journal of Personality and Social Psychology. 28*, 301-312.
92. Montoya, R., & Horton, R. S. (2004). On the importance of cognitive evaluation as a determinant of interpersonal attraction. *Journal of Personality and Social Psychology, 86*, 696-712.
93. Byrne, D., & Clore, G. L. (1970). A reinforcement model of evaluative responses. *Personality: An International Journal Vol 1(2) Sum 1970, 103-128.*
94. Byrne, D., & Clore, G. L. (1970). A reinforcement model of evaluative responses. *Personality: An International Journal Vol 1(2) Sum 1970, 118.*
95. Aronson, E., & Worchel, P. (1966). Similarity versus liking as determinants of interpersonal attractiveness. *Psychonomic Science, 5*, 157-158.
96. Condon, J. W., & Crano, W. D. (1988). Inferred evaluation and the relation between attitude similarity and interpersonal attraction. *Journal of Personality and Social Psychology, 54*, 789-797.
97. Schachter, S. (1959). *The psychology of affiliation: Experimental studies of the sources of gregariousness.* Oxford, England: Stanford University Press.
98. Byrne, D. (1961). Interpersonal attraction as a function of affiliation need and attitude similarity. *Human Relations, 14*, 283-289.
99. Baumeister, R. F., & Leary, M. R. (1995). The need to belong: Desire for interpersonal attachments as a fundamental human motivation. *Psychological Bulletin, 117*(3), 497-529.

CHAPTER THREE

1. Allport, G. A. (1954). *The nature of prejudice.* Cambridge, MA: Addison-Wesley.
2. Pettigrew, T. F. (1986). The contact hypothesis revisited. In M. Hewstone & R. Brown (Eds.), *Contact and Conflict in Intergroup Encounters* (pp. 169-195). Oxford, UK: Blackwell.
3. Pettigrew, T. F. & Tropp, L. R. (2006). A meta-analytic test of intergroup contact theory. *Journal of Personality and Social Psychology, 90*, 751-783.
4. Wilder, D. A. & Thompson, J. E. (1988). Assimilation and contrast effects in the judgments of outgroup. *Journal of Personality and Social Psychology, 54*, 62-73.
5. Sherif, M. (1958). Superordinate goals in the reduction of intergroup conflict. *American Journal of Sociology, 63*, 349-350.
6. Sherif, M., Harvey, O. J. White, B. J., Hood, W. R., & Sherif, C. W. (1961). *Intergroup conflict and cooperation: The Robbers Cave experiment.* Norman, OK: University of Oklahoma Book Exchange.
7. Sherif, M., Harvey, O. J. White, B. J., Hood, W. R., & Sherif, C. W. (1961). *Intergroup conflict and cooperation: The Robbers Cave experiment.* Norman, OK: University of Oklahoma Book Exchange.
8. Sherif, M., Harvey, O. J. White, B. J., Hood, W. R., & Sherif, C. W. (1961). *Intergroup conflict and cooperation: The Robbers Cave experiment.* Norman, OK: University of Oklahoma Book Exchange.
9. Aronson, E., & Worchel, P. (1966). Similarity versus liking as determinants of interpersonal attractiveness. *Psychonomic Science, 5*, 157-158.
10. Desforges, D. M., Lord, C. G., Ramsey, S. L., Mason, J. A., Van Leeuwen, M. D., & West, S. C., et al. (1991). Effects of structured cooperative contact on changing negative attitudes toward stigmatized social groups. *Journal of Personality and Social Psychology, 60*, 531-544.
11. Sherif, M. (1958). Superordinate goals in the reduction of intergroup conflict. *American Journal of Sociology, 63*, 349-350.
12. Dovidio, J. F., Gaertner, S. L., Hodson, G., Riek, B. M., Johnson, K. M., & Houlette, M. (2006). Recategorization and crossed categorization: The implications of group salience and representations for reducing bias. In R. J. Crisp & M. Hewstone (Eds.), *Multiple Social Categorization: Processes, Models, and Applications* (pp. 65-89). New York, NY: Psychology Press.

13. Sherif, M. (1958). Superordinate goals in the reduction of intergroup conflict. *American Journal of Sociology, 63*, 349-350.
14. Deschamps, J. C. & Brown, R. (1983). Superordinate goals and intergroup conflict. *British Journal of Social Psychology, 22*, 189-195.
15. Hewstone, M. & Brown, R. (1986). Contact is not enough: An intergroup perspective on the 'contact hypothesis.'. In M. Hewstone & R. Brown (Eds.). Contact and Conflict in Intergroup Encounters. Social Psychology and Society (pp. 1-44). Cambridge, MA: Basil Blackwell.
16. Kennedy, J. & Stephan, W. G. (1977). The effects of cooperation and competition on ingroup-outgroup bias. Journal of Applied Social Psychology, 7, 115-130.
17. Tajfel, H., & Turner, J. C. (1979). An integrative theory of intergroup conflict. In W. C. Austin & S. Worchel, (Eds.), The Social Psychology of Intergroup Relations (pp. 33-47), Montery, CA: Brooks/Cole.
18. van Knippenberg, D., Platow, M. J., Haslam, S. A. (2007). Unity through diversity: Value-in-diversity beliefs as moderator of the relationship between work group diversity and group identification. *Group Dynamics, 11*, 207-222.
19. Levin, S., Federico, C. M., Sidanius, J., & Rabinowitz, J. L. (2002). Social dominance orientation and intergroup bias: The legitimation of favoritism for high-status groups. *Personality and Social Psychology Bulletin, 28*, 144-157.
20. van Knippenberg, D., Platow, M. J., Haslam, S. A. (2007). Unity through diversity: Value-in-diversity beliefs as moderator of the relationship between work group diversity and group identification. *Group Dynamics, 11*, 207-222.
21. van Knippenberg, D., Platow, M. J., Haslam, S. A. (2007). Unity through diversity: Value-in-diversity beliefs as moderator of the relationship between work group diversity and group identification. *Group Dynamics, 11*, 207-222.
22. Watson, D., Clark, L. A., & Tellegen, A. (1988). Development and validation of brief measures of positive and negative affect: The panas scales. *Journal of Personality & Social Psychology,4*, 1063-1070.
23. Mucchi-Fania, A., Costarelli, S., & Romoli, C. (2002). The effects of intergroup context of evaluation on ambivalence toward the ingroup and the outgroup. *European Journal of Social Psychology, 32*, 247-259.
24. Lott, A. J., Bright, M. A., Weinstein, P., & Lott, B. E. (1970). Liking for persons as a function of incentive and drive during acquisition. Journal of Personality and Social Psychology, 14, 66-76.

25. Lott, A. J., & Lott, B. E. (1968). A learning theory approach to interpersonal attitudes. In A. G. Greenwald, T. C. Brock, & T. M. Ostrom (Eds.), Psychological Foundations of Attitudes. (pp. ???). New York, New York: Academic Press.
26. Lott, A. J., Bright, M. A., Weinstein, P., & Lott, B. E. (1970). Liking for persons as a function of incentive and drive during acquisition. Journal of Personality and Social Psychology, 14, 66-76.
27. Dovidio, J. F., Gaertner, S. L., Hodson, G., Riek, B. M., Johnson, K. M., & Houlette, M. (2006). Recategorization and crossed categorization: The implications of group salience and representations for reducing bias. In R. J. Crisp & M. Hewstone (Eds.), Multiple Social Categorization: Processes, Models, and Applications (pp. 65-89). New York, NY: Psychology Press.
28. Dovidio, J. F., Gaertner, S. L., Hodson, G., Riek, B. M., Johnson, K. M., & Houlette, M. (2006). Recategorization and crossed categorization: The implications of group salience and representations for reducing bias. In R. J. Crisp & M. Hewstone (Eds.), Multiple Social Categorization: Processes, Models, and Applications (pp. 65-89). New York, NY: Psychology Press.
29. Allport, G. A. (1954). The Nature of Prejudice. Cambridge, MA: Addison-Wesley.
30. Dovidio, J. F., Gaertner, S. L., Hodson, G., Riek, B. M., Johnson, K. M., & Houlette, M. (2006). Recategorization and crossed categorization: The implications of group salience and representations for reducing bias. In R. J. Crisp & M. Hewstone (Eds.), Multiple Social Categorization: Processes, Models, and Applications (pp. 65-89). New York, NY: Psychology Press.
31. Perdue, C. W., Dovidio, J. F., Gurtman, M. B., & Tyler, R. B. (1990). Us and them: Social categorization and the process of intergroup bias. Journal of Personality and Social Psychology, 59, 475-486.
32. Brewer, M. B. & Gardner, W. (1996). Who is this we?: Levels of collective self-identity and self representations. Journal of Personality and Social Psychology, 71, 83-93.
33. Fitzsimmons, G. M. & Kay, A. C. (2004). Language and interpersonal cognition: Causal effects of variation in pronoun usage on perceptions of closeness. Personality and Social Psychology Bulletin, 30, 547-557.
34. Deschamps, J. C. & Brown, R. (1983). Superordinate goals and intergroup conflict. British Journal of Social Psychology, 22, 189-195.

35. van Knippenberg, D., Platow, M. J., Haslam, S. A. (2007). Unity through diversity: Value-in-diversity beliefs as moderator of the relationship between work group diversity and group identification. *Group Dynamics, 11*, 207-222.
36. Steiner, I.D. (1972). Group Process and Productivity. New York: Academic Press.
37. Hogg, M. A., & Abrams, D. (1999). Social identity and social cognition: Historical background and current trends. In D. Abrams and M. A. Hogg (Eds.), *Social identity and social cognition* (pp. 1-25). Malden, MA: Blackwell.
38. Deschamps, J. C. & Brown, R. (1983). Superordinate goals and intergroup conflict. British Journal of Social Psychology, 22, 189-195.
39. van Knippenberg, D., Platow, M. J., Haslam, S. A. (2007). Unity through diversity: Value-in-diversity beliefs as moderator of the relationship between work group diversity and group identification. *Group Dynamics, 11*, 207-222.

CHAPTER FOUR

1. Hewstone, M., Rubin, M. & Willis, H. (2002). Intergroup bias. *Annual Review of Psychology, 53,* 575-604.
2. Sherif, M., Harvey, O. J. White, B. J., Hood, W. R., & Sherif, C. W. (1961). *Intergroup conflict and cooperation: The Robbers Cave experiment.* Norman, OK: University of Oklahoma Book Exchange.
3. Billig, M. & Tajfel, H. (1973). Social categorization and similarity in intergroup behavior. *European Journal of Social Psychology, 3,* 27-52.
4. Tajfel, H., & Turner, J. C. (1979). An integrative theory of intergroup conflict. In W. G. Austin & S. Worchel (Eds.), *The social psychology of intergroup relations* (pp. 33-47). Monterey, CA: Brooks/Cole.
5. Topalova, V. (1984). Cognitive bias in the representations of social structures. *Studia Psychologica, 26,* 219-226.
6. Tajfel, H., & Turner, J. C. (1979). An integrative theory of intergroup conflict. In W. G. Austin & S. Worchel (Eds.), *The social psychology of intergroup relations* (pp. 33-47). Monterey, CA: Brooks/Cole.
7. Brown, R., & Turner, J. (1979). The criss-cross categorization effect in intergroup discrimination. *British Journal of Social and Clinical Psychology, 18,* 371-383.
8. Billig, M. & Tajfel, H. (1973). Social categorization and similarity in intergroup behavior. *European Journal of Social Psychology, 3,* 27-52.
9. Tajfel, H. (1969). Cognitive aspects of prejudice. *Journal of Social Issues, 25,* 79-97.
10. Hogg, M. A., & Abrams, D. (1988). *Social identifications: A social psychology of intergroup relations and group processes.* New York: Routledge.
11. Hogg, M. A., & Abrams, D. (1988). *Social identifications: A social psychology of intergroup relations and group processes.* New York: Routledge.
12. Mackie, D. & Hamilton, J. (1993). *Affect, cognition and stereotyping: Interactive processes in group perception.* San Diego, CA: Academic Press.
13. Hewstone, M., Rubin, M. & Willis, H. (2002). Intergroup bias. *Annual Review of Psychology, 53,* 575-604.
14. Hewstone, M., Rubin, M. & Willis, H. (2002). Intergroup bias. *Annual Review of Psychology, 53,* 575-604.
15. Adorno, T. W., Frenkel-Brunswick, E., Levinson, D. J., & Sanford, R. N. (1950). *The authoritarian personality.* New York: Harper & Brothers.

16. Tajfel, H. (1969). Cognitive aspects of prejudice. *Journal of Social Issues, 25,* 90.
17. Rabbie, J. M., & Horowitz, M. (1969). Arousal of ingroup-outgroup bias by a chance win or loss. *Journal of Personality and Social Psychology, 13,* 269-277.
18. Blanz, M., Mummendey, A., & Otten, S. (1995). Positive-negative asymmetry in social discrimination: The impact of stimulus valence and status differentials on intergroup evaluations. *British Journal of Social Psychology, 34,* 409-419.
19. Tajfel, H., Billig, M. G., Bundy, R. F., & Flament, C. (1971). Social categorization and intergroup behavior. *European Journal of Social Psychology, 1,* 149-177.
20. Brewer, M. B. (1979). Ingroup bias in the minimal intergroup situation: A cognitive motivational analysis. *Psychological Bulletin, 86,* 307-324.
21. Gaertner, L., & Schopler, J. (1998). Perceived ingroup entitativity and intergroup bias: an interconnection of self and others. *European Journal of Social Psychology, 28,* 963-980.
22. Simon, B., & Brown, R. (1987). Perceived intragroup homogeneity in minority-majority contexts. *Journal of Personality and Social Psychology, 53,* 703-711.
23. Gerard, H. B. & Hoyt, M. F. (1974). Distinctiveness of social categorization and attitude toward ingroup members. *Journal of Personality and Social Psychology, 26,* 309-320.
24. Reichl (1997). Ingroup favouritism and outgroup favouritism in low status minimal groups: Differential responses to status-related and status-unrelated measures. Thinking and Feeling *European Journal of Social Psychology, 27,* 617-633.
25. Thompson, L. L., & Crocker, J. (1990). Downward social comparison in the minimal intergroup situation: A test of a self-enhancement interpretation. *Journal of Applied Social Psychology, 20,* 1166-1184.
26. Brewer, M. B. (1979). Ingroup bias in the minimal intergroup situation: A cognitive motivational analysis. *Psychological Bulletin, 86,* 307-324.
27. Anderson, N. H. (1968). Likeableness ratings of 555 personality-trait words. *Journal of Personality and Social Psychology, 9,* 272,279.
28. Whissel, C. M. (1989). The dictionary of affect in language. In R. Plutchik & H. Kellerman (Eds.), *The measurement of emotions* (pp. 113-131). San Diego, CA: Academic.

29. Brewer, M. B. (1979). Ingroup bias in the minimal intergroup situation: A cognitive motivational analysis. *Psychological Bulletin, 86,* 307-324.
30. Bettencourt, B. A., Dorr, N., Charlton, K., & Hume, D. L. (2001). Status differences and in-group bias: A meta-analytic examination of the effects of status stability, status legitimacy, and group permeability. *Psychological Bulletin, 127,* 520-542.
31. Mullen, B., Brown, R., & Smith, C. (1992). Ingroup bias as a function of salience, relevance, and status: An integration. *European Journal of Social Psychology, 22,* 103-122.
32. Bettencourt, B. A., Dorr, N., Charlton, K., & Hume, D. L. (2001). Status differences and in-group bias: A meta-analytic examination of the effects of status stability, status legitimacy, and group permeability. *Psychological Bulletin, 127,* 520-542.
33. Shaw, M. E. (1981). *Group dynamics: The psychology of small group behavior* (3rd ed.). New York: McGraw-Hill.
34. Mullen, B., Brown, R., & Smith, C. (1992). Ingroup bias as a function of salience, relevance, and status: An integration. *European Journal of Social Psychology, 22,* 103-122.
35. Mullen, B., & Hu, L. (1989). Social projection as a function of cognitive mechanisms: Two meta-analytic integrations. *British Journal of Social Psychology, 27,* 333-356.
36. Mullen, B. Johnson, C., & Salas, E. (1991). Productivity loss in brainstorming groups: A meta-analytic integration. *Basic and Applied Social Psychology, 12,* 3-23.
37. Mullen, B., & Copper, C. (1994). The relation between group cohesiveness and performance: An integration. *Psychological Bulletin, 115,* 210-227.
38. Mullen, B., Brown, R., & Smith, C. (1992). Ingroup bias as a function of salience, relevance, and status: An integration. *European Journal of Social Psychology, 22,* 103-122.
39. Mullen, B. Johnson, C., & Salas, E. (1991). Productivity loss in brainstorming groups: A meta-analytic integration. *Basic and Applied Social Psychology, 12,* 3-23.
40. Mullen, B. Johnson, C., & Salas, E. (1991). Productivity loss in brainstorming groups: A meta-analytic integration. *Basic and Applied Social Psychology, 12,* 12.
41. Mullen, B. Johnson, C., & Salas, E. (1991). Productivity loss in brainstorming groups: A meta-analytic integration. *Basic and Applied Social Psychology, 12,* 3-23.

42. Brewer, M. B. (1979). Ingroup bias in the minimal intergroup situation: A cognitive motivational analysis. *Psychological Bulletin, 86,* 307-324.
43. Brewer, M. B. (1979). Ingroup bias in the minimal intergroup situation: A cognitive motivational analysis. *Psychological Bulletin, 86,* 479.
44. Sidanius, J., & Pratto, F. (1999). *Social Dominance: An Intergroup Theory of Social Hierarchy and Oppression.* New York: Cambridge University Press.
45. Sidanius, J., & Pratto, F. (1999). *Social Dominance: An Intergroup Theory of Social Hierarchy and Oppression.* New York: Cambridge University Press.
46. Crocker, J. & Luhtanen, R. (1990). Collective self-esteem and ingroup bias. *Journal of Personality and Social Psychology, 58,* 60-67.
47. Brewer, M. B. (1979). Ingroup bias in the minimal intergroup situation: A cognitive motivational analysis. *Psychological Bulletin, 86,* 307-324.
48. Mullen, B., Brown, R., & Smith, C. (1992). Ingroup bias as a function of salience, relevance, and status: An integration. *European Journal of Social Psychology, 22,* 103-122.
49. Brewer, M. B. (1979). Ingroup bias in the minimal intergroup situation: A cognitive motivational analysis. *Psychological Bulletin, 86,* 307-324.
50. Bettencourt, B. A., Dorr, N., Charlton, K., & Hume, D. L. (2001). Status differences and in-group bias: A meta-analytic examination of the effects of status stability, status legitimacy, and group permeability. *Psychological Bulletin, 127,* 520-542.
51. Berger, J., & Zeldtich, M. (1998). *Status, power, and legitimacy: Strategies and theories.* New Brunswick, NJ: Transaction.
52. Ridgeway, C. L., & Bourg, C. (2004). Gender as status: An expectation states theory approach. In A. H. Eagly, A. E. Beall, & R. J. Sternberg (Eds.), *The Psychology of Gender.* New York: Guilford Press.
53. Tajfel, H., & Turner, J. C. (1986). The social identity theory of intergroup behaviour. In Worchel, S., and Austin, W. G. (Eds.), *Psychology of Intergroup Relations.* Chicago: Nelson-Hall.
54. Jost, J. T., & Banaji, M. R. (1994). The role of stereotyping in system-justification and the production of false consciousness. *British Journal of Social Psychology, 33,* 1-27.
55. Brewer, M. B. (1979). Ingroup bias in the minimal intergroup situation: A cognitive motivational analysis. *Psychological Bulletin, 86,* 307-324.

56. Wilson, W., & Robinson, C. (1968). Selective intergroup bias in both authoritarians and non-authoritarians after playing a modified prisoner's dilemma game. *Perceptual and Motor Skills, 27,* 1051-1058.
57. Brewer, M. B., Manzi, J. M., & Shaw, J. S. (1993). In-group identification as a function of depersonalization, distinctiveness, and status. *Psychological Science, 4,* 88-92.
58. Mullen, B., Brown, R., & Smith, C. (1992). Ingroup bias as a function of salience, relevance, and status: An integration. *European Journal of Social Psychology, 22,* 103-122.
59. Tversky, A. (1977). Features of similarity. *Psychological Review, 84,* 327-352.
60. Tversky, A. (1977). Features of similarity. *Psychological Review, 84,* 327-352.
61. Tajfel, H., & Wilkes, A. L., (1963). Classification and quantitative judgment. *British Journal of Psychology, 54,* 101-114.
62. Tajfel, H., & Turner, J. C. (1986). The social identity theory of intergroup behaviour. In Worchel, S., and Austin, W. G. (Eds.), *Psychology of Intergroup Relations.*Chicago: Nelson-Hall.
63. Tajfel, H., & Turner, J. C. (1986). The social identity theory of intergroup behaviour. In Worchel, S., and Austin, W. G. (Eds.), *Psychology of Intergroup Relations.*Chicago: Nelson-Hall.
64. Tarrant, M., & North, A. C. (2004). Explanations for positive and negative behavior: The intergroup attribution bias in achieved groups. *Current Psychology: Developmental, Learning, Personality, Social, 23 (2),* 161-172.
65. Tajfel, H., & Turner, J. C. (1986). The social identity theory of intergroup behaviour. In Worchel, S., and Austin, W. G. (Eds.), *Psychology of Intergroup Relations.*Chicago: Nelson-Hall.
66. Ellemers, N., Wilke, H., & van Knippenberg, A. (1993). Effects of the legitimacy of low group or individual status on individual and collective status-enhancement strategies. *Journal of Personality and Social Psychology, 64,* 766-788.
67. Bettencourt, B. A., Dorr, N., Charlton, K., & Hume, D. L. (2001). Status differences and in-group bias: A meta-analytic examination of the effects of status stability, status legitimacy, and group permeability. *Psychological Bulletin, 127,* 520-542.
68. Brewer, M. B. (1991). The social self: On being the same and different at the same time. *Personality and Social Psychology Bulletin, 17,* 475-482.

69. Brewer, M. B. (1991). The social self: On being the same and different at the same time. *Personality and Social Psychology Bulletin, 17,* 475-482.
70. Brewer, M. B. (1991). The social self: On being the same and different at the same time. *Personality and Social Psychology Bulletin, 17,* 475-482.
71. Brewer, M. B. (1991). The social self: On being the same and different at the same time. *Personality and Social Psychology Bulletin, 17,* 478.
72. Tajfel, H., & Turner, J. C. (1986). The social identity theory of intergroup behaviour. In Worchel, S., and Austin, W. G. (Eds.), *Psychology of Intergroup Relations.*Chicago: Nelson-Hall.
73. Tajfel, H., & Turner, J. C. (1986). The social identity theory of intergroup behaviour. In Worchel, S., and Austin, W. G. (Eds.), *Psychology of Intergroup Relations.*Chicago: Nelson-Hall.
74. Tajfel, H., Billig, M. G., Bundy, R. F., & Flament, C. (1971). Social categorization and intergroup behavior. *European Journal of Social Psychology, 1,* 149-177.
75. Reynolds, K. J., Turner, J. C., & Haslam, S. A. (2000). When are we better than them and they worse than us? A closer look at social discrimination in positive and negative domains. *Journal of Personality and Social Psychology, 78,* 64-80.
76. Gaertner, L., & Schopler, J. (1998). Perceived ingroup entitativity and intergroup bias: an interconnection of self and others. *European Journal of Social Psychology, 28,* 963-980.
77. Doise, W., & Sinclair, A. (1973). The categorization process in intergroup relations. *European Journal of Social Psychology, 3,* 145-157.
78. Gerard, H. B. & Hoyt, M. F. (1974). Distinctiveness of social categorization and attitude toward ingroup members. *Journal of Personality and Social Psychology, 26,* 309-320.
79. Bodenhausen, G. V. (1993). Emotions, arousal, and stereotypic judgments: A heuristic model of affect and stereotyping. In D. M. Mackie & D. L. Hamilton (Eds.), *Affect, cognition, and stereotyping: Interactive processes in group perception* (pp. 13-37). San Diego, CA: Academic Press.
80. Bodenhausen, G. V. (1993). Emotions, arousal, and stereotypic judgments: A heuristic model of affect and stereotyping. In D. M. Mackie & D. L. Hamilton (Eds.), *Affect, cognition, and stereotyping: Interactive processes in group perception* (pp. 13-37). San Diego, CA: Academic Press.

81. Bodenhausen, G. V. (1993). Emotions, arousal, and stereotypic judgments: A heuristic model of affect and stereotyping. In D. M. Mackie & D. L. Hamilton (Eds.), *Affect, cognition, and stereotyping: Interactive processes in group perception* (pp. 13-37). San Diego, CA: Academic Press. 14
82. Rubin, M., Hewstone, M., & Voci, A. (2001). Stretching the boundaries: Strategic perceptions of intragroup variability. *European Journal of Social Psychology, 31,* 413-429.
83. Rabbie, J. M., Benoist, F., Oosterbaan, H., & Visser, L. (1974). Differential power and effects of expected competitive and cooperative intergroup interaction on intragroup and outgroup attitudes. *Journal of Personality and Social Psychology, 30,* 46-56.
84. Rabbie, J. M., Benoist, F., Oosterbaan, H., & Visser, L. (1974). Differential power and effects of expected competitive and cooperative intergroup interaction on intragroup and outgroup attitudes. *Journal of Personality and Social Psychology, 30,* 46-56.
85. Eurich-Fulcer, R., Schofield, J. W. (1995). Correlated versus uncorrelated social categorizations: The effect on intergroup bias. *Personality and Social Psychology Bulletin, 21,* 149-159.
86. Brown, R., & Turner, J. (1979). The criss-cross categorization effect in intergroup discrimination. *British Journal of Social and Clinical Psychology, 18,* 371-383.
87. Brown, R., & Turner, J. (1979). The criss-cross categorization effect in intergroup discrimination. *British Journal of Social and Clinical Psychology, 18,* 371-383.
88. Andreopoulou, A., & Houston, D. M. (2002). The impact of collective self-esteem on intergroup evaluation: Self-protection and self-enhancement. *Current Research in Social Psychology, 7,* 243-256.
89. Dion, K. L. (1973). Cohesiveness as a determinant of ingroup-outgroup bias. *Journal of Personality and Social Psychology, 28,* 163-171.
90. Eagly, A. H., & Chaiken, S. (1993). *The psychology of attitudes.* Orlando, FL: Harcourt Brace Jovanovich.
91. Fiske, S. T., & Taylor, S. E. (1991). *Social cognition (2nd edition).* New York: McGraw-Hill.
92. Averill, J. R. (1990). Emotions as episodic dispositions, cognitive schemas, and transitory social roles: Steps toward an integrated theory of emotion. In D. J. Ozer, J. M. Healy, Jr., & A. J. Stewart (Eds.), *Perspectives in personality: Vol. 3a. Self and emotion* (pp. 137-165). Greenwich, CT. JAI Press.

93. Holyoak, K. J. & Gordon, P. C. (1984). Information processing and social cognition. In R. S. Wyer, Jr., & T. K. Srull (Eds.), *Handbook of social cognition* (Vol. 1, pp. 39-70). Hillsdale, NJ: Erlbaum.
94. Fiske, S. T., & Taylor, S. E. (1991). *Social cognition (2nd edition).* New York: McGraw-Hill.
95. Esses, V. M., Haddock, G., & Zanna, M. P. (1993). Values, stereotypes, and emotions as determinants of intergroup attitudes. In D. M. Mackie & D. L. Hamilton (Eds.), *Affect, cognition, and stereotyping: Interactive processes in group perception* (pp. 137-166). New York: Academic Press.
96. Zajonc, R. B. (1980). Feeling and thinking: Preferences need no inferences. *American Psychologist, 35,* 151-175.
97. Eagly, A. H., & Chaiken, S. (1993). *The psychology of attitudes.* Orlando, FL: Harcourt Brace Jovanovich.
98. Stephan, W. G., & Stephan, C. W. (1993). Cognition and affect in stereotyping: Parallel interactive networks. In D. M. Mackie & D. L. Hamilton (Eds.), *Affect, cognition, and stereotyping: Interactive processes in group perception* (pp. 111-136). New York: Academic Press. 117.
99. Esses, V. M., Haddock, G., & Zanna, M. P. (1993). Values, stereotypes, and emotions as determinants of intergroup attitudes. In D. M. Mackie & D. L. Hamilton (Eds.), *Affect, cognition, and stereotyping: Interactive processes in group perception* (pp. 137-166). New York: Academic Press.
100. Hogg, M. A., & Abrams, D. (1999). Social identity and social cognition: Historical background and current trends. In D. Abrams and M. A. Hogg (Eds.), *Social identity and social cognition* (pp. 1-25). Malden, MA: Blackwell.
101. Bodenhausen, G. V. (1993). Emotions, arousal, and stereotypic judgments: A heuristic model of affect and stereotyping. In D. M. Mackie & D. L. Hamilton (Eds.), *Affect, cognition, and stereotyping: Interactive processes in group perception* (pp. 13-37). San Diego, CA: Academic Press. 14
102. Jussim, L., Nelson, T. E., Manis, M. & Soffin, S. (1995). Prejudice, stereotypes, and labeling effects: Sources of bias in person perception. *Journal of Personality and Social Psychology, 68,* 228-246.
103. Jussim, L., Nelson, T. E., Manis, M. & Soffin, S. (1995). Prejudice, stereotypes, and labeling effects: Sources of bias in person perception. *Journal of Personality and Social Psychology, 68,* 228-246.

104. Jussim, L., Nelson, T. E., Manis, M. & Soffin, S. (1995). Prejudice, stereotypes, and labeling effects: Sources of bias in person perception. *Journal of Personality and Social Psychology, 68,* 228-246.
105. Johnson, C., & Mullen, B. (1993). The determinants of differential group evaluations in distinctiveness-based illusory correlations in stereotyping. *British Journal of Social Psychology, 32,* 253-263.
106. Johnson, C., & Mullen, B. (1993). The determinants of differential group evaluations in distinctiveness-based illusory correlations in stereotyping. *British Journal of Social Psychology, 32,* 253-263.
107. Johnson, C., Mullen, B., Carlson, D., & Southwick, S. (2001). The affective and memorial components of distinctiveness-based illusory correlations. *British Journal of Social Psychology, 40,* 337-358.
108. Zanna, M. P., Haddock, G., & Esses, V. M. (1990). *On the nature of prejudice.* Paper presented at the Nags Head Conference on Stereotypes and Intergroup Relations, Nags Head Conference Center, Kill Devil Hills, N. C.
109. Zanna, M. P., Haddock, G., & Esses, V. M. (1990). *On the nature of prejudice.* Paper presented at the Nags Head Conference on Stereotypes and Intergroup Relations, Nags Head Conference Center, Kill Devil Hills, N. C.
110. Stangor, C., Sullivan, L. A., & Ford, T. E. (1991). Affective and cognitive determinants of prejudice. *Social Cognition, 9,* 359-380.
111. Verkuyten, M. (1991). Self-definition and ingroup formation among ethnic minorities in the Netherlands. *Social Psychology Quarterly, 54,* 280-286.
112. Verkuyten, M. (1991). Self-definition and ingroup formation among ethnic minorities in the Netherlands. *Social Psychology Quarterly, 54,* 280-286.

CHAPTER FIVE

1. Lauer, M. (Host). (2004, September 8). Powell Calls for Perseverance in Iraq Despite Military Losses. *NBC's Today Show with Matt Lauer*. NBC. Transcript retrieved November 11, 2006, from: http://iraq.usembassy.gov/iraq/040908_persevere.html
2. Fischhoff, B. (1975). Hindsight ≠ foresight: The effect of outcome knowledge on judgment under uncertainty. *Journal of Experimental Psychology: Human Perception & Performance, 1,* 288-299.
3. Ricks, T. E., & Wright, R. (2004). Powell Advised Bush to Add Iraq Troops. *The Washington Post.* Retrieved November 11, 2006, from http://www.washingtonpost. com/wp-dyn/ articles/A23381-2004Dec23.html
4. Lehrer, J. (2005, January 13). Newsmaker: Colin Powell. *News Hour with Jim Lehrer.* Public Broadcasting Service. Transcript retrieved November 11, from: http://www. pbs.org/newshour/bb/fedagencies/jan-june05/powell_1-13.html van Dijk, W. W., & Zeelenberg, M. (2002). What do we talk about when we talk about disappointment? *Cognition and Emotion, 16,* 787-807.
5. Lazarus, R. S. 1991. *Emotion and adaptation.* New York: Oxford University Press.
6. O'Rorke, P., & Ortony, A. (1994). Explaining emotions. *Cognitive Science, 18,* 283-323.
7. van Dijk, W. W., & Zeelenberg, M. (2002). What do we talk about when we talk about disappointment? *Cognition and Emotion, 16,* 787-807.
8. Fischhoff, B. (1975). Hindsight ≠ foresight: The effect of outcome knowledge on judgment under uncertainty. *Journal of Experimental Psychology: Human Perception & Performance, 1,* 288-299.
9. Guilbault, R. L., Bryant, F. B., Brockway, J. H., & Posava, E. J. (2004). A meta-analysis of research on hindsight bias. *Basic and Applied Social Psychology, 26,* 103-117.
10. Slovic, P. & Fischhoff, B. (1977). On the psychology of experimental surprises. *Journal of Experimental Psychology: Human Perception and Performance, 3,* 544-551.
11. Renner, B. (2003). Hindsight bias after receiving self-relevant health risk information: A motivational perspective. *Memory, 11,* 455-472.
12. Wasserman, D., Lampert, R. O., & Hastie, R. (1991). Hindsight and causality. *Personality & Social Psychology Bulletin, 17,* 30-35.

13. Hoffrage, U., Hertwig, R., & Gigerenzer, G. (2000). Hindsight bias: A by-product of knowledge updating? *Journal of Experimental Psychology: Learning, Memory, & Cognition, 26,* 566-581.
14. Scherer, K. R. (2003). Introduction: Cognitive components of emotion. In R. J. Davidson, H. Goldsmith, K. R. Scherer (Eds.), *Handbook of the Affective Sciences* (pp. 563-571). New York and Oxford: Oxford University Press.
15. Henriksen, K. & Kaplan, H. (2003). Hindsight bias, outcome knowledge and adaptive learning. *Quality and Safety in Health Care, 12,* 46-50.
16. Louie, T. A. (1999). Decision makers' hindsight bias after receiving favorable and unfavorable feedback. *Journal of Applied Psychology, 84,* 29-41.
17. Sanna, L. J., Schwarz, N., & Stocker, S. L. (2002) b. When debiasing backfires: Assessible content and assessibility experiences in debiasing hindsight. *Journal of Experimental Psychology: Learning, Memory, & Cognition, 28,* 497-502.
18. Schwarz, N., Sanna, L. J., Skurnik, I., & Yoon, C. (2007). The intricacies of setting people straight: Implications for debiasing and public information campaigns. *Advances in Experimental Social Psychology, 39,* 127-161.
19. Schwarz, N., & Clore, G. L. (2007). Feelings and phenomenal experiences. In E. T.
20. Higgins & A. Kruglanski (eds.), *Social psychology. Handbook of basic principles* (2nd ed.; pp. 385-407). New York: Guilford.
21. Elster, J. (1998). Emotions and economic theory. *Journal of Economic Literature, 36,* 47-74.
22. Lerner, J. S., & Tiedens L. Z. (2006). Portrait of the angry decision maker: How appraisal tendencies shape anger's influence on cognition. *Journal of Behavioral Decision Making, 19,* 115-137.
23. Frijda, N. H. (1986). *The emotions.* Cambridge, England: Cambridge University Press.
24. Rucker, D. D., & Petty, R. E. (2004). An Emotion Specificity Approach to Consumer Decision Making. *Motivation and Emotion, 28,* 3-21.
25. Keltner, D., Ellsworth, P. C., & Edwards, K. (1993). Beyond simple pessimism: Effects of sadness and anger on social perception. *Journal of Personality and Social Psychology, 64,* 740-752.
26. DeSteno, D., Petty, R. E., Rucker, D. D, Wegener, D. T., & Braverman, J. (2004). Discrete emotions and persuasion: The role of emotion-induced expectancies. *Journal of Personality & Social Psychology 86,* 43-56.

27. Tiedens, L. Z. (2001). The effect of anger on the hostile inferences of aggressive and nonaggressive people: Specific emotions, cognitive processing, and chronic accessibility. *Motivation and Emotion, 25,* 233-251.
28. Roese, N. J. (1997). Counterfactual thinking. *Psychological Bulletin, 121,* 133-148.
29. Kahneman, D. & Miller, D. T. (1986). Norm theory: Comparing reality to its alternatives. *Psychological Review, 93,* 136-153.
30. Roseman, I. J., Antoniou, A. A., & Jose, P. E. (1996). Appraisal determinants of emotions: Constructing a more accurate and comprehensiv e theory. *Cognition and Emotion, 10,*241-277.
31. Roseman, I. J., Antoniou, A. A., & Jose, P. E. (1996). Appraisal determinant s of emotions: Constructing a more accurate and comprehensive theory. *Cognition and Emotion, 10,* 241-277.
32. van Dijk, W. W., & Zeelenberg, M. (2002). What do we talk about when we talk about disappointment? *Cognition and Emotion, 16,* 787-807.
33. Roseman, I. J. (2001). A model of appraisal in the emotion system: Integrating theory, research, and applications. In K. R. Scherer & A. Schorr (Eds)., *Appraisal processes in emotion: Theory, methods, research* (pp. 68-91). New York: Oxford University Press.
34. Zeelenberg, M., van Dijk, W. W., & Manstead, A. S. R. (1998). Reconsidering the relation between regret and responsibility. *Organizational Behavior and Human Decision Processes, 74,* 254-272.
35. Zeelenberg, M., van Dijk, W. W., & Manstead, A. S. R. (1998). Reconsidering the relation between regret and responsibility. *Organizational Behavior and Human Decision Processes, 74,* 254-272.
36. Zeelenberg, M., & Pieters, F. G. M. (2004). Beyond valence in customer dissatisfaction: A review and new findings on behavioral responses to regret and disappointment in failed services. *Journal of Business Research, 57,* 445-455.
37. Roseman, I. J. (2001). A model of appraisal in the emotion system: Integrating theory, research, and applications. In K. R. Scherer & A. Schorr (Eds)., *Appraisal processes in emotion: Theory, methods, research* (pp. 68-91). New York: Oxford University Press.
38. O'Rorke, P., & Ortony, A. (1994). Explaining emotions. *Cognitive Science, 18,* 283-323.
39. Roseman, I. J. (2001). A model of appraisal in the emotion system: Integrating theory, research, and applications. In K. R. Scherer & A.

Schorr (Eds)., *Appraisal processes in emotion: Theory, methods, research* (pp. 68-91). New York: Oxford University Press.
40. Oliver, R. L. (1997). *Satisfaction: A behavioral perspective on the consumer.* New York: Irwin/McGraw-Hill.
41. Roseman, I. J. (2001). A model of appraisal in the emotion system: Integrating theory, research, and applications. In K. R. Scherer & A. Schorr (Eds)., *Appraisal processes in emotion: Theory, methods, research* (pp. 68-91). New York: Oxford University Press. 68.
42. Roseman, I. J. (2001). A model of appraisal in the emotion system: Integrating theory, research, and applications. In K. R. Scherer & A. Schorr (Eds)., *Appraisal processes in emotion: Theory, methods, research* (pp. 68-91). New York: Oxford University Press. 69.
43. Roseman, I. J. (2001). A model of appraisal in the emotion system: Integrating theory, research, and applications. In K. R. Scherer & A. Schorr (Eds)., *Appraisal processes in emotion: Theory, methods, research* (pp. 68-91). New York: Oxford University Press.
44. van Dijk, W. W., & Zeelenberg, M. (2002). What do we talk about when we talk about disappointment? *Cognition and Emotion, 16,* 787-807.
45. Zeelenberg, M., van Dijk, W. W., & Manstead, A. S. R. (2000). Regret and responsibility resolved? Evaluating Ordóñez and Connolly's (2000) conclusions. *Organizational Behavior and Human Decision Processes, 81,* 143-154.
46. Connolly, T., Ordóñez, L. D., & Coughlan, R. (1997). Regret and responsibility in the evaluation of decision outcomes. *Organizational Behavior and Human Decision Processes, 70,* 73-85.
47. Zeelenberg, M., van Dijk, W. W., & Manstead, A. S. R. (2000). Regret and responsibility resolved? Evaluating Ordóñez and Connolly's (2000) conclusions. *Organizational Behavior and Human Decision Processes, 81,* 143-154.
48. Tykocinski, O. E., Pick, D., & Kedmi, D. (2002). Retroactive pessimism: A different kind of hindsight bias. *European Journal of Social Psychology. 32,* 577-588.
49. Pezzo, M. V., & Pezzo, S. P. (2007). Making sense of failure: A motivated model of hindsight bias. *Social Cognition, 25,* 147-164.
50. Pezzo, M. V., & Pezzo, S. P. (2007). Making sense of failure: A motivated model of hindsight bias. *Social Cognition, 25,* 147-164.
51. Pezzo, M. V. (2003). Surprise, defence, or making sense: What removes the hindsight bias? *Memory, 11,* 421-441.

52. Tykocinski, O.E., Pick, D., & Kedmi, D. (2002). Retroactive pessimism: A different kind of hindsight bias. *European Journal of Social Psychology. 32,* 577-588.
53. Louie, T. A. (1999). Decision makers' hindsight bias after receiving favorable and unfavorable feedback. *Journal of Applied Psychology, 84,* 29-41.
54. Louie, T. A. (1999). Decision makers' hindsight bias after receiving favorable and unfavorable feedback. *Journal of Applied Psychology, 84,* 29-41.
55. Louie, T. A. (1999). Decision makers' hindsight bias after receiving favorable and unfavorable feedback. *Journal of Applied Psychology, 84,* 29-41.
56. Mark, M. M., Boburka, R. R., Eyssell, K. M., Cohen, L. L., & Mellor, S. (2003). "I couldn't have seen it coming": The impact of negative self-relevant outcomes on retrospections about foreseeability. *Memory, 11,* 443-454.
57. Mark, M. M., Boburka, R. R., Eyssell, K. M., Cohen, L. L., & Mellor, S. (2003). "I couldn't have seen it coming": The impact of negative self-relevant outcomes on retrospections about foreseeability. *Memory, 11,* 443-454.
58. Mark, M. M., Boburka, R. R., Eyssell, K. M., Cohen, L. L., & Mellor, S. (2003). "I couldn't have seen it coming": The impact of negative self-relevant outcomes on retrospections about foreseeability. *Memory, 11,* 443-454.

CHAPTER SIX

1. Shanteau, J. (1992). Competence in experts: The role of task characteristics. *Organizational Behavior and Human Decision Processes, 53,* 252-266.
2. Camerer, C. F., & Johnson, E. J. (1997). The process-performance paradox in expert judgment: How can experts know so much and predict so badly? In W. M. Goldstein, & R. M. Hogarth (Eds.), *Research on judgment and decision making: Currents, connections, and controversies* (pp. 342-364). New York, NY: Cambridge University Press.
3. Spilich, G. J., Vesonder, G. T., Chiesi, H. L., & Voss, J. F. (1979). Text processing of domain-related information for individuals with high and low domain knowledge. *Journal of Verbal Learning and Verbal Behavior, 18,* 275-290.
4. Spilich, G. J., Vesonder, G. T., Chiesi, H. L., & Voss, J. F. (1979). Text processing of domain-related information for individuals with high and low domain knowledge. *Journal of Verbal Learning and Verbal Behavior, 18,* 275-290.
5. Spilich, G. J., Vesonder, G. T., Chiesi, H. L., & Voss, J. F. (1979). Text processing of domain-related information for individuals with high and low domain knowledge. *Journal of Verbal Learning and Verbal Behavior, 18,* 275-290.
6. Spilich, G. J., Vesonder, G. T., Chiesi, H. L., & Voss, J. F. (1979). Text processing of domain-related information for individuals with high and low domain knowledge. *Journal of Verbal Learning and Verbal Behavior, 18,* 275-290.
7. Larkin, J., McDermott, J., Simon, D. P., & Simon, H. A. (1980). Expert and novice performance in solving physics problems. *Science, 208,* 1335-1342.
8. Spilich, G. J., Vesonder, G. T., Chiesi, H. L., & Voss, J. F. (1979). Text processing of domain-related information for individuals with high and low domain knowledge. *Journal of Verbal Learning and Verbal Behavior, 18,* 275-290.
9. Shanteau, J. (1992). Competence in experts: The role of task characteristics. *Organizational Behavior and Human Decision Processes, 53,* 252-266.
10. Tversky, A., & Kahneman, D. (1974). Judgment under uncertainty: Heuristics and biases. *Science, 185,* 1124-1131.

11. Poses, R. M., & Anthony, M. (1991). Availability, wishful thinking, and physicians' diagnostic judgments for patients with suspected bacteremia. *Medical Decision Making, 11,* 159-168.
12. Casscells, W., Schoenberger, A., & Graboys, T. (1978) Interpretation by physicians of clinical laboratory results. *New England Journal of Medicine, 299,* 999-1001.
13. Caplan, R. A., Posner, K. L., & Cheney, F. W. (1991). Effect of outcome on physician judgments of appropriateness of care. *Journal of the American Medical Association, 265,* 1957-1960.
14. Chapman, G. B., & Elstein, A. S. (2000). Cognitive processes and biases in medical decision making. In G. B. Chapman & F. A. Sonnenberg (Eds.), *Decision Making in Health Care: Theory, Psychology, and Applications* (pp. 183-210). New York, NY: Cambridge University Press
15. Guthrie, C., Rachlinski, J. J., & Wistrich, A. J. (2001). Inside the judicial mind. *Cornell Law Review, 86,* 777-830.
16. Arkes, H. R., & Freedman, M. R. (1984). A demonstration of the costs and benefits of expertise in recognition memory. *Memory & Cognition, 12,* 84-89.
17. Arkes, H. R., Faust, D., Guilmette, T. J., & Hart, K. (1988). Eliminating the hindsight bias. *Journal of Applied Psychology, 73,* 305-307.
18. Arkes, H. R., & Freedman, M. R. (1984). A demonstration of the costs and benefits of expertise in recognition memory. *Memory & Cognition, 12,* 84-89.
19. Arkes, H. R., & Freedman, M. R. (1984). A demonstration of the costs and benefits of expertise in recognition memory. *Memory & Cognition, 12,* 84-89.
20. Arkes, H. R., & Freedman, M. R. (1984). A demonstration of the costs and benefits of expertise in recognition memory. *Memory & Cognition, 12,* 84-89.
21. Arkes, H. R., & Harkness, A. R. (1980). The effect of making a diagnosis on subsequent recognition of symptoms. *Journal of Experimental Psychology: Human Learning and Memory, 6,* 568-575.
22. Arkes, H. R., & Freedman, M. R. (1984). A demonstration of the costs and benefits of expertise in recognition memory. *Memory & Cognition, 12,* 84-89.
23. Bradley, J. V. (1981). Overconfidence in ignorant experts. *Bulletin of the Psychonomic Society, 17(2),* 82-84.
24. Bradley, J. V. (1981). Overconfidence in ignorant experts. *Bulletin of the Psychonomic Society, 17(2),* 82-84.

25. Nickerson, R. S. (1999). How we know—and sometimes misjudge—what others know: Imputing one's own knowledge to others. *Psychological Bulletin, 125,* 737-759.
26. Nickerson, R. S. (1999). How we know—and sometimes misjudge—what others know: Imputing one's own knowledge to others. *Psychological Bulletin, 125,* 737-759.
27. Nickerson, R. S., Baddeley, A., & Freeman, B. (1987). Are people's estimates of what other people know influenced by what they themselves know? *Acta Psychologica, 64,* 245-259.
28. Nickerson, R. S. (1999). How we know—and sometimes misjudge—what others know: Imputing one's own knowledge to others. *Psychological Bulletin, 125,* 737-759.
29. Hinds, P. J. (1999). The curse of expertise: The effects of expertise and debiasing methods on predictions of novice performance. *Journal of Experimental Psychology: Applied, 5,* 205-221.
30. Tversky, A., & Kahneman, D. (1973). Availability: A heuristic for judging frequency and probability. *Cognitive Psychology, 5,* 207-232.
31. Hinds, P. J. (1999). The curse of expertise: The effects of expertise and debiasing methods on predictions of novice performance. *Journal of Experimental Psychology: Applied, 5,* 205-221.
32. Tversky, A., & Kahneman, D. (1973). Availability: A heuristic for judging frequency and probability. *Cognitive Psychology, 5,* 207-232.
33. Hinds, P. J. (1999). The curse of expertise: The effects of expertise and debiasing methods on predictions of novice performance. *Journal of Experimental Psychology: Applied, 5,* 205-221.
34. Fischhoff, B. (1975). Hindsight ≠ foresight: The effect of outcome knowledge on judgment under uncertainty. *Journal of Experimental Psychology: Human Perception and Performance, 1,* 288-299.
35. Hinds, P. J. (1999). The curse of expertise: The effects of expertise and debiasing methods on predictions of novice performance. *Journal of Experimental Psychology: Applied, 5,* 205-221.
36. Blank, H., Fischer, V., & Erdfelder, E. (2003). Hindsight bias in political elections. *Memory, 11,* 491-504.
37. LaBine, S. J., & LaBine, G. (1996). Determinations of negligence and the hindsight bias. *Law and Human Behavior, 20,* 501-516.
38. Guthrie, C., Rachlinski, J. J., & Wistrich, A. J. (2001). Inside the judicial mind. *Cornell Law Review, 86,* 777-830.
39. Guthrie, C., Rachlinski, J. J., & Wistrich, A. J. (2001). Inside the judicial mind. *Cornell Law Review, 86,* 777-830.

40. Casper, J. D., Benedict, K., & Kelly, J. R. (1988). Cognitions, attitudes, and decision-making in search and seizure cases. *Journal of Applied Social Psychology, 18,* 93-113.
41. Berlin, L. (2000). Hindsight bias. *American Journal of Roentgenology, 175,* 597-601.
42. LaBine, S. J., & LaBine, G. (1996). Determinations of negligence and the hindsight bias. *Law and Human Behavior, 20,* 501-516.
43. Dawson, N. V., Arkes, H. R., Siciliano, C., Blinkhorn, R., Lakshmanan, M., & Petrelli, M. (1988). Hindsight bias: An impediment to accurate probability estimation in clinicopathologic conferences. *Medical Decision Making, 8,* 259-264.
44. Dawson, N. V., Arkes, H. R., Siciliano, C., Blinkhorn, R., Lakshmanan, M., & Petrelli, M. (1988). Hindsight bias: An impediment to accurate probability estimation in clinicopathologic conferences. *Medical Decision Making, 8,* 259-264.
45. Dawson, N. V., Arkes, H. R., Siciliano, C., Blinkhorn, R., Lakshmanan, M., & Petrelli, M. (1988). Hindsight bias: An impediment to accurate probability estimation in clinicopathologic conferences. *Medical Decision Making, 8,* 259-264.
46. Gray, R., Beilock, S. L., & Carr, T. H. (2007). "As soon as the bat met the ball, I knew it was gone": Outcome prediction, hindsight bias, and the representation and controlof action in expert and novice baseball players. *Psychonomic Bulletin & Review, 14,* 669-675.
47. Shanteau, J. (1992). Competence in experts: The role of task characteristics. *Organizational Behavior and Human Decision Processes, 53,* 252-266.
48. Harley, E. M., Carlsen, K. A., & Loftus, G. R. (2004). The "saw-it-all-along" effect: Demonstrations of visual hindsight bias. *Journal of Experimental Psychology: Learning, Memory, and Cognition, 30,* 960-968.
49. Guthrie, C., Rachlinski, J. J., & Wistrich, A. J. (2001). Inside the judicial mind. *Cornell Law Review, 86,* 777-830.
50. Guthrie, C., Rachlinski, J. J., & Wistrich, A. J. (2007). Blinking on the bench: How judges decide cases. *Cornell Law Review, 93,* 1-44.
51. Guthrie, C., Rachlinski, J. J., & Wistrich, A. J. (2001). Inside the judicial mind. *Cornell Law Review, 86,* 777-830.
52. Guthrie, C., Rachlinski, J. J., & Wistrich, A. J. (2007). Blinking on the bench: How judges decide cases. *Cornell Law Review, 93,* 1-44.
53. Guthrie, C., Rachlinski, J. J., & Wistrich, A. J. (2007). Blinking on the bench: How judges decide cases. *Cornell Law Review, 93,* 1-44.

54. Lichtenstein, S., & Fischhoff, B. (1977). Do those who know more also know more about how much they know? *Organizational Behavioral and Human Performance, 20,* 159-183.
55. Smith, J. F., & Kida, T. (1991). Heurstics and biases: Expertise and task realism. *Psychological Bulletin, 109,* 472-489.
56. Christensen-Szalanski, J. J. J., & Willham, C. F. (1991). The hindsight bias: A meta-analysis. *Organizational Behavior and Human Decision Processes, 48,* 175-168.
57. Dawson, N. V., Arkes, H. R., Siciliano, C., Blinkhorn, R., Lakshmanan, M., & Petrelli, M. (1988). Hindsight bias: An impediment to accurate probability estimation in clinicopathologic conferences. *Medical Decision Making, 8,* 259-264.
58. McKenzie, C. R. M., Liersch, M. J., & Yaniv, I. (2008). Overconfidence in interval estimates: What does expertise buy you? *Organizational Behavior and Human Decision Processes, 107,* 179-191.
59. Dawson, N.V., Connors, A. F., Speroff, T., Kemka, A., Shaw, P., & Arkes, H. (1993). Hemodynamic assessment in managing the critically ill: Is physician confidence warranted? *Medical Decision Making, 13,* 258-266.
60. Bradley, J. V. (1981). Overconfidence in ignorant experts. *Bulletin of the Psychonomic Society, 17(2),* 82-84.
61. Bradley, J. V. (1981). Overconfidence in ignorant experts. *Bulletin of the Psychonomic Society, 17(2),* 84.
62. Werth, L., & Strack, F. (2003). An inferential approach to the knew-it-all-along phenomenon. *Memory, 11,* 411-419.
63. Werth, L., & Strack, F. (2003). An inferential approach to the knew-it-all-along phenomenon. *Memory, 11,* 411-419.
64. Werth, L., & Strack, F. (2003). An inferential approach to the knew-it-all-along phenomenon. *Memory, 11,* 411-419.
65. Werth, L., & Strack, F. (2003). An inferential approach to the knew-it-all-along phenomenon. *Memory, 11,* 411-419.
66. Werth, L., & Strack, F. (2003). An inferential approach to the knew-it-all-along phenomenon. *Memory, 11,* 411-419.
67. Werth, L., & Strack, F. (2003). An inferential approach to the knew-it-all-along phenomenon. *Memory, 11,* 411-419.
68. McKenzie, C. R. M., Liersch, M. J., & Yaniv, I. (2008). Overconfidence in interval estimates: What does expertise buy you? *Organizational Behavior and Human Decision Processes, 107,* 179-191.
69. Marks, M. A. Z., & Arkes, H. R. (2010). The effects of mental contamination on the hindsight bias: Source confusion determines

success in disregarding knowledge. *Journal of Behavioral Decision, 23*(2), 131-160.
70. Wilson, T. D., & Brekke, N. (1994). Mental contamination and mental correction: Unwanted influences on judgments and evaluations. *Psychological Bulletin, 116,* 117-142.
71. Marks, M. A. Z., & Arkes, H. R. (2010). The effects of mental contamination on the hindsight bias: Source confusion determines success in disregarding knowledge. *Journal of Behavioral Decision, 23*(2), 131-160.
72. Marks, M. A. Z., & Arkes, H. R. (2010). The effects of mental contamination on the hindsight bias: Source confusion determines success in disregarding knowledge. *Journal of Behavioral Decision, 23*(2), 131-160.
73. Guilbault, R. L., Bryant, F. B., Brockway, J. H., & Posavac, E. J. (2004). A meta-analysis of research on hindsight bias. *Basic and Applied Social Psychology, 26,* 103-117.

CHAPTER SEVEN

1. Ellsworth, P. (1989). Are twelve heads better than one? Law and Contemporary Problems, 52, 205-224.
2. Hans, V., & Appel, A. (1999). The jury on trial. In W. Abbott & J. Batt (Eds.), A handbook of jury research. Philadelphia, PA: The American Law Institute.
3. Casper, J., Benedict, K., & Perry, J. (1989). Juror decision making, attitudes, and the hindsight bias. Law and Human Behavior, 13, 291-310.
4. Ostrom, T., Saks, M., & Werner, C. (1978). An integration theory of analysis of jurors' presumptions of guilt or innocence. Journal of Personality and Social Psychology, 36(4), 436-450.
5. Packer, H. L. (1964). Two models of the criminal process. University of Pennsylvania Law Review, 113(1), 1-68.
6. Ellsworth, P. (1989). Are twelve heads better than one? Law and Contemporary Problems, 52, 205-224.
7. Holstein, J. (1985). Jurors' interpretations and jury decision making. Law and Human Behavior, 9(1), 83-100.
8. Holstein, J. (1985). Jurors' interpretations and jury decision making. Law and Human Behavior, 9(1), 83-100.
9. Holstein, J. (1985). Jurors' interpretations and jury decision making. Law and Human Behavior, 9(1), 83-100.
10. Kalven, H., & Zeisel, H. (1966). The American jury. Boston, MA: Little, Brown.
11. Kalven, H., & Zeisel, H. (1966). The American jury. Boston, MA: Little, Brown.
12. Caretta, T., & Moreland, R. (1983). The direct and indirect effects of inadmissable evidence. Journal of Applied Social Psychology, 13, 291-309.
13. Kerr, N., Niedermeier, K., & Kaplan, M. (1999). Bias in jurors vs. bias in juries: New evidence from the SDS perspective. Organizational Behavior and Human Performance, 80(1), 70-86.
14. Kerr, N., Niedermeier, K., & Kaplan, M. (1999). Bias in jurors vs. bias in juries: New evidence from the SDS perspective. Organizational Behavior and Human Performance, 80(1), 70-86.
15. Kerr, N., Niedermeier, K., & Kaplan, M. (1999). Bias in jurors vs. bias in juries: New evidence from the SDS perspective. Organizational Behavior and Human Performance, 80(1), 70-86.

16. Wrightsman, L., Greene, E., Nietzel, M., & Fortune, W. (2002). Psychology and the legal system (5th ed.). Belmont, CA: Wadsworth.
17. De la Fuente, L., De la Fuente, E., & Garcia, J. (2003). Effects of pretrial juror bias, strength of evidence and deliberation process on juror decisions: New validity evidence of the juror bias scale scores. Psychology, Crime & Law, 9(2), 197-209.
18. Kalven, H., & Zeisel, H. (1966). The American jury. Boston, MA: Little, Brown.
19. Kalven, H., & Zeisel, H. (1966). The American jury. Boston, MA: Little, Brown.
20. Kalven, H., & Zeisel, H. (1966). The American jury. Boston, MA: Little, Brown.
21. Kalven, H., & Zeisel, H. (1966). The American jury. Boston, MA: Little, Brown.
22. Kalven, H., & Zeisel, H. (1966). The American jury. Boston, MA: Little, Brown.
23. Kalven, H., & Zeisel, H. (1966). The American jury. Boston, MA: Little, Brown.
24. Visher, C. (1987). Juror decision making: The importance of evidence. Law and Human Behavior, 11(1), 1-17.
25. De la Fuente, L., De la Fuente, E., & Garcia, J. (2003). Effects of pretrial juror bias, strength of evidence and deliberation process on juror decisions: New validity evidence of the juror bias scale scores. Psychology, Crime & Law, 9(2), 197-209.
26. Narby, D., Cutler, B., & Moran, G. (1993). A meta-analysis of the association between authoritarianism on jurors' perceptions of defendant culpability. Journal of Applied Social Psychology, 78, 34-42.
27. Lieberman, J., & Sales, B. (2007). Scientific jury selection. Washington, DC: American Psychological Association.
28. Moran, G., Cutler, B., & Loftus, E. (1990). Jury selection in major controlled substance trials: The need for extended voir dire. Forensic Reports, 3, 331-348.
29. Vidmar, N., & Schuller, R. (1989). Juries and expert evidence: Social framework testimony. Law and Contemporary Problems, 52, 133-176.
30. Ajzen, I., & Fishbein, M. (2005). The influence of attitudes on behavior. In D. Albarracin, B. Johnson & M. Zanna (Eds.), The handbook of attitudes (pp. 173-221). Mahwah, NJ: Lawrence Erlbaum Associates.

31. Wicker, A. (1969). Attitudes versus actions: The relationship of verbal and overt behavioral responses to attitude objects. Journal of Social Issues, 25, 41-78.
32. Ajzen, I., & Fishbein, M. (2005). The influence of attitudes on behavior. In D. Albarracin, B. Johnson & M. Zanna (Eds.), The handbook of attitudes (pp. 173-221). Mahwah, NJ: Lawrence Erlbaum Associates.
33. Kraus, S. (1995). Attitudes and the prediction of behavior: A meta-analysis of the empirical literature. Personality and Social Psychology Bulletin, 21(1), 58-75.
34. Kaplan, M., & Kemmerick, G. (1974). Juror judgment as information integration: Combining evidential and nonevidential information. Journal of Personality and Social Psychology, 30, 493-499.
35. Kaplan, J., & Miller, L. (1978). Reducing the effects of juror bias. Journal of Personality and Social Psychology, 36(12), 1433-1455.
36. Ajzen, I., & Fishbein, M. (2005). The influence of attitudes on behavior. In D. Albarracin, B. Johnson & M. Zanna (Eds.), The handbook of attitudes (pp. 173-221). Mahwah, NJ: Lawrence Erlbaum Associates.
37. Rotter, J. (1966). Generalized expectancies for internal versus external control of reinforcement. Psychological Monographs, 80(609).
38. Phares, E., & Wilson, K. (1972). Responsibility attribution: Role of outcome severity, situational ambiguity, and internal-external control. Journal of Personality, 40, 392-406.
39. Lerner, M., & Simmons, C. (1966). Observer's reaction to the "innocent victim": Compassion or rejection? Journal of Personality and Social Psychology, 4, 203-210.
40. Moran, G., & Comfort, J. (1982). Scientific jury selection: Sex as a moderator of demographic and personality predictors of impaneled felony juror behavior. Journal of Personality and Social Psychology, 43, 1052-1063.
41. Summers, G., & Feldman, N. (1984). Blaming the victim versus blaming the perpetrator: An attribution analysis of spouse abuse. Journal of Social and Clinical Psychiatry, 2, 339-347.
42. Gerbasi, K., Zuckerman, M., & Reis, H. (1977). Justice needs a new blindfold: A review of mock jury research. Psychological Bulletin, 84, 323-345.
43. Adorno, T., Frenkel-Brunswik, E., Levinson, D., & Sanford, N. (1950). The authoritarian personality. New York: Harper.

44. Narby, D., Cutler, B., & Moran, G. (1993). A meta-analysis of the association between authoritarianism on jurors' perceptions of defendant culpability. Journal of Applied Social Psychology, 78, 34-42.
45. Narby, D., Cutler, B., & Moran, G. (1993). A meta-analysis of the association between authoritarianism on jurors' perceptions of defendant culpability. Journal of Applied Social Psychology, 78, 34-42.
46. Olsen-Fulero, L., & Fulero, S. (1997). Commonsense rape judgments: An empathy complexity theory of rape juror story making. Psychology, Public Policy, and the Law, 3, 402-427.
47. Garcia, L., & Griffitt, W. (1978). Authoritarianism-situation interactions in the determination of punitiveness: Engaging authoritarian ideology. Journal of Research in Personality, 12, 469-478.
48. Lieberman, J., & Sales, B. (2007). Scientific jury selection. Washington, DC: American Psychological Association.
49. Thompson, W., Cowan, C., Ellsworth, P., & Harrington, J. (1984). Death penalty attitudes and conviction proneness: The translation of attitudes into verdicts. Law and Human Behavior, 8(1/2), 95-114.
50. Witherspoon v. Illinois, 391 U.S. 510 1968.
51. Fitzgerald, R., & Ellsworth, P. (1984). Due process vs. crime control: Death qualification and jury attitudes. Law and Human Behavior, 8(1/2), 31-51.
52. Fitzgerald, R., & Ellsworth, P. (1984). Due process vs. crime control: Death qualification and jury attitudes. Law and Human Behavior, 8(1/2), 31-51.
53. Packer, H. L. (1968). The limits of the criminal sanction. Stanford, CA: Stanford University Press.
54. Packer, H. L. (1964). Two models of the criminal process. University of Pennsylvania Law Review, 113(1), 1-68.
55. Packer, H. L. (1964). Two models of the criminal process. University of Pennsylvania Law Review, 113(1), 1-68.
56. Packer, H. L. (1964). Two models of the criminal process. University of Pennsylvania Law Review, 113(1), 1-68.
57. Fitzgerald, R., & Ellsworth, P. (1984). Due process vs. crime control: Death qualification and jury attitudes. Law and Human Behavior, 8(1/2), 31-51.
58. Fitzgerald, R., & Ellsworth, P. (1984). Due process vs. crime control: Death qualification and jury attitudes. Law and Human Behavior, 8(1/2), 31-51.

59. Fitzgerald, R., & Ellsworth, P. (1984). Due process vs. crime control: Death qualification and jury attitudes. Law and Human Behavior, 8(1/2), 31-51.
60. Packer, H. L. (1964). Two models of the criminal process. University of Pennsylvania Law Review, 113(1), 1-68.
61. Fitzgerald, R., & Ellsworth, P. (1984). Due process vs. crime control: Death qualification and jury attitudes. Law and Human Behavior, 8(1/2), 31-51.
62. Liu, J., & Shure, G. (1993). Due process orientation does not always mean political liberalism. Law and Human Behavior, 17(3), 343-360.
63. Liu, J., & Shure, G. (1993). Due process orientation does not always mean political liberalism. Law and Human Behavior, 17(3), 343-360.
64. Fitzgerald, R., & Ellsworth, P. (1984). Due process vs. crime control: Death qualification and jury attitudes. Law and Human Behavior, 8(1/2), 31-51.
65. Liu, J., & Shure, G. (1993). Due process orientation does not always mean political liberalism. Law and Human Behavior, 17(3), 343-360.
66. Liu, J., & Shure, G. (1993). Due process orientation does not always mean political liberalism. Law and Human Behavior, 17(3), 343-360.
67. Packer, H. L. (1964). Two models of the criminal process. University of Pennsylvania Law Review, 113(1), 20.
68. Liu, J., & Shure, G. (1993). Due process orientation does not always mean political liberalism. Law and Human Behavior, 17(3), 343-360.
69. Casper, J., Benedict, K., & Perry, J. (1989). Juror decision making, attitudes, and the hindsight bias. Law and Human Behavior, 13, 291-310.
70. Packer, H. L. (1964). Two models of the criminal process. University of Pennsylvania Law Review, 113(1), 1-68.
71. Kerlinger, F. (1984). Liberalism and conservatism: The nature and structure of social attitudes. Hillsdale, NJ: Lawrence Erlbaum Associates.
72. Kerlinger, F. (1984). Liberalism and conservatism: The nature and structure of social attitudes. Hillsdale, NJ: Lawrence Erlbaum Associates.
73. Thompson, W., Cowan, C., Ellsworth, P., & Harrington, J. (1984). Death penalty attitudes and conviction proneness: The translation of attitudes into verdicts. Law and Human Behavior, 8(1/2), 95-114.

CHAPTER EIGHT

1. Ayres, I., & Siegelman, P. (1995). Race and gender discrimination in bargaining for a new car. *The American Economic Review, 85,* 304-321.
2. Eagly, A. H., & Carli, L. L. (2007). *Through the labyrinth: The truth about how women become leaders.* Boston: Harvard Business School Press.
3. Eagly, A. H., & Mladinic, A. (1989). Gender stereotypes and attitudes towards women and men. *Personality and Social Psychology Bulletin, 15,* 543-558.
4. Fazio, R. H., Jackson, J. R., Dunton, B. C., & Williams, C. J. (1995). Variability in automatic activation as an unobtrusive measure of racial attitudes: A bona fide pipeline? *Journal of Personality and Social Psychology, 69,* 1013-1028
5. Gallese, V., Keysers, C., & Rizzolatti, G. (2004). A unifying view of the basis of social cognition. *Trends in Cognitive Sciences, 8,* 396-403.
6. Jackman, M. R. (1994). *The velvet glove: Paternalism and conflict in gender, class, and race relations.* Berkeley and Los Angeles: University of California Press.
7. Healey, J. F. (2009). *Race, Ethnicity, Gender, and Class.* Thousand Oaks, CA: Pine Forge Press.
8. Eagly, A. H., & Koenig, A. M. (2008). Gender prejudice: On the risks of occupying incongruent roles. In E. Borgida & S. T. Fiske (Eds.), *Beyond common sense: Psychological science in the courtroom* (pp. 63-81). Malden, MA: Blackwell.
9. Bayard, K., Hellerstein, J., Neumark, D., & Troske, K. (2003). New evidence on sex segregation and sex differences in wages from matched employee-employer data. *Journal of Labor Economics, 21,* 887-922.
10. Ilies, R., Hauserman, N., Schwochau, S., & Stibal, J. (2003). Reported incidence rates of work-related sexual harassment in the United States: Using meta-analysis to explain reported rate disparities. *Personnel Psychology, 56,* 607-651.
11. Kolbert, E. (1991). Sexual harassment at work is pervasive. *New York Times, October 10,* A1, A17.
12. Tosi. H., & Einbender, S. (1985). The effects of the type and amount of information in sex discrimination: A meta-analysis. *Academy of Management Journal, 28,* 712-723.

13. Copus, D. (2005). A lawyer's view: Avoiding junk science. In Landy, F.(Ed.), *Employment Discrimination Litigation: Behavioral, Quantitative, and Legal Perspectives.* Jossey-Bass, San Francisco, 450-462.
14. Heilman, M. E., Wallen, A.S., Fuchs, D., & Tamkins, M.M. (2004). Penalties for Success: Reactions to Women Who Succeed at Male Gender-Typed Tasks. *Journal of Applied Psychology, 89,* 416-427.
15. Greenwald, A. G., Pickrell, J. E., & Farnham, S. D., (2002). Implicit partisanship: Taking sides for no reason. *Journal of Personality and Social Psychology, 83,* 367-379.
16. Shiffrin, R. M., & Schneider, W. (1977). Controlled and automatic human information processing: II. Perceptual learning, automatic attending and a general theory. *Psychological Review, 84,* 127-190.
17. Greenwald, A. G., McGhee, D. E., & Schwartz, L. K. (1998). Measuring individual differences in implicit cognition: The implicit association task. *Journal of Personality and Social Psychology, 74,* 1464-1480.
18. Rudman, L. A., & Glick, P. (1999). Feminized management and backlash towards agentic women: The hidden costs to women of a kinder, gentler image of middle managers. *Journal of Personality and Social Psychology, 77,* 1004-1010.
19. Greenwald, A. G., Pickrell, J. E., & Farnham, S. D., (2002). Implicit partisanship: Taking sides for no reason. *Journal of Personality and Social Psychology, 83,* 367-379.
20. Greenwald, A. G., McGhee, D. E., & Schwartz, L. K. (1998). Measuring individual differences in implicit cognition: The implicit association task. *Journal of Personality and Social Psychology, 74,* 1464-1480.
21. Eagly, A. H., & Karau, S. J. (2002). Role congruity theory of prejudice towards female leaders. *Psychological Review, 109,* 573-598.
22. Landy, F. (2008). Stereotypes, bias and personnel decisions: Strange and stranger. *Industrial and Organizational Psychology: Perspectives on Science and Practice, 1,* 379-392.
23. Copus, D. (2005). A lawyer's view: Avoiding junk science. In Landy, F.(Ed.), *Employment Discrimination Litigation: Behavioral, Quantitative, and Legal Perspectives.* Jossey-Bass, San Francisco, 450-462.

24. Landy, F. (2008). Stereotypes, bias and personnel decisions: Strange and stranger. *Industrial and Organizational Psychology: Perspectives on Science and Practice, 1,* 379-392.
25. Hilton, J. L., & Hippel, W. V. (1996). Stereotypes. *Annual Review of Psychology, 47,* 237-271.
26. Merton, R. (1948). The self-fulfilling prophecies. *Antioch Review, 8,* 193-210.
27. Deaux, K., & Major, B. (1987). Putting gender into context: An interactive model of gender-related behavior. *Psychological Review, 94,* 369-389.
28. Fiske, S. T., & Depret, E. (1996). Control, interdependence and power: Understanding social cognition in its social context. In W. Stroebe & M. Hewstone (Eds.) *European Review of social psychology* (Vl. 7, pp. 31-61). New York: Wiley.
29. Merton, R. (1948). The self-fulfilling prophecies. *Antioch Review, 8,* 193-210.
30. Nosek, B. A., & Banaji, M. R. (2001). The go/no-go association task. *Social Cognition, 19,* 625-666.
31. Schmader, T., Johns, M., & Barquissau, M. (2004). The cost of accepting gender differences: The role of stereotype endorsement in women's experience in the math domain. *Sex Roles: A Journal of Research 50,* 835-851.
32. Oswald, D. L., & Harvey, R. D. (2000). Hostile environments, stereotype threat, and math performance among undergraduate women. *Current Psychology 19,* 338-352.
33. Fraizer, P., Cochran, C., & Olson, A. (1995). Social science research on lay definitions of sexual harassment. *Journal of Social Issues, 51,* 21-38.
34. Oswald, D. L., & Harvey, R. D. (2000). Hostile environments, stereotype threat, and math performance among undergraduate women. *Current Psychology 19,* 338-352.
35. Walton, G. M., & Cohen, G. L. (2003). Stereotype Lift. *Journal of Experimental Social Psychology, 39,* 456-46.
36. Steele, C. M. (1997). A threat in the air: How stereotypes shape intellectual identity and performance. *American Psychologist, 52,* 613-629.
37. Steele, C. M., & Aronson, J. (1995). Stereotype threat and the intellectual test performance of African Americans. *Journal of Personality and Social Psychology, 69,* 797-811.

38. Katz, J., Joiner, T. E., & Kwon, P. (2002). Membership in a devalued social group and emotional well-being: Developing a model of personal self-esteem, collective self-esteem, and group socialization. *Sex Roles: A Journal of Research*, 419-432.
39. Lockwood, P. (2002). Could it happen to you? Predicting the impact of downward comparisons on the self. *Journal of Personality and Social Psychology, 82*, 343-358.
40. Luhtanen, R., & Crocker, J. (1992). A collective self-esteem scale: Self-evaluation of one's social identity. *Personality and Social Psychology Bulletin, 18*, 302-318.
41. Katz, J., Joiner, T. E., & Kwon, P. (2002). Membership in a devalued social group and emotional well-being: Developing a model of personal self-esteem, collective self-esteem, and group socialization. *Sex Roles: A Journal of Research*, 419-432.
42. Katz, J., Joiner, T. E., & Kwon, P. (2002). Membership in a devalued social group and emotional well-being: Developing a model of personal self-esteem, collective self-esteem, and group socialization. *Sex Roles: A Journal of Research*, 419-432.
43. Trafimow, D., Armendariz, M. L., & Madson, L. (2004). A test of whether attributions provide for self-enhancement or self-defense. *The Journal of Social Psychology, 144*, 453-464.
44. Swann, W. B., Jr. (1983). Self-verification: Bringing social reality into harmony with the self. In J. Suls & A. G. Greenwald (Eds.), *Social psychological perspectives on the self* (pp. 33-66). Hillsdale, NJ: Erlbaum.
45. Swann, W. B., & Ely, R. J. (1984). A battle of wills: Self-verification verses behavioral confirmation. *Journal of Personaility and Social Psychology, 46*, 1287-1302.
46. Higgins, E. T. (1987). Self-discrepancy: A theory relating self and affect. *Psychological Review, 94*, 319-340.
47. Madon, S., Smith, A., Jussim, L., Russell, D. W., Eccles, J., Palumbo, P., & Walkiewicz, M. (2001). Am I as you see me or do you see me as I am? Self-fulfilling prophecies and self-verification. *Personality and Social Psychology Bulletin, 27*, 1214-1224.
48. Ditto, P. H., & Griffin, J. (1993). The value of uniqueness: Self-evaluation and the perceived prevalence of valenced characteristics. *Journal of Social Behavior and Personality, 8*, 221-240.
49. Crocker, J., & Major, B. (1989). Social Stigma and self-esteem: The self-protective properties of stigma. *Psychology Review, 96*, 608-630.

50. Blanton, H., Crocker, J., & Miller, D. T. (2000). The effects of in-group versus outgroup social comparison on self-esteem in the context of a negative stereotype. *Journal of Experimental Social Psychology, 36,* 519-530.
51. Lockwood, P. (2002). Could it happen to you? Predicting the impact of downward comparisons on the self. *Journal of Personality and Social Psychology, 82,* 343-358.
52. Lockwood, P. (2002). Could it happen to you? Predicting the impact of downward comparisons on the self. *Journal of Personality and Social Psychology, 82,* 343-358.
53. Martinot, D., Redersdorff, S., Guimond, S., & Dif, S. (2002). Ingroup versus outgroup comparisons and self-esteem: The role of group status and ingroup identification. *Personality and Social Psychology Bulletin, 28,* 1586-1600.
54. Martinot, D., Redersdorff, S., Guimond, S., & Dif, S. (2002). Ingroup versus outgroup comparisons and self-esteem: The role of group status and ingroup identification. *Personality and Social Psychology Bulletin, 28,* 1586-1600.
55. Buunk, B., Collins, R., Taylor, S., Dakof, G., & Yperen, N. (1990). The affective consequences of social comparison: Either direction has its ups and downs. *Journal of Personality and Social Psychology, 59,* 1238-1249.
56. Buunk, B., Collins, R., Taylor, S., Dakof, G., & Yperen, N. (1990). The affective consequences of social comparison: Either direction has its ups and downs. *Journal of Personality and Social Psychology, 59,* 1238-1249.
57. Rudman, L. A., & Glick, P. (2001). Prescriptive gender stereotypes and backlash towards agentic women. *Journal of Social Issues, 57,* 743-762.
58. Steele, C. M. (1997). A threat in the air: How stereotypes shape intellectual identity and performance. *American Psychologist, 52,* 613-629.
59. Sudman, S., & Bradburn, N. M. (1982). *Asking Questions.* San Francisco, CA: Jossey-Bass.
60. Greenwald, A. G., McGhee, D. E., & Schwartz, L. K. (1998). Measuring individual differences in implicit cognition: The implicit association task. *Journal of Personality and Social Psychology, 74,* 1464-1480.
61. Greenwald, A. G., Nosek, B. A., & Banaji, M. R., (2003). Understanding and using the implicit association test: I. an improved

scoring algorithm. *Journal of Personality and Social Psychology, 85,* 197-216.
62. Shiffrin, R. M., & Schneider, W. (1977). Controlled and automatic human information processing: II. Perceptual learning, automatic attending and a general theory. *Psychological Review, 84,* 127-190.
63. Shiffrin, R. M., & Schneider, W. (1977). Controlled and automatic human information processing: II. Perceptual learning, automatic attending and a general theory. *Psychological Review, 84,* 127-190.
64. Shiffrin, R. M., & Schneider, W. (1977). Controlled and automatic human information processing: II. Perceptual learning, automatic attending and a general theory. *Psychological Review, 84,* 127-190.
65. Stroop, J. R. (1935). Studies of interference in serial verbal reaction. *Journal of Experimental Psychology, 18,* 643-662.
66. Bargh, J. A. (1999). The cognitive monster: The case against the controllability of automatic stereotype effects. In S. Chaiken & Y. Trope (Eds.), *Dual-process theories in social psychology* (pp. 361-382). New York: Guilford Press.
67. Reisberg, R. (2001). *Cognition: Exploring the science of the mind.* New York: W. W. Norton & Company.
68. Shiffrin, R. M., & Schneider, W. (1984). Automatic and controlled processes revisited. *Psychological Review, 91,* 269-276.
69. Goldstein, E. B. (2005). *Cognitive Psychology: Connecting mind, research, and everyday experience. Belmont.* CA: Thomson Wadsworth.
70. Nosek, B. A., Greenwald, A. G., & Banaji, M. R. (2005). Understanding and using the implicit association test: II. Method variables and construct validity. *Personality and Social Psychology Bulletin, 31,* 166-180.
71. Goldstein, E. B. (2005). *Cognitive Psychology: Connecting mind, research, and everyday experience. Belmont.* CA: Thomson Wadsworth.
72. Nosek, B. A., Greenwald, A. G., & Banaji, M. R. (2005). Understanding and using the implicit association test: II. Method variables and construct validity. *Personality and Social Psychology Bulletin, 31,* 166-180.
73. Banaji, M. R., & Greenwald, A. G. (1995). Implicit gender stereotyping in judgments of fame. *Journal of Personality and Social Psychology, 68,* 181-198.
74. Davison, H. K., & Burke, M. J. (2000). Sex discrimination in simulated employment contexts: A meta-analytic investigation. *Journal of Vocational Behavior, 56,* 225-248.

75. Davison, H. K., & Burke, M. J. (2000). Sex discrimination in simulated employment contexts: A meta-analytic investigation. *Journal of Vocational Behavior, 56,* 225-248.
76. Davison, H. K., & Burke, M. J. (2000). Sex discrimination in simulated employment contexts: A meta-analytic investigation. *Journal of Vocational Behavior, 56,* 225-248.
77. Eagly, A. H., & Karau, S. J. (2002). Role congruity theory of prejudice towards female leaders. *Psychological Review, 109,* 573-598.
78. Fiske, S. T., & Stevens, L. E. (1993). What's so special about sex? Gender stereotyping and discrimination. In S. Oskamp & M. Costanzo (Eds.), *Gender issues in contemporary society: Applied social psychology annual* (pp. 173-196). Newbury Park, CA: Sage.
79. Schein, V. E., & Mueller, R. (1992). Sex-role stereotyping and requisite management characteristics: A cross cultural look. *Journal of Organizational Behavior, 13,* 439-447.
80. Schein, V. E., & Mueller, R. (1992). Sex-role stereotyping and requisite management characteristics: A cross cultural look. *Journal of Organizational Behavior, 13,* 439-447.
81. Schien, V. E., Mueller, R., Lituchy, T., & Liu, J. (1996). Think manager-think male: A global phenomenon? *Journal of Organizational Behavior, 17,* 33-41.
82. Duehr, E. E., & Bono, J. E. (2006). Men, women, and managers: Are stereotypes finally changing? *Personnel Psychology, 59,* 815-846.
83. Eagly, A. H., & Karau, S. J. (2002). Role congruity theory of prejudice towards female leaders. *Psychological Review, 109,* 573-598.
84. Eagly, A. H., & Karau, S. J. (2002). Role congruity theory of prejudice towards female leaders. *Psychological Review, 109,* 573-598.
85. Eagly, A. H., & Karau, S. J. (2002). Role congruity theory of prejudice towards female leaders. *Psychological Review, 109,* 573-598.
86. Eagly, A. H., & Mitchell, A. A. (2004). Social role theory of sex differences and similarities: Implications for the sociopolitical attitudes of women and men, In M. Paludi (Ed.), *The psychology of gender* (pp. 183-206).
87. Rudman, L. A., & Glick, P. (1999). Feminized management and backlash towards agentic women: The hidden costs to women of a kinder, gentler image of middle managers. *Journal of Personality and Social Psychology, 77,* 1004-1010.
88. Rudman, L. A., & Glick, P. (1999). Feminized management and backlash towards agentic women: The hidden costs to women of a

kinder, gentler image of middle managers. *Journal of Personality and Social Psychology, 77,* 1004-1010.
89. Eagly, A. H., & Koenig, A. M. (2008). Gender prejudice: On the risks of occupying incongruent roles. In E. Borgida & S. T. Fiske (Eds.), *Beyond common sense: Psychological science in the courtroom* (pp. 63-81). Malden, MA: Blackwell.
90. Heilman, M. E. (1983). Sex bias in work settings: The lack of fit model. *Research in Organizational Behavior, 5,* 269-298.
91. Heilman, M. E. & Haynes, M. C. (2008). Subjectivity in the appraisal process: A facilitator of gender bias in work settings. In E. Borgida & S. T. Fiske (Eds.), *Beyond common sense: Psychological science in the courtroom* (pp. 63-81). Malden, MA: Blackwell.
92. Eagly, A. H., & Koenig, A. M. (2008). Gender prejudice: On the risks of occupying incongruent roles. In E. Borgida & S. T. Fiske (Eds.), *Beyond common sense: Psychological science in the courtroom* (pp. 63-81). Malden, MA: Blackwell.
93. Burgess, D., & Borgida, E. (1999). Who women are, who women should be: Descriptive and prescriptive gender stereotyping in sex discrimination. *Psychology, Public Policy, and Law, 5,* 665-692.
94. Eagly, A. H., & Koenig, A. M. (2008). Gender prejudice: On the risks of occupying incongruent roles. In E. Borgida & S. T. Fiske (Eds.), *Beyond common sense: Psychological science in the courtroom* (pp. 63-81). Malden, MA: Blackwell.
95. Davison, H. K., & Burke, M. J. (2000). Sex discrimination in simulated employment contexts: A meta-analytic investigation. *Journal of Vocational Behavior, 56,* 225-248.
96. Neumark, D., Bank, R. J., & Van Nort, K. D. (1996). Sex discrimination in restaurant hiring: An audit study. *Quarterly Journal of Economics, 111,* 915-941.
97. Glick, P., & Fiske, S. T. (1996). The ambivalent sexism inventory: Differentiating hostile and benevolent sexism. *Journal of Personality and Social Psychology, 70,* 491-512.
98. Glick, P., & Fiske, S. T. (1996). The ambivalent sexism inventory: Differentiating hostile and benevolent sexism. *Journal of Personality and Social Psychology, 70,* 491-512.
99. Glick, P., Fiske, S. T., Mladinic, A., Saiz, J. L., Abrams, D. & Masser, B. (2000) Beyond prejudice as simple antipathy: Hostile and benevolent sexism across cultures. *Journal of Personality and Social Psychology, 79,* 763-75.

100. Carli, L. L., LaFleur, S., & Loeber, C. C. (1995). Nonverbal behavior, gender, and influence. *Journal of Personality and Social Psychology, 68,* 1030-1041.
101. Rudman, L. A. (1998). Self-promotion as a risk factor for women: The cost and benefits of counter-stereotypical impression management. *Journal of Personality and Social Psychology, 74,* 629-645.
102. Rudman, L. A., & Glick, P. (2001). Prescriptive gender stereotypes and backlash towards agentic women. *Journal of Social Issues, 57,* 743-762.
103. Wiley, M. G., & Eskilson, A. (1985). Speech style, gender stereotypes, and corporate success: What of women talk more like men? *Sex Roles, 12,* 993-1007.
104. Rudman, L. A., & Glick, P. (2001). Prescriptive gender stereotypes and backlash towards agentic women. *Journal of Social Issues, 57,* 743-762.
105. Jackman, M. R. (1994). *The velvet glove: Paternalism and conflict in gender, class, and race relations.* Berkeley and Los Angeles: University of California Press.
106. Glick, P., & Fiske, S. T. (1996). The ambivalent sexism inventory: Differentiating hostile and benevolent sexism. *Journal of Personality and Social Psychology, 70,* 491-512.
107. Spence, J. T. & Bucker, C. E. (2000). Instrumental and expressive traits, trait stereotypes, and sexist attitudes: What do they signify? *Psychology of Women Quarterly, 24,* 44-62.
108. Eagly, A. H., & Makhijani, M. G., & Klonsky, B. G. (1992). Gender and the evaluation of leaders: A meta-analysis. *Psychological Bulletin, 111,* 3-22.
109. Eagly, A. H., & Mladinic, A. (1989). Gender stereotypes and attitudes towards women and men. *Personality and Social Psychology Bulletin, 15,* 543-558.
110. Glick, P., & Fiske, S. T. (1996). The ambivalent sexism inventory: Differentiating hostile and benevolent sexism. *Journal of Personality and Social Psychology, 70,* 491-512.
111. Rudman, L. A. (1998). Self-promotion as a risk factor for women: The cost and benefits of counter-stereotypical impression management. *Journal of Personality and Social Psychology, 74,* 629-645.
112. Rudman, L. A., & Kilianski, S. E. (2000). Implicit and explicit attitudes toward female authority. *Personality and Social Psychology Bulletin, 26,* 1315-1328.

113. Glick, P., & Fiske, S. T. (1996). The ambivalent sexism inventory: Differentiating hostile and benevolent sexism. *Journal of Personality and Social Psychology, 70,* 491-512.

114. Rudman, L. A., & Kilianski, S. E. (2000). Implicit and explicit attitudes toward female authority. *Personality and Social Psychology Bulletin, 26,* 1315-1328.

115. Diekman, A. B., & Eagly, A. H. (2000). Stereotypes as dynamic constructs: Women and men of the past, present, and future. *Personality and Social Psychology Bulletin, 26,* 1171-1181.

116. Twenge, J. M. (2001). Changes in women's assertiveness response to status and roles: A cross-temporal meta-analysis, 1931-1993. *Journal of Personality and Social Psychology, 81,* 133-145.

117. Offerman, L. R., & Leibold, J. M. (1990). Organizations of the future: Changes and challenges. *American psychologist, 45,* 95-108.

118. Bass, B. M., Avolio, B. J., & Atwater, L (2008). The transformational and transactional leadership of men and women. *Applied Psychology, 45,* 5-34.

119. Eagly, A. H., & Carli, L. L. (2007). *Through the labyrinth: The truth about how women become leaders.* Boston: Harvard Business School Press.

120. Phelan, J. E., Moss-Racusin, C. A., & Rudman, L. A. (2008). Competent yet out in the cold: Shifting criteria for hiring reflect backlash towards agentic women. *Psychology of Women Quarterly, 32,* 406-413.

121. Phelan, J. E., Moss-Racusin, C. A., & Rudman, L. A. (2008). Competent yet out in the cold: Shifting criteria for hiring reflect backlash towards agentic women. *Psychology of Women Quarterly, 32,* 406-413.

122. Glick, P., & Fiske, S. T. (1996). The ambivalent sexism inventory: Differentiating hostile and benevolent sexism. *Journal of Personality and Social Psychology, 70,* 491-512.

123. Diekman, A. B., & Eagly, A. H. (2000). Stereotypes as dynamic constructs: Women and men of the past, present, and future. *Personality and Social Psychology Bulletin,26,* 1171-1181.

124. Diekman, A. B., & Eagly, A. H. (2000). Stereotypes as dynamic constructs: Women and men of the past, present, and future. *Personality and Social Psychology Bulletin,26,* 1171-1181

125. Schriesheim, C.A., Cogliser, C. C., Neider, L. L., Fleishman, E. A., & James, L. (1998). The Ohio State model. In F. Dansereau & F.

J. Yammarino (Eds.), *Leadership—The multiple-level approaches: Classical and new wave* (Monographs in Organizational Behavior and Industrial Relations, Vol. 24, pp. 3-71). Stamford, CT: JAI Press.
126. Schriesheim, C.A., Cogliser, C. C., Neider, L. L., Fleishman, E. A., & James, L. (1998). The Ohio State model. In F. Dansereau & F. J. Yammarino (Eds.), *Leadership—The multiple-level approaches: Classical and new wave* (Monographs in Organizational Behavior and Industrial Relations, Vol. 24, pp. 3-71). Stamford, CT: JAI Press.
127. Schriesheim, C.A., Cogliser, C. C., Neider, L. L., Fleishman, E. A., & James, L. (1998). The Ohio State model. In F. Dansereau & F. J. Yammarino (Eds.), *Leadership—The multiple-level approaches: Classical and new wave* (Monographs in Organizational Behavior and Industrial Relations, Vol. 24, pp. 3-71). Stamford, CT: JAI Press.
128. Scesny, S. (2003). A closer look beneath the surface: Various facets of the think manager-think-male stereotype. *Sex Roles, 49,* 353-363.
129. O'Shea, P. G., & Bush, D. F. (2002). Negotiation for starting salary: Antecedents and outcomes among recent college graduates. *Journal of Business and Psychology, 16,* 365-383.
130. Kray, L. J., & Thompson, L. (2005). Gender stereotypes and negotiation performance: A review of theory and research. In B. M. Staw & R. Kramer (Eds.), *Research in organizational behavior series* (Vol. 26, pp. 103-182). Greenwich, CT: JAI Press.
131. Stuhlmacher, A. F., & Walters, A. E. (1999). Gender differences in negotiation outcome: A meta-analysis. *Personnel Psychology, 52,* 653-677.
132. Nash, J. (1950). The bargaining problem. *Econometrica, 18,* 155-162.
133. Kray, L. J., & Thompson, L. (2005). Gender stereotypes and negotiation performance: A review of theory and research. In B. M. Staw & R. Kramer (Eds.), *Research in organizational behavior series* (Vol. 26, pp. 103-182). Greenwich, CT: JAI Press.
134. Andreoni, J., & Vesterlund, L. (2001). Which is the fairer sex? Gender differences in altruism. *Quarterly Journal of Economics, 116,* 293-312.
135. Buchan, N. R., Croson, R. T. A., & Solnick, S. (2008). Trust and gender: An examination of behavior and beliefs in the investment game. *Journal of Economic Behavior & Organizations, 68,* 466-476.
136. Kray, L. J., Galinsky, A., & Thompson, L. (2002). Reversing the gender gap in negotiation: An exploration of stereotype regeneration.

Organization Behavior and Human Decision-making Processes, 87, 386-409.
137. Kray, L. J., Thompson, L., & Galinsky, A. (2001). Battle of the sexes: Gender stereotype confirmation and reactance in negotiations. *Journal of Personality and Social Psychology, 80,* 942-958.
138. Small, D. A., Gelfand, M., Babcock, L., & Gettman, H. (2007). Who goes to the bargaining table? The influence of gender and framing on the initiation of negotiation. *Journal of Personality and Social Psychology, 93,* 600-613.
139. Stuhlmacher, A. F., Citera, M., & Willis, T. (2007). Gender differences in virtual negotiation: Theory and research. *Sex Roles, 57,* 329-339.
140. Stevens, C. K., Bavetta, A. G., & Gist, M. E. (1993). Gender differences in the acquisition of salary negotiation skills: The role of goals, self-efficacy, and perceived control. *Journal of Applied Psychology, 78,* 723-735.
141. Stuhlmacher, A. F., Citera, M., & Willis, T. (2007). Gender differences in virtual negotiation: Theory and research. *Sex Roles, 57,* 329-339.
142. Stevens, C. K., Bavetta, A. G., & Gist, M. E. (1993). Gender differences in the acquisition of salary negotiation skills: The role of goals, self-efficacy, and perceived control. *Journal of Applied Psychology, 78,* 723-735.
143. Babcock, L., Gelfand, M., Small, D., & Stayn, H. (2006). Gender differences in the propensity to initiate negotiations. *Social Psychology and Economics, 39,* 239-259.
144. Kray, L. J., & Thompson, L. (2005). Gender stereotypes and negotiation performance: A review of theory and research. In B. M. Staw & R. Kramer (Eds.), *Research in organizational behavior series* (Vol. 26, pp. 103-182). Greenwich, CT: JAI Press.
145. Guadagno, R. E., & Cialdini, R. B. (2007). Gender differences in impression management in organizations: A qualitative review. *Sex Roles, 56,* 483-494.
146. Eagly, A. H., & Karau, S. J. (2002). Role congruity theory of prejudice towards female leaders. *Psychological Review, 109,* 573-598.
147. Bowles, H. R., Babcock, L., & Lai, L. (2007). Social incentives for gender differences in the propensity to initiate negotiation: Sometimes it does hurt to ask. *Organizational Behavior and Human Decision Processes, 103,* 84-101
148. Copus, D. (2005). A lawyer's view: Avoiding junk science. In Landy, F.(Ed.), *Employment Discrimination Litigation: Behavioral,*

Quantitative, and Legal Perspectives. Jossey-Bass, San Francisco, 450-462.

149. Copus, D. (2005). A lawyer's view: Avoiding junk science. In Landy, F.(Ed.), *Employment Discrimination Litigation: Behavioral, Quantitative, and Legal Perspectives.* Jossey-Bass, San Francisco, 450-462.

150. Landy, F. (2008). Stereotypes, bias and personnel decisions: Strange and stranger. *Industrial and Organizational Psychology: Perspectives on Science and Practice, 1,* 379-392.

151. Copus, D. (2005). A lawyer's view: Avoiding junk science. In Landy, F.(Ed.), *Employment Discrimination Litigation: Behavioral, Quantitative, and Legal Perspectives.* Jossey-Bass, San Francisco, 450-462.

152. Fiske, S. T., Bersoff, D. N., Borgida, E., Deaux, K., & Heilman, M. E. (1991). Social Science research on trial. *American Psychologist, 46,* 1049-1060.

153. Landy, F. (2008). Stereotypes, bias and personnel decisions: Strange and stranger. *Industrial and Organizational Psychology: Perspectives on Science and Practice, 1,* 379-392.

154. Landy, F. (2008). Stereotypes, bias and personnel decisions: Strange and stranger. *Industrial and Organizational Psychology: Perspectives on Science and Practice, 1,* 379-392.

155. Lyness, K. S., & Heilman, M. E. (2006). When fit is fundamental: Performance evaluations and promotions of upper-level female and male managers. *Journal of Applied Psychology, 91,* 777-785.

156. Martell, R. F., Lane, D. M., & Emrich, C. G. (1996). Male-female differences: A computer simulation. *American Psychologist, 51,* 157-158.

157. Nelson, D. L., & Campbell Q. J. (2009). *Organizational Behavior.* Mason, OH: South-Western Cengage Learning.

158. Eagly, A. H., & Carli, L. L. (2007). *Through the labyrinth: The truth about how women become leaders.* Boston: Harvard Business School Press.

159. Eagly, A. H., & Carli, L. L. (2007). *Through the labyrinth: The truth about how women become leaders.* Boston: Harvard Business School Press.

160. Ryan, M. K., & Haslam, S. A. (2005). The glass cliff: Evidence that women are overrepresented in precarious leadership positions. *British Journal of Management, 16,* 81-90.

161. Fiske, S. T., & Neuberg, S. L. (1990). A continuum of impression formation, from category-based to individuating processes: Influences of information and motivation on attention and interpretation. In M. P. Zanua (Ed.), *Advances in experimental social Psychology* (Vol. 23, pp. 1-74). San Diego, CA: Academic Press.
162. Landy, F. (2008). Stereotypes, bias and personnel decisions: Strange and stranger. *Industrial and Organizational Psychology: Perspectives on Science and Practice, 1,* 379-392.
163. Kunda, Z., & Thagard, P. (1996). Forming impressions from stereotypes, traits, and behaviors: A parallel-constraint-satisfaction theory. *Psychological Review 102,* 284-308.
164. Landy, F. (2008). Stereotypes, bias and personnel decisions: Strange and stranger. *Industrial and Organizational Psychology: Perspectives on Science and Practice, 1,* 379-392.
165. Fiske, S. T., Bersoff, D. N., Borgida, E., Deaux, K., & Heilman, M. E. (1991). Social Science research on trial. *American Psychologist, 46,* 1049-1060.
166. Hunt, J.S., Borgida, E., Kelly, K.A., & Burgess, D. (2002). Gender stereotyping: Scientific status. In D. Faigman, D.H. Kaye, M.J. Saks, & J. Sanders (Eds.), *Modern scientific evidence: The law and science of expert testimony.* (pp.374-426). St. Paul, MN: West Publishing Co.
167. Welle, B., & Heilman, M. E. (2005). Formal and informal discrimination against women at work. In D. Steiner, S. W. Gilliland, & D. Skarlicki (Eds.) *Research in social issues in management: Managing Social and Ethical Issues in Organizations* (pp. 24-39). Westport, CT: Information Age Publishing.
168. Borgida, E., Hunt, C., & Kim, A. (2005). On the use of gender stereotyping research in sex discrimination litigation. *Journal of Law and Policy, 13,* 613-628.
169. Swim, J., Borgida, E., Maruyama, G., & Myers, D. (1989). McKay vs. McKay: Is there a case for gender biased evaluations? *Psychological Bulletin, 105,* 409-429.
170. Wason, P. C. (1960). On the failure to eliminate hypotheses in a conceptual task. *Quarterly Journal of Experimental Psychology, 12,* 129-140.
171. Marks, M. J., & Fraley, R. C. (2006). Confirmation bias and the sexual double standard. *Sex Roles, 54,* 19-26.
172. Milhausen, R. R., & Herold, E. S. (2001). Reconceptualizing the sexual double standard. *Journal of Psychology and Human Sexuality, 13,* 63-83.

173. Marks, M. J., & Fraley, R. C. (2006). Confirmation bias and the sexual double standard. *Sex Roles, 54,* 19-26.
174. Cook, M. B., & Smallman, H. S. (2008). Human factors of the confirmation bias in intelligence analysis: Decision support from graphical evidence landscapes. *Human Factors: The Journal of the Human Factors and Ergonomics Society, 50,* 745-754.
175. Olivetti, C., & Petrongolo, B. (2008) Unequal pay or unequal employment? A cross country analysis of gender gaps. *Journal of Labor Economics 26,* 621-654.
176. Adams, S. M., Gupta, A., Haughton, D. M., & Leeth, J. D. (2008). Gender differences in CEO compensation: Evidence from the USA. *Women in Management Review, 22,* 208-224.
177. Jones, A. S., & Frick, K. D. (2008). Gender bias in economic evaluation methods time costs and productivity loss. *Women's Health Issues, 18,* 1-3.
178. Jones, A. S., & Frick, K. D. (2008). Gender bias in economic evaluation methods time costs and productivity loss. *Women's Health Issues, 18,* 1-3.
179. Eagly, A. H., & Karau, S. J. (2002). Role congruity theory of prejudice towards female leaders. *Psychological Review, 109,* 573-598.
180. Gill, M. J. (2004). When information does not deter stereotyping: Prescriptive stereotyping can foster bias under conditions that deter description stereotyping. *Journal of Experimental Social Psychology, 40,* 619-632.
181. Heilman, M. E., Wallen, A.S., Fuchs, D., & Tamkins, M.M. (2004). Penalties for Success: Reactions to Women Who Succeed at Male Gender-Typed Tasks. *Journal of Applied Psychology, 89,* 416-427.

CHAPTER NINE

1. Gray, J. (1992). *Men are from Mars, Women are from Venus: A practical guide for improving communication and getting what you want in your relationships.* New York: HarperCollins.
2. Gray, J. (2006). About John Gray: Men are from Mars, women are from Venus [web site]. MarsVenus.com: http://www.marsvenus.com/JohnGrayProfile.php. [accessed March 2006, April 2007].
3. Tannen, D. (1990). *You just don't understand: Women and men in conversation.* New York: William Morrow & Co.
4. Baron-Cohen, S. (2003). *The essential difference: The truth about the male and female brain.* New York: Perseus Books Group.
5. Becker, R. (Writer). (1991). *Defending the caveman* [Broadway play]. United States: Theater Mogul NA, Inc.
6. Epinions (2000). Epinions.com—Defending the caveman [web site]. Shopping.com, Inc.: *http://www.epinions.com/trvl-review-201D-4562E89D-3A4BAE9C-prod3.*
7. Seidman, S. A. (1992). An investigation of sex-role stereotyping in music videos. *Journal of Broadcasting and Electronic Media, 36*(2), 209-216.
8. Billings, A. C., Angelini, J. R., & Eastman, S. T. (2005). Diverging discourses: Gender d Thompson, T. L., & Zerbinos, E. (1995). Gender roles in animated cartoons: Has the picture changed in 20 years? *Sex Roles, 32,* 651-673.
9. Thompson, T. L., & Zerbinos, E. (1995). Gender roles in animated cartoons: Has the picture changed in 20 years? *Sex Roles, 32,* 651-673.
10. Dundes, L. (2001). Disney's modern heroine Pocahontas: Revealing age-old gender stereotypes and role discontinuity under a façade of liberation. *The Social Science Journal, 38*(3), 353-365.
11. Canary, D. J., & Emmers-Sommer, T. M. (with Faulkner, S.) (1997). *Sex and gender differences in personal relationships.* New York: Guilford Press.
12. Wester, S. R., Vogel, D. L., Pressley, P. K., & Heesacker, M. (2002). Sex differences in emotion: A critical review of the literature and implications for counseling psychology. *The Counseling Psychologist, 30*(4), 630-652.
13. Canary, D. J., & Emmers-Sommer, T. M. (with Faulkner, S.) (1997). *Sex and gender differences in personal relationships.* New York: Guilford Press.

14. Simon, R. W., & Nath, L. E. (2004). Gender and Emotion in the United States: Do men and women differ in self-reports of feelings and expressive behavior? *American Journal of Sociology 109*(5), 1166.
15. Lively, K. J., & Heise, D. R. (2004). Sociological realms of emotional experience. *American Journal of Sociology 109*(5), 1120.
16. Simpson, P. A., & Stroh, L. K. (2004). Gender differences: Emotional expression and feelings of personal inauthenticity. *Journal of Applied Psychology, 89*(4), 715-721.
17. Vogel, D. L., Wester, S. R., Heesacker, M., & Madon, S. (2003). Confirming gender stereotypes: A social role perspective. *Sex Roles 48*(11-12), 519-528.
18. LaFrance, M., Hecht, M. A., & Paluck, E.L. (2003). The contingent smile: A meta-analysis of sex differences in smiling. *Psychological bulletin, 129*(2), 305-334.
19. Ekman, P. (1993). Facial expression and emotion. *American Psychologist, 48*(4), 384-392.
20. Philippot, P., Feldman, R. S., & Coats, E. J. (2003). The role of nonverbal behavior in clinical settings: Introduction and overview. In P. Phillipot, R. S. Feldman, & E. J. Coats (Eds.), *Nonverbal behavior in clinical settings.* New York: Oxford University Press.
21. Plant, E. A., Hyde, J. S., Keltner, D., & Devine, P. G. (2000). The gender stereotyping of emotions. *Psychology of Women Quarterly, 24*(1), 81-92.
22. Algoe, S. B., Buswell, B. N., & DeLamater, J. D. (2000). Gender and job status as contextual cues for the interpretation of facial expression of emotion. *Sex Roles, 42*(3-4), 183-208.
23. Major, B., Carnevale, P. J., & Deaux, K. (1981). A different perspective on androgyny: Evaluations of masculine and feminine personality characteristics. *Journal of Personality and Social Psychology, 41*(5), 988-1001.
24. Plant, E. A., Hyde, J. S., Keltner, D., & Devine, P. G. (2000). The gender stereotyping of emotions. *Psychology of Women Quarterly, 24*(1), 81-92.
25. Plant, E. A., Kling, K. C., & Smith, G. L. (2004). The influence of gender and social role on the interpretation of facial expressions. *Sex Roles, 51*(3-4), 187-196.
26. Hess, U., Adams, R. B. Jr., & Kleck, R. E. (2004). Facial appearance, gender, and emotion expression. *Emotion 4*(4), 378-388.
27. Buck, R., Miller, R. E., & Caul, W. F. (1974). Sex, personality, and physiological variables in the communication of affect via

facial expression. *Journal of Personality and Social Psychology, 30*(4), 587-596.
28. Buck, R., Miller, R. E., & Caul, W. F. (1974). Sex, personality, and physiological variables in the communication of affect via facial expression. *Journal of Personality and Social Psychology, 30*(4), 593.
29. Zuckerman, M., Lipets, M. S., Koivumaki, J. H., & Rosenthal, R. (1975). Encoding and decoding nonverbal cues of emotion. *Journal of Personality and Social Psychology, 32*(6), 1068-1076.
30. Condry, J., & Condry, S. (1976). Sex differences: A study of the eye of the beholder. *Child Development, 47*(3), 812-819.
31. Condry, J., & Condry, S. (1976). Sex differences: A study of the eye of the beholder. *Child Development, 47*(3), 816.
32. Eiland, R., & Richardson, D. (1976). The influence of race, sex, and age on judgments of emotion portrayed in photographs. *Communication Monographs, 43*(3), 167-175.
33. Eiland, R., & Richardson, D. (1976). The influence of race, sex, and age on judgments of emotion portrayed in photographs. *Communication Monographs, 43*(3), 14-175.
34. Felleman, E. S., Barden, R. C., Carlson, C. R., Rosenberg, L., & Masters, J. C. (1983). Children's and adults' recognition of spontaneous and posed emotional expressions in young children. *Developmental Psychology, 19*(3), 405-413.
35. Knudsen, H. R., & Muzekari, L. H. (1983) The effects of verbal statements of context on facial expressions of emotion. *Journal of Nonverbal Behavior, 7*(4), 202-212.
36. Condry, J., & Condry, S. (1976). Sex differences: A study of the eye of the beholder. *Child Development, 47*(3), 812-819.
37. Thompson, J. K. (1983). Visual field, exposure duration, and sex as factors in the perception of emotional facial expressions. *Cortex, 19*(3), 293-308.
38. Wagner, H. L., MacDonald, C. J., & Manstead, A. S. (1986). Communication of individual emotions by spontaneous facial expressions. *Journal of Personality and Social Psychology, 50*(4), 737-743.
39. Rotter, N. G., & Rotter, G. S. (1988). Sex differences in the encoding and decoding of negative facial emotions. *Journal of Nonverbal Behavior, 12*(2), 139-148.
40. Rotter, N. G., & Rotter, G. S. (1988). Sex differences in the encoding and decoding of negative facial emotions. *Journal of Nonverbal Behavior, 12*(2), 14-147.

41. Wallbott, H. G. (1988). Big girls don't frown, big boys don't cry—Gender differences of professional actors in communicating emotion via facial expression. *Journal of Nonverbal Behavior, 12*(2), 98-106.
42. Ekman, P., Friesen, W. V., & Ellsworth, P. (1972) *Emotion in the human face: Guidelines for research and an integration of findings.* Oxford: Pergamon Press.
43. Erwin, R. J., Gur, R. C., Gur, R. E., Skolnick, B., Mawhinney-Hee, M., & Samalis, J. (1992). Facial emotion discrimination: I. Task construction and behavioral findings in normal subjects. *Psychiatry Research, 42*(3), 231-240.
44. Keltner, D. (1995). Signs of appeasement: Evidence for the distinct displays of embarrassment, amusement, and shame. *Journal of Personality and Social Psychology, 68*(3), 441-454.
45. Keltner, D. (1995). Signs of appeasement: Evidence for the distinct displays of embarrassment, amusement, and shame. *Journal of Personality and Social Psychology, 68*(3), 441-454.
46. Baron-Cohen, S., Wheelwright, S., & Jolliffe, T. (1997). Is there a 'language of the eyes'? Evidence from normal adults, and adults with autism or Asperger syndrome. *Visual Cognition, 4*(3), 311-331.
47. Hess, U., Blairy, S., Kleck, R. E. (1997). The intensity of emotional facial expressions and decoding accuracy. *Journal of Nonverbal Behavior, 21*(4), 241-257.
48. Hess, U., Blairy, S., Kleck, R. E. (1997). The intensity of emotional facial expressions and decoding accuracy. *Journal of Nonverbal Behavior, 21*(4), 255.
49. Algoe, S. B., Buswell, B. N., & DeLamater, J. D. (2000). Gender and job status as contextual cues for the interpretation of facial expression of emotion. *Sex Roles, 42*(3-4), 183-208.
50. Dimitrovsky, L., Spector, H., & Levy-Shiff, R. (2000). Stimulus gender and emotional difficulty level: Their effect on recognition of facial expressions of affect in children with and without LD. *Journal of learning Disabilities, 33*(5), 410-416.
51. Dimitrovsky, L., Spector, H., & Levy-Shiff, R. (2000). Stimulus gender and emotional difficulty level: Their effect on recognition of facial expressions of affect in children with and without LD. *Journal of learning Disabilities, 33*(5), 414.
52. Hess, U., Blairy, S., Kleck, R. E. (2000). The influence of facial emotion displays, gender, and ethnicity on judgments of dominance and affiliation. *Journal of Nonverbal Behavior, 24*(4), 265-283.

53. Hess, U., Blairy, S., Kleck, R. E. (2000). The influence of facial emotion displays, gender, and ethnicity on judgments of dominance and affiliation. *Journal of Nonverbal Behavior, 24*(4), 281.
54. Plant, E. A., Hyde, J. S., Keltner, D., & Devine, P. G. (2000). The gender stereotyping of emotions. *Psychology of Women Quarterly, 24*(1), 81-92.
55. Ekman, P., & Friesen, W. V. (1976). Measuring facial movement. *Environmental Psychology & Nonverbal Behavior, 1*(1), 56-75.
56. Condry, J., & Condry, S. (1976). Sex differences: A study of the eye of the beholder. *Child Development, 47*(3), 812-819.
57. Thayer, J. F., & Johnsen, B. H. (2000). Sex differences in judgment of facial affect: A multivariate analysis of recognition errors. *Scandinavian Journal of Psychology, 41*(3), 243-246.
58. Pell, M. D. (2002). Evaluation of nonverbal emotion in face and voice: Some preliminary findings on a new battery of tests. *Brain and Cognition, 48*(2-3), 499-504.
59. Pell, M. D. (2002). Evaluation of nonverbal emotion in face and voice: Some preliminary findings on a new battery of tests. *Brain and Cognition, 48*(2-3), 504.
60. Widen, S. C., & Russell, J. A. (2002). Gender and preschoolers' perception of emotion. *Merrill-Palmer Quarterly, 48*(3), 248-262.
61. Mignault, A., & Chaudhuri, A. (2003). The many faces of a neutral face: Head tilt and perception of dominance and emotion. *Journal of Nonverbal Behavior, 27*(2), 111-132.
62. Mignault, A., & Chaudhuri, A. (2003). The many faces of a neutral face: Head tilt and perception of dominance and emotion. *Journal of Nonverbal Behavior, 27*(2), 117.
63. Mignault, A., & Chaudhuri, A. (2003). The many faces of a neutral face: Head tilt and perception of dominance and emotion. *Journal of Nonverbal Behavior, 27*(2), 128.
64. Hess, U., Adams, R. B. Jr., & Kleck, R. E. (2004). Facial appearance, gender, and emotion expression. *Emotion 4*(4), 378-388.
65. Hess, U., Adams, R. B. Jr., & Kleck, R. E. (2004). Facial appearance, gender, and emotion expression. *Emotion 4*(4), 378-388.
66. Palermo, R., & Coltheart, M. (2004). Photographs of facial expression: Accuracy, response times, and ratings of intensity. *Behavior Research Methods, Instruments, & Computers 36*(4), 634-638.
67. Plant, E. A., Kling, K. C., & Smith, G. L. (2004). The influence of gender and social role on the interpretation of facial expressions. *Sex Roles, 51*(3-4), 187-196.

68. Hess, U., Adams, R. B. Jr., & Kleck, R. E. (2004). Facial appearance, gender, and emotion expression. *Emotion 4*(4), 378-388.
69. Rahman, Q., Wilson, G. D., & Abrahams, S. (2004). Sex, sexual orientation, and identification of positive and negative facial affect. *Brain and Cognition, 54*(3), 179-185.
70. Atkinson, A. P., Tipples, J., & Burt, D. M. (2005). Asymmetric interference between sex and emotion in face perception. *Perception & Psychophysics, 67*(7), 1199-1213.
71. Hess, U., Adams, R. B. Jr., & Kleck, R. E. (2005). Who may frown and who should smile? Dominance, affiliation, and the display of happiness and anger. *Cognition & Emotion, 19*(4), 515-536.
72. Hess, U., Adams, R. B. Jr., & Kleck, R. E. (2005). Who may frown and who should smile? Dominance, affiliation, and the display of happiness and anger. *Cognition & Emotion, 19*(4), 534.
73. Hugenberg, K., & Sczesny, S. (2006). On wonderful women and seeing smiles: Social categorization moderates the happy face response latency advantage. *Social Cognition, 24*(5), 516-539.
74. Becker, D. V., Kenrick, D. T., Neuberg, S. L., Blackwell, K. C., & Smith, D. M. (2007) The confounded nature of angry men and happy women. *Journal of Personality and Social Psychology, 92*(2), 179-190.
75. Becker, D. V., Kenrick, D. T., Neuberg, S. L., Blackwell, K. C., & Smith, D. M. (2007) The confounded nature of angry men and happy women. *Journal of Personality and Social Psychology, 92*(2), 181.
76. Becker, D. V., Kenrick, D. T., Neuberg, S. L., Blackwell, K. C., & Smith, D. M. (2007) The confounded nature of angry men and happy women. *Journal of Personality and Social Psychology, 92*(2), 187.
77. Condry, J., & Condry, S. (1976). Sex differences: A study of the eye of the beholder. *Child Development, 47*(3), 812-819.
78. Hess, U., Adams, R. B. Jr., & Kleck, R. E. (2005). Who may frown and who should smile? Dominance, affiliation, and the display of happiness and anger. *Cognition & Emotion, 19*(4), 515-536.

CHAPTER TEN

1. Pruitt, D. G., & Kim, S. H. (2004). *Social conflict: Escalation, stalemate, and settlement* (3rd ed.). New York: McGraw-Hill.
2. Bronfenbrenner, U. (1961). The mirror image in Soviet-American relations: A social psychologist's report. *Journal of Social Issues, 17,* 45-56.
3. De Dreu, C. K. (1995). Coercive power and concession making in bilateral negotiation. *Journal of Conflict Resolution, 39,* 646-670.
4. Jervis, R. (1976). *Perception and misperception in international politics.* Princeton, NJ: Princeton University Press.
5. Pruitt, D. G., & Kim, S. H. (2004). *Social conflict: Escalation, stalemate, and settlement* (3rd ed.). New York: McGraw-Hill.
6. Kydd, A. H. (2005). *Trust and mistrust in international relations.* Princeton, NJ: Princeton University Press.
7. Kydd, A. H. (2000). Arms races and arms control: Modeling the hawk perspective. *American Journal of Political Science, 44,* 222-238.
8. Zhang, L. & Baumeister, R. F. (2006). Your money or your elf-esteem: Threatened egoism promotes costly entrapment in losing endeavors. *Personality and Social Psychology Bulletin, 32,* 881-893.
9. Bazerman, M. H. (2002). *Judgment in managerial decision making* (5th ed.). New York: Wiley.
10. Staw, B. M. (1976). Knee-deep in the big muddy: A study of escalating commitment to a chosen course of action. *Organizational Behavior and Human Performance, 16,* 27-44.
11. Elms, D. K. (2004). Large costs, small benefits: Explaining trade dispute outcomes. *Political Psychology, 25,* 241-270.
12. Platt, J. (1973). Social traps. *American Psychologist, 28,* 641-651.
13. Holsti, O. R. (1971). Crisis, stress, and decisionmaking. In R. A. Falk & S. S. Kim (Eds.), *The war system: An interdisciplinary approach* (pp. 491-508). Boulder, CO: Westview Press.
14. McCauley, C., & Segal, M. (1987). Social psychology of terrorist groups. In C. Hendrick (Ed.), *Review of personality and social psychology* (Vol. 9, pp. 231-256). Beverly Hills, CA: Sage.
15. Haslam, N. (2006). Dehumanization: An integrative review. *Personality and Social Psychology Review, 10,* 252-264.
16. Scheepers, D., Spears, R., Doosje, B., & Manstead, A. S. R (2006). The social functions of ingroup bias: Creating, confirming, or changing social reality. *European Journal of Social Psychology, 17,* 359-396.

17. Castano, E., & Giner-Sorollo, R. (2006). Not quite human: Infrahumanization in response to collective responsibility for intergroup killing. *Journal of Personality and Social Psychology, 90*, 804-818.
18. Bandura, A., Underwood, B., & Fromson, M. E. (1975). Disinhibition of aggression through diffusion of responsibility and dehumanization of victims. *Journal of Research in Personality, 9*, 253-269.
19. Osofsky, M. J., Bandura, A., & Zimbardo, P. G. (2005). The role of moral disengagement in the execution process. *Law and Human Behavior, 29*, 371-393.
20. Struch, N., & Schwartz, S. H. (1989). Intergroup aggression: Its predictors and distinctiveness from in-group bias. *Journal of Personality and Social Psychology, 56*, 364-373.
21. Harris, L. T., & Fiske, S. T. (2006). Dehumanizing the lowest of the low: Neuroimaging responses to extreme out-groups. *Psychological Science, 17*, 847-853.
22. Pronin, E., Lin, D. Y., & Ross, L. (2002). The bias blind spot: Perceptions of bias in self versus others. *Personality and Social Psychology Bulletin, 28*, 369-381.
23. Ross, L., & Ward, A. (1995). Psychological barriers to dispute resolution. In M. Zanna (Ed.), *Advances in experimental social psychology* (Vol. 27, pp. 255-304). San Diego: Academic Press.
24. Wilson, T. D., Centerbar, D. B., & Brekke, N. (2002). Mental contamination and the debiasing problem. In D. Kahneman, T. Gilovich, & D. Griffin (Eds.), *Heuristics and biases: The psychology of intuitive judgment*, New York: Cambridge University Press.
25. Pronin, E., & Kugler, M. B. (2007). Valuing thoughts, ignoring behavior: The introspection illusion as a source of the bias blind spot. *Journal of Experimental Social Psychology, 43*, 565-578.
26. Vivian, J. E., & Berkowitz, N. H. (1992). Anticipated bias from an outgroup: An attributional analysis. *European Journal of Social Psychology, 22*, 415-424.
27. Kruger, J., & Gilovich, T. (1999). "Naïve cynicism" in everyday theories of responsibility assessment: On biased assumptions of bias. *Journal of Personality and Social Psychology, 76*, 743-753.
28. Miller, D. T., & Ratner, R. K. (1998). The disparity between the actual and assumed power of self-interest. *Journal of Personality and Social Psychology, 74*, 53-62.

29. Cohen, G. L. (2003). Party over policy: The dominating impact of group influence on political beliefs. *Journal of Personality and Social Psychology, 85,* 808-822.
30. Robinson, R. J., Keltner, D., Ward, A., & Ross, L. (1995). Actual versus assumed differences in construal: "Naïve realism" in intergroup perception and conflict. *Journal of Personality and Social Psychology, 68,* 404-417.
31. Ehrlinger, J., Gilovich, T., & Ross, L. (2005). Peering into the bias blind spot: People's assessments of bias in themselves and others. *Personality and Social Psychology Bulletin, 31,* 680-692.
32. Nesselroade, K. P., Williams, J. K., Nam, R. K., & McBride, D. M. (2006). Self-enhancement of opinion objectivity: Effects of perceived moral weight. *Journal of Psychology and Christianity, 25,* 27-33.
33. Chambers, J. R., Baron, R. S., & Inman, M. L. (2006). Misperceptions in intergroup conflict: Disagreeing about what we disagree about. *Psychological Science, 17,* 38-45.
34. Frantz, C. M. (2006). I AM being fair: The bias blind spot as a stumbling block to seeing both sides. *Basic and Applied Social Psychology, 28,* 157-167.
35. Pronin, E., Gilovich, T., & Ross, L. (2004). Objectivity in the eye of the beholder: Divergent perceptions of bias in self versus others. *Psychological Review, 111,* 781-799.
36. Pronin, E., Lin, D. Y., & Ross, L. (2002). The bias blind spot: Perceptions of bias in self versus others. *Personality and Social Psychology Bulletin, 28,* 369-381.
37. Pronin, E., Gilovich, T., & Ross, L. (2004). Objectivity in the eye of the beholder: Divergent perceptions of bias in self versus others. *Psychological Review, 111,* 781-799.
38. Reeder, G. D., Pryor, J. B., Wohl, M. J. A., & Griswell, M. L. (2005). On attributing negative motives to others who disagree with our opinions. *Personality and Social Psychology Bulletin, 31,* 1498-1510.
39. Pronin, E., Kennedy, K., & Butsch, S. (2006). Bombing versus negotiating: How preferences for combating terrorism are affected by perceived terrorist rationality. *Basic and Applied Social Psychology, 28,* 385-392.
40. Blake, R. R., & Mouton, J. S. (1964). The *managerial grid.* Houston: Gulf.

41. Deutsch, M. (2000). Cooperation and competition. In M. Deutsch, & P. T. Coleman, (Eds.), *The handbook of conflict resolution: Theory and practice* (pp. 21-40). San Francisco: Jossey-Bass.
42. Jervis, R. (1976). *Perception and misperception in international politics.* Princeton, NJ: Princeton University Press.
43. Pronin, E., Kennedy, K., & Butsch, S. (2006). Bombing versus negotiating: How preferences for combating terrorism are affected by perceived terrorist rationality. *Basic and Applied Social Psychology, 28,* 385-392.
44. Merari, A. (2004). Suicide terrorism in the context of the Israeli-Palestinian conflict. Paper commissioned for *Suicide Terrorism Conference.* Washington, DC: National Institute of Justice.
45. Fisher, R. (1983). Negotiating power. *American Behavioral Scientist, 27,* 149-166.
46. Galinsky, A. D., Leonardelli, G. J., Okhuysen, G. A., & Mussweiler, T. (2005). Regulatory focus at the bargaining table: Promoting distributive and integrative success. *Personality and Social Psychology Bulletin, 31,* 1087-1098.
47. Kydd, A. H. (2005). *Trust and mistrust in international relations.* Princeton, NJ: Princeton University Press.
48. Pronin, E., Olivola, C. Y., & Kennedy, K. A. (2008). Doing unto future selves as you would do unto others: Psychological distance and decision making. *Personality and Social Psychology Bulletin, 34,* 224-236.
49. Raiffa, H. (1982). *The art and science of negotiation.* Cambridge, MA: Harvard University Press.
50. Lord, C. G., Ross, L., & Lepper, M. R. (1979). Biased assimilation and attitude polarization: The effects of prior theories on subsequently considered evidence. *Journal of Personality and Social Psychology, 37,* 2098-2109.
51. Liberman N., Trope, Y., & Stephan, E. (2007). Psychological distance. In E. T. Higgins & A. W. Kruglanski (Eds.), *Social psychology: Handbook of basic principles* (Vol. 2, pp. 323-381). New York: Guilford Press.
52. Nussbaum, S., Trope, Y., & Liberman, N. (2003). Creeping dispositionalism: The temporal dynamics of behavior prediction. *Journal of Personality and Social Psychology, 84,* 485-497.
53. Lang, F., Floyd, M. R., & Beine, K. L. (2000). Clues to patients explanations and concerns about their illness. *Archives of Family Medicine, 9,* 222-227.
54. Churchill, D. (1993). *Negotiation tactics.* New York: University Press of America.

55. Rogers, C. (1955). *Active listening*. Chicago: The Industrial Relations Center of the University of Chicago.
56. Worchel, S., & Simpson, J. A. (1993). *Conflict between people and groups*. Chicago: Nelson Hall.
57. Kunda, Z. (1990). The case for motivated reasoning. *Psychological Bulletin, 108,* 480-498.
58. Hochberg, J. (1981). Perceptual organization. In M. Kubovy & J. R. Pomerantz (eds.), *Perceptual organization*. Hillsdale, NJ: Lawrence Erlbaum.
59. Rock, I. (1986). The description and analysis of object and event perception. In K.R. Boff, L. Kaufmenn, & J. P. Thomas (eds.), *Handbook of perception and human performance. Volume II: Cognitive processes and performance*. New York, John Wiley.
60. Hastorf, A. H., & Cantril, H. (1954). They saw a game: A case study. *Journal of Abnormal and Social Psychology, 49,* 129-134.
61. Giner-Sorolla, R., & Chaiken, S. (1994). The causes of hostile media judgments. *Journal of Experimental Social Psychology, 30,* 165-180.
62. Nickerson, R. S. (1998). Confirmation bias: A ubiquitous phenomenon in many guises. *Review of General Psychology, 2,* 175-220.
63. Darley, J. M., & Gross, P. H. (1983). A hypothesis-confirming bias in labeling effects. *Journal of Personality and Social Psychology, 44,* 20-33.
64. Jussim, L., & Eccles, J. (1995). Naturally occurring interpersonal expectancies. *Review of Personality and Social Psychology, 15,* 74-108.
65. Lord, C. G., Ross, L., & Lepper, M. R. (1979). Biased assimilation and attitude polarization: The effects of prior theories on subsequently considered evidence. *Journal of Personality and Social Psychology, 37,* 2098-2109.
66. Kelley, H. H., & Stahelski, A. J. (1970). Social interaction basis of cooperators' and competitors' beliefs about others. *Journal of Personality and Social Psychology, 16,* 66-91.
67. Babcock, L., Loewenstein, G., Issacharoff, S., & Camerer, C. (1995). Biased judgments of fairness in bargaining. *The American Economic Review, 85,* 1337-1343.
68. Kelley, H. H. (1950). The warm-cold variable in first impressions of persons. *Journal of Personality, 18,* 431-439.
69. Hovland, C. I., & Weiss, W. (1951). The influence of source credibility on communication effectiveness. *Public Opinion Quarterly, 15,* 635-650.
70. Pronin, E., Olivola, C. Y., & Kennedy, K. A. (2008). Doing unto future selves as you would do unto others: Psychological distance and decision making. *Personality and Social Psychology Bulletin, 34,* 224-236.

71. Henderson, M. D., Trope, Y., & Carnevale, P. J. (2006). Negotiation from a near and distant time perspective. *Journal of Personality and Social Psychology, 91*, 712-729.
72. Ainslie, G., & Haslam, N. (1992). Hyperbolic discounting. In Loewenstein & Elster (Eds.), *Choice over time*. New York: Russell Sage.
73. Loewenstein, G., Read, D., & Baumeister, R. (2003). *Time and decision: Economic and psychological perspectives on intertemporal choice*. New York: Russel Sage.
74. Loewenstein, G., & Thaler, R. H. (1989). Intertemporal choice. *Journal of Economic Perspectives, 3*, 181-193.
75. Simonson, I. (1990). The effect of purchase quantity and timing on variety seeking behavior. *Journal of Marketing Research, 27*, 150-162.
76. Schelling, T. (1984). Self-command in practice, in policy, and in a theory of rational choice. *American Economic Review, 74*, 1-11.
77. De Dreu, C. K. (2003). Time pressure and closing of the mind in negotiation. *Organizational Behavior and Human Decision Processes, 91*, 280-295.
78. Okhuysen, G. A., Galinsky, A. D., & Uptigrove, T. A. (2003). Saving the worst for last: The effect of time horizon on the efficiency of negotiating benefits and burdens. *Organizational Behavior and Human Decision Processes, 91*, 269-279.
79. Ainslie, G. (1992). *Picoeconomics: The strategic interaction of successive motivational states within the person*. New York: Cambridge.
80. Thaler, R. H., & Shefrin, H. M. (1981). An economic theory of self-control. *The Journal of Political Economy, 89*, 392-406.
81. Schelling, T. (1984). Self-command in practice, in policy, and in a theory of rational choice. *American Economic Review, 74*, 1-11.
82. Ariely, D. & Wertenbroch, K. (2002). Procrastination, deadlines, and performance: Self-control by precommittment. *Psychological Science, 13*, 219-224.
83. Bazerman, M. H., Tenbrunsel, A. E., & Wade-Benzoni, K. (1998). Negotiating with yourself and losing: Making decisions with competing internal preferences. *The Academy of Management Review, 23*, 225-241.
84. Markus, H., & Nurius, P. (1986). Possible selves. *American Psychologist, 41*, 954-969.
85. Liberman N., Trope, Y., & Stephan, E. (2007). Psychological distance. In E. T. Higgins & A. W. Kruglanski (Eds.), *Social psychology: Handbook of basic principles* (Vol. 2, pp. 323-381). New York: Guilford Press.

86. Liberman, N., & Trope, Y. (2008). The psychology of transcending the here and now. *Science, 322,* 1201-1205.
87. Trope, Y., & Liberman, N. (2003). Temporal construal. *Psychological Review, 110,* 403-421.
88. Liberman, N., & Trope, Y. (2008). The psychology of transcending the here and now. *Science, 322,* 1201-1205.
89. Ersner-Hershfield, H., Wimmer, G. E., & Knutson, B. (2009). Saving for the future self: Neural measures of future self-continuity predict temporal discounting. *Social Cognitive and Affective Neuroscience, 4,* 85-92.
90. Ersner-Hershfield, H., Wimmer, G. E., & Knutson, B. (2009). Saving for the future self: Neural measures of future self-continuity predict temporal discounting. *Social Cognitive and Affective Neuroscience, 4,* 85-92.
91. Nussbaum, S., Trope, Y., & Liberman, N. (2003). Creeping dispositionalism: The temporal dynamics of behavior prediction. *Journal of Personality and Social Psychology, 84,* 485-497.
92. Pronin, E., & Ross, L. (2006). Temporal differences in trait self ascription: When the self is seen as an other. *Journal of Personality and Social Psychology, 90,* 197-209.
93. Pronin, E., Olivola, C. Y., & Kennedy, K. A. (2008). Doing unto future selves as you would do unto others: Psychological distance and decision making. *Personality and Social Psychology Bulletin, 34,* 224-236.

CHAPTER ELEVEN

1. Green, D. P., McFalls, L. H., & Smith, J. K. (2001). Hate crime: An emergent research agenda. Annual Review of Sociology, 27, 479-504. In D. Canter & L. Alison (Eds.), The Social Psychology of Crime: Offender Profiling Series III). Aldershot: Ashgate Publishing.
2. Allport, G. W. (1954). The nature of prejudice. New York: Doubleday Books.
3. Federal Bureau of Investigation (FBI) (1999). (Annual) Uniform crime reports: Hate crime reporting statistics. Washington, DC: Author.
4. Green, D., Strolovitch, D., Bailey R., and Wong, J. (2001). Measuring gay population density and the incidence of anti-gay hate crime. Social Science Quarterly, 82, 281-296.
5. Reasons, C. and Hughson, Q. (2000). Violence against gays and lesbians. In Race, Ethnicity, Sexual Orientation and Violent Crime: The Realities and the Myths. The Haworth Press, 137-159.
6. Reasons, C. and Hughson, Q. (2000). Violence against gays and lesbians. In Race, Ethnicity, Sexual Orientation and Violent Crime: The Realities and the Myths. The Haworth Press, 137-159.
7. Federal Bureau of Investigation (FBI) (2006). (Annual) Uniform crime reports: Hate crime reporting statistics. Washington, DC: Author.
8. Federal Bureau of Investigation (FBI) (2003, 2004, 2005, 2006). (Annual) Uniform crime reports: Hate crime reporting statistics. Washington, DC: Author.
9. Federal Bureau of Investigation (FBI) (2004). (Annual) Uniform crime reports: Hate crime reporting statistics. Washington, DC: Author.
10. Federal Bureau of Investigation (FBI) (2004). (Annual) Uniform crime reports: Hate crime reporting statistics. Washington, DC: Author.
11. Maxwell, C. and Maxwell, S. (1995). Youth participation in hate-motivated crimes: Research and Policy Implications. Center for the Study and Prevention of Violence. University of Colorado, Boulder.
12. Comstock, G. (1991). Violence Against Lesbians and Gay Men. New York: Columbia University Press.
13. Green, D., Strolovitch, D., Bailey R., and Wong, J. (2001). Measuring gay population density and the incidence of anti-gay hate crime. Social Science Quarterly, 82, 281-296.

14. Biderman, A. D. and Lynch, J. (1991). Understanding Crime Incidence Statistics: Why the UCR Diverges from the NCS? New York: Springer Verlag, 1991.
15. Maxwell, C. and Maxwell, S. (1995). Youth participation in hate-motivated crimes: Research and Policy Implications. Center for the Study and Prevention of Violence. University of Colorado, Boulder.
16. Strom, K. (2001). Hate crime reported in NIBRS, 1997-1999. U.S. Department of Justice, Office of Justice Programs. Washington, DC.
17. Adams, H., Wright, Jr., L., & Lohr, B. (1996). Is homophobia associated with homosexual arousal? Journal of Abnormal Psychology, 105, 440-445.
18. Ituarte, S. (2000). Inside the mind of hate. UMI Dissertation.
19. Bufkin, J. (1999). Bias crime as gendered behavior. Social Justice, 26, 155-176.
20. Bernat, J. A., Calhoun, R. S., Adams, H. E., and Zeichner, A. (2001). Homophobia and physical aggression toward homosexual and heterosexual individuals. Journal of Abnormal Psychology, 110, 179-188.
21. Bufkin, J. (1999). Bias crime as gendered behavior. Social Justice, 26, 158.
22. Cotton, P. (1992). Attacks on homosexual persons may be increasing, but many 'bashings' still aren't reported. The Journal of the American Medical Association, 267, 3000.
23. Maxwell, C. and Maxwell, S. (1995). Youth participation in hate-motivated crimes: Research and Policy Implications. Center for the Study and Prevention of Violence. University of Colorado, Boulder. 36.
24. Maxwell, C. and Maxwell, S. (1995). Youth participation in hate-motivated crimes: Research and Policy Implications. Center for the Study and Prevention of Violence. University of Colorado, Boulder.
25. Reasons, C. and Hughson, Q. (2000). Violence against gays and lesbians. In Race, Ethnicity, Sexual Orientation and Violent Crime: The Realities and the Myths. The Haworth Press, 137-159.
26. Bufkin, J. (1999). Bias crime as gendered behavior. Social Justice, 26, 161.
27. Craig, K. (2002). Examining hate-motivated aggression: A review of the social-psychology literature on hate crimes as a distinct form of aggression. Aggression & Violent Behavior, 7, 89.

28. Maxwell, C. and Maxwell, S. (1995). Youth participation in hate-motivated crimes: Research and Policy Implications. Center for the Study and Prevention of Violence. University of Colorado, Boulder.
29. Craig, K. (2002). Examining hate-motivated aggression: A review of the social-psychology literature on hate crimes as a distinct form of aggression. Aggression & Violent Behavior, 7, 85-99.
30. Maxwell, C. and Maxwell, S. (1995). Youth participation in hate-motivated crimes: Research and Policy Implications. Center for the Study and Prevention of Violence. University of Colorado, Boulder.
31. Reasons, C. and Hughson, Q. (2000). Violence against gays and lesbians. In Race, Ethnicity, Sexual Orientation and Violent Crime: The Realities and the Myths. The Haworth Press, 140.
32. Reasons, C. and Hughson, Q. (2000). Violence against gays and lesbians. In Race, Ethnicity, Sexual Orientation and Violent Crime: The Realities and the Myths. The Haworth Press, 140.
33. Franklin, K. (2000). Antigay behaviors among young adults: Prevalence, patterns, and motivators in a noncriminal population. Journal of Interpersonal Violence, 15, 346.
34. Kuehnle, K. & Sullivan, A. (2001). Patterns of anti-gay violence: An analysis of incident characteristics and victims reporting. Journal of Interpersonal Violence, 16, 928-943.
35. Craig, K. (2002). Examining hate-motivated aggression: A review of the social-psychology literature on hate crimes as a distinct form of aggression. Aggression & Violent Behavior, 7, 85-99.
36. Franklin, K. (2000). Antigay behaviors among young adults: Prevalence, patterns, and motivators in a noncriminal population. Journal of Interpersonal Violence, 15, 346.
37. Franklin, K. (2000). Antigay behaviors among young adults: Prevalence, patterns, and motivators in a noncriminal population. Journal of Interpersonal Violence, 15, 347.
38. Comstock, G. (1991). Violence Against Lesbians and Gay Men. New York: Columbia University Press.
39. Bufkin, J. (1999). Bias crime as gendered behavior. Social Justice, 26, 162.
40. Levin, J. & McDevitt, J. (1993). Hate Crimes: The Rising Tide of Bigotry and Bloodshed. New York: Plenum Press
41. Bufkin, J. (1999). Bias crime as gendered behavior. Social Justice, 26, 163.

42. Maxwell, C. and Maxwell, S. (1995). Youth participation in hate-motivated crimes: Research and Policy Implications. Center for the Study and Prevention of Violence. University of Colorado, Boulder.
43. American Psychological Association. (2004). Hate crimes today: An age-old foe in modern dress. Part of the series, Clarifying the debate: Psychology Examines the Issues. Washington, DC.
44. Anderson, J., Dyson, L., and Brooks, Jr., W. (2002). Preventing hate crime and profiling hate crime offenders. The Western Journal of Black Studies, 26, 2002.
45. Reasons, C. and Hughson, Q. (2000). Violence against gays and lesbians. In Race, Ethnicity, Sexual Orientation and Violent Crime: The Realities and the Myths. The Haworth Press, 137-159.
46. Reasons, C. and Hughson, Q. (2000). Violence against gays and lesbians. In Race, Ethnicity, Sexual Orientation and Violent Crime: The Realities and the Myths. The Haworth Press, 137-159.
47. Dunbar, E. (2003). Symbolic, relational, and ideological signifiers of bias-motivated offenders: Toward a strategy of assessment. American Journal of Orthopsychiatry, 73(2), 203-211.
48. Dunbar, E. (2003). Symbolic, relational, and ideological signifiers of bias-motivated offenders: Toward a strategy of assessment. American Journal of Orthopsychiatry, 73(2), 203-211.
49. Allport, G. W. (1954). The nature of prejudice. New York: Doubleday Books.
50. Ehrlich, H. (1990). The ecology of anti-gay violence. Journal of Interpersonal Violence, 5, 359-365.
51. Fiske, S. (2002). What we know now about bias and intergroup conflict, the problem of the century. Current Directions in Psychological Science, 11, 123-128.
52. Dunbar, E. (2003). Symbolic, relational, and ideological signifiers of bias-motivated offenders: Toward a strategy of assessment. American Journal of Orthopsychiatry, 73(2), 203-211.
53. Dunbar, E. (2003). Symbolic, relational, and ideological signifiers of bias-motivated offenders: Toward a strategy of assessment. American Journal of Orthopsychiatry, 73(2), 203-211.
54. Canter, D., Alison, L., Alison, E., and Wentink, N. (2004). The organized/disorganized typology of serial murder: Myth or Model? Psychology, Public Policy, and the Law, 10(3), 293-320.

55. Fiske, S. (2002). What we know now about bias and intergroup conflict, the problem of the century. Current Directions in Psychological Science, 11, 123-128.
56. Abrams, K. (2002). "Fighting fire with fire:" Rethinking the role of disgust in hate crimes. California Law Review, 90, 1423-1465.
57. Dunbar, E. (2003). Symbolic, relational, and ideological signifiers of bias-motivated offenders: Toward a strategy of assessment. American Journal of Orthopsychiatry, 73(2), 203-211.
58. Dunbar, E. (2003). Symbolic, relational, and ideological signifiers of bias-motivated offenders: Toward a strategy of assessment. American Journal of Orthopsychiatry, 73(2), 203-211.
59. Dunbar, E. (2003). Symbolic, relational, and ideological signifiers of bias-motivated offenders: Toward a strategy of assessment. American Journal of Orthopsychiatry, 73(2), 203-211.
60. Ituarte, S. (2000). Inside the mind of hate. UMI Dissertation.
61. Levin, J., & McDevitt, J. (2002). Hate crimes revisited: Americas' war on those who are different. Boulder, CO: Westview.
62. Perry, B. (2001). In the Name of Hate: Understanding Hate Crimes. New York: Routledge.
63. Dunbar, E. (2003). Symbolic, relational, and ideological signifiers of bias-motivated offenders: Toward a strategy of assessment. American Journal of Orthopsychiatry, 73(2), 203-211.
64. Hegland, S. & Rix, M. (1990). Aggression and assertiveness in kindergarten children differing in day care experiences. Early Childhood Research Quarterly, 5(1), 105-116.
65. Shoda, Y. (1999). A united framework for the study of behavioral consistency: bridging the person/situation interaction and the consistency paradox. European Journal of Personality, 13(5), 361-387.
66. Toch, H. (1969). Violent men: An inquiry into the psychology of violence. Chicago: Aldine.
67. Berkowitz, L. (1993). Aggression: Its causes, consequences and control. Philadelphia: Temple University Press.
68. Fesbach, S. (1964). The function of aggression and the regulation of aggressive drive. Psychological Review, 71, 257-272.
69. Toch, H. (1969). Violent men: An inquiry into the psychology of violence. Chicago: Aldine.
70. Cornell, D.G. (1990). Prior adjustment of violent juvenile offenders. Law and Human Behavior, 14, 569-478.

71. Berkowitz, L. (1993). Aggression: Its causes, consequences and control. Philadelphia: Temple University Press.
72. Cornell, D.G., Warren, J., Hawk, G., Stafford, E., Oram, G., & Pine, D. (1996). Psychopathy in instrumental and reactive violent offenders. Journal of Consulting and Clinical Psychology, 64, 783-790.
73. Salfati, C. G. and Canter, D. V. (1999). Differentiating stranger murders: Profiling offender characteristics from behavioral styles. Journal of Behavioral Sciences and the Law, 1, 391-406.
74. Federal Bureau of Investigation (FBI) (2004). (Annual) Uniform crime reports: Hate crime reporting statistics. Washington, DC: Author.
75. Block, R. (1977). Violent Crime. Lexington, MA: Lexington Books/D.C. Heath.
76. Glaser, D., Kenefich, D., & O'Leary, V. (1968). The Violent Offender. Washington, DC: US Department of Health, Education and Welfare, Social Rehabilitation Service, Office of Juvenile Delinquency and Youth Development.
77. Canter, D., Alison, L., Alison, E., and Wentink, N. (2004). The organized/disorganized typology of serial murder: Myth or Model? Psychology, Public Policy, and the Law, 10(3), 293-320.
78. Buss, D. M., & Shackelford, T. K. (1997). Human aggression in evolutionary psychological perspective. Clinical Psychology Review, 17, 605-619.
79. Salfati, C. G. (2000). The nature of expressiveness and instrumentality in homicide. Homicide Studies, 4, 265-293.
80. Salfati, C. G. (2000). The nature of expressiveness and instrumentality in homicide. Homicide Studies, 4, 265-293.
81. Wolfgang, M. E. (1958). Patterns in Criminal Homicide. Philadelphia: University of Pennsylvania Press.
82. Gillis, A. R. (1986). Domesticity, divorce, and deadly quarrels: An exploratory study of integration-regulation and homicide. In T. Hartnagel & R. Silverman (Eds.), Critique and explanation: Essays in honor of Gwynne Nettler (pp. 133-147). New Brunswick, NJ: Transaction.
83. Salfati, C. G. and Canter, D. V. (1999). Differentiating stranger murders: Profiling offender characteristics from behavioral styles. Journal of Behavioral Sciences and the Law, 1, 391-406.
84. Shye, S., Elizur, D., and Hoffman, M. (1994). Introduction to Facet Theory: Content Design an Intrinsic Data Analysis in Behavioral Research. Thousand Oaks, CA: Sage.

85. McAndrew, D. (1999). The Structural Analysis of Criminal Networks. In D. Canter & L. Alison (Eds.), The Social Psychology of Crime: Offender Profiling Series III. Burlington, VT: Ashgate Publishing.
86. Farrington, D. P. (1991). Antisocial personality from childhood to adulthood. The Psychologist, 4, 389-394.
87. Donald, I. & Wilson, A. (1999). Ram Raiding: Criminals working in groups. In The Social Psychology of Crime: Groups, Teams and Networks. (Eds. D. Canter & L. Alison). Ashgate: Aldershot, pp. 189-246.
88. Salfati, C. G. & Taylor, P. (2006). Differentiating sexual violence: A comparison of sexual homicide and rape. Psychology, Crime & Law, 12(2), 107-125.
89. Salfati, C. G. (2000). The nature of expressiveness and instrumentality in homicide. Homicide Studies, 4, 265-293.
90. Berkowitz, L. (1993). Aggression: Its causes, consequences and control. Philadelphia: Temple University Press.
91. Abrams, K. (2002). "Fighting fire with fire:" Rethinking the role of disgust in hate crimes. California Law Review, 90, 1423-1465.
92. D'Augelli A. (1998). Developmental implications of victimization of lesbian, gay, and bisexual youths. In: Herek GM, ed. Stigma and sexual orientation: Understanding prejudice against lesbians, gay men, and bisexuals. Thousand Oaks, CA: Sage Publications, 1998:198.
93. Griffin, J. (1997). Anti-lesbian and gay violence in schools. In Homophobic Violence (Eds. G. Mason & S. Tamsen). Hawkins Press.
94. Ituarte, S. (2000). Inside the mind of hate. UMI Dissertation.
95. Franklin, K. (2000). Antigay behaviors among young adults: Prevalence, patterns, and motivators in a noncriminal population. Journal of Interpersonal Violence, 15, 339-362.
96. Canter, D. & Alison, L. (1999). The social psychology of crime: Groups, Teams and Networks. In D. Canter & L. Alison (Eds.), The Social Psychology of Crime: Offender Profiling Series III (pp. 1-20). Aldershot: Ashgate Publishing.
97. Salfati, C. G. and Haratsis, E. (2001). Greek homicide: A behavioral examination of offender crime-scene actions. Homicide Studies, 5, 335-362.
98. Cheatwood, D. (1996). Interactional patterns in multiple-offender homicides. Justice Quarterly, 13(1), 107-128.

99. Porter, L. E. and Alison, L. J. (2006). Leadership and hierarchies in criminal groups: Scaling degrees of leader behavior in group robbery. Legal and Criminological Psychology, 11, 245-265.
100. Porter, L.E. & Alison, L.J. (2004). Behavioural coherence in violent group activity: An interpersonal model of sexually violent gang behaviour. Aggressive Behavior, 30(6): 449-468.
101. Cheatwood, D. (1992). Notes on the Empirical, Theoretical, and Policy Significance of Multiple Offender Homicides. Homicide: The Victim/Offender Connection, edited by Anna Wilson. Cincinnati: Anderson.
102. Cheatwood, D. (1996). Interactional patterns in multiple-offender homicides. Justice Quarterly, 13(1), 107-128.
103. Cheatwood, D. (1996). Interactional patterns in multiple-offender homicides. Justice Quarterly, 13(1), 107-128.
104. 104. Warr, M. (1996). Organization and instigation in delinquent groups. *Criminology*, 34, 11-37.
105. 105. Porter, L.E. & Alison, L.J. (2004). Behavioural coherence in violent group activity: An interpersonal model of sexually violent gang behaviour. Aggressive Behavior, 30(6): 449-468.
106. 106. Cheatwood, D. (1996). Interactional patterns in multiple-offender homicides. Justice Quarterly, 13(1), 107-128.
107. 107. Canter, D. & Heritage, R. (1990). A multivariate model of sexual offence behavior: Developments in offender profiling: Part 1. Journal of Forensic Psychiatry, 1, 185-212.
108. 108. Franklin, K. (2000). Antigay behaviors among young adults: Prevalence, patterns, and motivators in a noncriminal population. Journal of Interpersonal Violence, 15, 339-362.
109. 109. Porter, L.E. & Alison, L.J. (2004). Behavioural coherence in violent group activity: An interpersonal model of sexually violent gang behaviour. Aggressive Behavior, 30(6): 449-468.
110. 110. Porter, L.E. & Alison, L.J. (2004). Behavioural coherence in violent group activity: An interpersonal model of sexually violent gang behaviour. Aggressive Behavior, 30(6): 467.
111. 111. Cheatwood, D. (1996). Interactional patterns in multiple-offender homicides. Justice Quarterly, 13(1), 107-128.
112. 112. Canter, D., Alison, L., Alison, E., and Wentink, N. (2004). The organized/disorganized typology of serial murder: Myth or Model? Psychology, Public Policy, and the Law, 10(3), 293-320.

113. 113. Canter, D. (1995). Psychology of offender profiling. In R. Bull & D. Carson (Eds.), Handbook of Psychology in Legal Contexts (pp. 335-343). New York: John Wiley and Sons.
114. 114. Canter, D., Alison, L., Alison, E., and Wentink, N. (2004). The organized/disorganized typology of serial murder: Myth or Model? Psychology, Public Policy, and the Law, 10(3), 293-320.

Printed in Great Britain
by Amazon.co.uk, Ltd.,
Marston Gate.